Tom Penders and Ten Years at the University of Texas

BY KYLE DALTON

Lenexa, KS

Published by Addax Publishing Group, Inc.

Edited by An Beard
Designed by Randy Breeden
Cover Designed by Laura Bolter

For Information address:
Addax Publishing Group, Inc.
8643 Hauser Drive, Suite 235, Lenexa, KS 66215

ISBN: 1-886110-92-1

Printed in the USA

1 3 5 7 9 10 8 6 4 2

Library of Congress Cataloging-in-Publication Data

Dalton, Kyle
Burned orange : Tom Penders and 10 years at the University of Texas / by Kyle Dalton.
p.cm.
ISBN 1-886110-92-1 (pbk.)
1. Penders, Tom. 2. Basketball coaches—United States—Biography. 3. University of Texas at Austin—Basketball—History. I. Title.

GV884.P43 D24 2000
796.323'092—dc21
[B] 99-088287

DEDICATION

To my beautiful wife and daughter, and my family, all of whom have offered their unwavering support and understanding during the past two years which allowed their husband, dad, son, and brother to work on "The Book."

TABLE OF CONTENTS

Acknowledgments

This book would have not been possible without the help and guidance from many different people. Thanks to Rebecca and Michael for their help in getting everything rolling, Cliff for his editorial guidance, Ed and Mickey for pointing me in the right direction, Frank, my agent, for believing in the project, and An, my editor, for patiently guiding me through the entire process. A special thanks to all those who gave up countless hours of their time to talk with me and discuss their time with Tom Penders and the University of Texas.

Introduction

When athletics and the University of Texas are mentioned in the same breath, it's more than likely the topic is football. Whether it's two older gentleman over coffee at a local diner in the middle of west Texas, or two radio broadcasters on a national sports talk show, football and the University of Texas go together like mashed potatoes and gravy. No doubt about it, in Texas, and specifically the University of Texas – football is, indeed, king.

Since the days of legendary football coach Darrell Royal and his national championship teams, fans of the Burnt Orange have followed football with such enthusiastic interest, a non-follower of the school might think these ardent supporters actually have sons playing in the games. However, in the last 15 years, the enthusiasm that once filled the former Memorial Stadium (now Darrell K. Royal-Texas Memorial Stadium) is guarded at best. Fans aren't sure what to expect one year to the next, and have endured a ride with more ups and downs than the Texas Hill Country.

Since Fred Akers left in 1986, Texas football hasn't come close to being considered the perennial power and national title contender it once was under Royal. Instead of the teams of the late 1960s and 70s that were consistently vying for the top spot in the nation, the football program is now consistent in only one respect – inconsistency. This lack of winning on a regular basis has not only turned the once stable atmosphere of Texas football into a coaching carousel (three head coaches in 12 years); it has also turned the stomachs of numerous fans. Many have decided to focus their interest and support elsewhere.

"One man's loss is another man's gain."
-Anonymous

Gaining support of those followers who left the confines of Memorial Stadium were those who held court, literally, across the street in the Erwin Center – the men's and women's basketball programs. If for no other reason than basketball fell next on the calendar.

For the women's program, this added fan support was just a bonus to their already impressive attendance numbers compared with other women's college basketball programs. For the men, however, it wasn't until the late 1980s when the migration of fans from Memorial Stadium to the Erwin Center became noticeable. Instead of the usual 4,000 or so fans attending each men's contest at the Erwin Center — a number regularly lower than the attendance at women's games — 10,000 or more supporters began filling the "Drum." At the time, the shift in fan support might have been attributed to fans trying to forget about another mediocre football season that had mercifully ended. But in the years to follow, it became obvious – the large crowds turning out at the Erwin Center from the late 1980s through the 1990s were not because of a waning interest in the football program, but because of an increasing interest in the successful basketball program. The once proud winning tradition found only a decade before in football, had switched from the grass to the hardwood. And fans took notice.

I. The Early Years

Chapter One

Opportunity Knocks

Kansas City's Kemper Arena was host site for the 1988 Final Four featuring two teams from the Big 8 in Kansas and Oklahoma, as well as perennial powerhouses Arizona and Duke. Fans of each school flocked to the Midwest with hopes of cheering their team on to victory. Coaches from around the country also converged on the city, not to watch the games, but to attend the annual National Association of Basketball Coaches (NABC) convention and trade show, held each year in the Final Four host city.

The NABC show, like any other professional convention, allows those attending a chance to mingle with their counterparts and find out the latest trends in the industry as well as the most recent advances in technology. Coaches attending the annual event regularly fill up sessions – often taught by nationally known coaches – which cover a variety of topics including offensive and defensive techniques and how to successfully use them. Although the backdrop for the show is one of learning about the profession including the Xs and Os, it also acts as a marketplace for the coaching industry, and a very prosperous one for those who are opportunistic.

It is not uncommon to see coaches visiting with other coaches or athletic directors on the trade show floor, in the hotel lobby, and sometimes even in the men's room. Whether it's in the capacity of head coach trying to find one or two assistants, or an up-and-coming coach trying to move up the ranks, coaches understand the importance of the NABC show and how it can provide quality employment opportunities not found any other time of the year. For coaches who have recently completed successful seasons, the number of opportunities can increase dramatically. In 1988, Tom Penders was a perfect example.

Penders, in just his second year as head coach, led the Rhode Island Rams to a 28-7 record and a berth in the Sweet 16, where they eventually lost by one point to Final Four participant Duke. Immediately following the season, the 42-year-old Penders became a hot commodity and his name was often mentioned as a possible candidate for numerous vacancies around the country.

One school on the fast track to acquire Penders' services was Rutgers, if for no other reason than the persistence of its athletic director Fred Gruninger, a close personal friend of Penders for more than 20 years. Gruninger was so intent on getting Penders to take over the job at Rutgers he made it a point to get Penders' ear before his Rhode Island squad earned its "Cinderella" status at the NCAA tournament and other suitors began knocking on his door. To do that, Gruninger approached Penders about the job at the Atlantic 10 Tournament that year. Although no hard figures were actually discussed, the amount was to be significantly higher than Penders' salary at Rhode Island of $47,500 base, and $25,000 from a shoe contract with Reebok. The two agreed they would officially discuss the matter at the upcoming Final Four in Kansas City once Penders received approval from his athletic director John Chuckran at

Rhode Island to talk with Rutgers.

Despite the considerable increase in salary he would receive if he took on the new position at the New Jersey school, Penders was still unsure of his decision. He loved Rhode Island. It was, after all, right next door to his home state of Connecticut, where he'd grown up and played basketball and baseball at the University of Connecticut. However, his business sense told him he should be rewarded for taking his team to the Sweet 16. By his own admission, he wasn't expecting the mother lode, but something that would take him out of the salary range he described as the "lower 10 percentile of college coaches in the entire country." When he left for Kansas City, he wasn't sure of what his decision was going to be, but he was leaning toward making the move to Rutgers.

Upon arrival in Kansas City, everything was going as planned. On Saturday, Penders attended the semifinal games. On Sunday, the day before the meeting with Gruninger, everything changed with one phone call. On the other end of the phone that day was University of Texas Athletic Director DeLoss Dodds.

Although there were rumors abounding in Austin as to who might replace former Texas coach Bob Weltlich, Dodds and the search committee had their sights set on Penders. According to one former athletic department administrator who spoke on the condition of anonymity, Penders was a perfect fit at the time for a variety of reasons. "If you really have a frame of reference of where the basketball program had been, there had been very little visibility nationally in terms of television. Texas basketball was not recognized nationally," the official said. "The attendance and the support of the program were not very significant at the time. Tom brought a lot of ingredients, a lot of expertise and experience in terms of building a basketball program that included national exposure and visibility. He knew it required a willingness to schedule, willingness to go on the road, and a willingness to play a game on television wherever. He could do that and then he would go and work the community and bring some excitement. In that regard, he had a lot of experience in doing that."

Dodds, never having met Penders before, was calling for a variety of reasons, the first of which was to introduce himself. After the salutation was done, Dodds cut to the chase and told Penders the real reasons he was calling. He informed Penders that there was a vacant head coaching position available at Texas. Before he made the call, Dodds wasn't even sure if Penders was aware of the Texas opening. Dodds then proceeded to probe and see if there was any interest from Penders.

After getting what he interpreted as positive feedback from Penders, Dodds got to his final reason for calling – the interview. Dodds asked Penders if he would come over to his hotel room for an interview during Final Four weekend. Caught by surprise and completely unaware the Texas position was available, Penders told Dodds he would have to get back with him. Dodds said he understood and gave Penders his hotel phone number. As soon as the two hung up, Penders was making a call back to Rhode Island to find out if the mystery man he had just spoken to was in fact, who he claimed to be.

"When he told me his name, I wrote it down because I had never heard the name before. I didn't know anybody down there," he said. "I called my secretary at home and asked her to look up his name in the college blue book. When she read me the name, I said, 'This guy must be legitimate.'" After verifying Dodds and his status, Penders called him back to set up a time for the interview. The meeting was scheduled on

Monday, the same day Penders was to interview with Gruninger.

On Monday morning, the same day of the national championship, which was scheduled for later that evening, Penders met with Dodds at the Hyatt. Upon arrival, Penders, without resume and dressed in only a warm-up suit (he had already worn his suit twice during the weekend), met Dodds and his assistant athletic director Craig Helwig for the first time.

Although Dodds and Helwig were formal in their dress wearing suits, the meeting itself was very informal. During the two-hour long session, Helwig asked most of the questions. At the conclusion of the interview Dodds told Penders he would get back to him later in the day. Penders left the hotel and headed off to his next interview with Rutgers.

After concluding his second interview of the day, Penders went back to his hotel to try and relax. The relaxation didn't last long and just after 3 p.m., Penders received another phone call from Dodds, who asked if Penders would fly down to Texas and meet with a committee made up of alumni, administrators and the university president. Penders, once again, caught somewhat off guard by Dodds' question, was frank with Dodds and fired back with a question of his own, "How much money are we talking about?" Penders asked. Dodds said it would be around $400,000. Penders would essentially be getting a $100,000 raise from the Rutgers position he had all intentions of taking. Now, he was faced with turning down one program and an athletic director he was very familiar with for another he had no previous notions about, and an athletic director he had met just days before.

Penders agreed to meet with the committee, but he and his wife had to first make arrangements for their two children to remain in Kansas City. (Ironically for Penders, his career at the University of Texas would come full circle 10 years later when he would coach his final game as University of Texas head basketball coach in the same city.)

After leaving their kids with relatives and altering the family plans, which included flying back to Rhode Island the next day, Penders and his wife were flown to the D/FW Airport Hyatt on the private jet of alum Mike Myers, a well-known supporter at UT who, in March 1999, had the new track and field complex named in his honor. In Dallas, Penders met with Dodds, Helwig and Myers, as well as legendary former football coach Darrell Royal, and Jay Arnette, a former standout basketball player at Texas.

Like the first encounter, the meeting was on the informal side, with each member of the committee asking questions of Penders. In retrospect, according to Penders, it was most likely the response to a question asked by Royal near the end of the meeting that got him the job.

In his dry, countrified manner, Royal asked Penders exactly what he knew about the University of Texas. Penders told the coach, whom he admired greatly and followed closely during his days as head coach for the football team, "I know the colors are orange and white. I know Tommy Nobis wore number 60, Earl Campbell wore number 20, and James Street wore number 16. I can also hum the fight song and I can do an imitation of Lindsey Nelson, the announcer at the Cotton Bowl."

Everyone in the room smiled.

Penders learned later that after he left the meeting room, all in attendance expressed how they were impressed with the coach, but some questioned his choice of jewelry, in particular, a ring on his pinky. One committee member even asked, "This guy wears a pinky ring. Do you think he'd fit the image at Texas?" Royal discounted the questioner by telling the group, "If he's going to recruit great players, then I don't think that's going to work against him." When told this story later, Penders admitted he was superstitious and had worn the championship fast-pitch softball ring because he had all season and it got them to the Sweet 16.

Back in his hotel room following the first meeting, Penders realized in the flurry of activity he hadn't even spoken to his athletic director at Rhode Island, John Chuckran, about the Texas job. With a break in the action, he had a chance to call. In the phone conversation, Penders asked Chuckran if interviewing with Texas was OK. Chuckran told him it was fine. He then instructed Penders not to sign anything until he had spoken with Rhode Island president, Ted Eddy. Soon after the conversation with Chuckran, Dodds called Penders and asked to meet with him.

Dodds made it to Penders' room and cut to the chase, "If we offered you the job would you take it?"

"You have to put something in writing and I still want to see the campus first," Penders answered.

Dodds immediately grabbed a piece of paper and wrote the basic salary, guarantees, shoe money, and television money – all totaling around $400,000. He then signed it. Penders unofficially accepted the job at that point in time, but insisted on seeing the campus and the city.

"I didn't know what Austin was about and I'd never seen the University of Texas on television," he would say later.

Soon after it was agreed, in principle, that Penders would accept the job, Penders' wife and Dodds' wife Mary Ann returned from an outing at the area shops. The four then left for a cocktail hour which university president William Cunningham had flown in to attend.

After a few minutes of mingling with the other guests, Penders and his wife were greeted by Cunningham. Soon after, Cunningham got the attention of those gathered in the room and offered a toast to the new head basketball coach. Although it was not official, it was the next best thing. Penders, if everything went as planned on the trip to Austin, would become the next head basketball coach at the University of Texas.

Penders, optimistic about the upcoming visit, wanted to make sure he had a clear mind. If something didn't feel right about the visit, it wasn't too late to back out. He also remembered back to the conversation he and SMU coach Dave Bliss had days before at the NCAA tournament. After being approached by Dodds about the position at Texas, Penders approached Bliss, knowing full well Bliss was familiar with the coaching situation at Texas because of his experience coaching in the same conference and his strong relationship with outgoing Texas coach Bob Weltlich.

During that visit Penders bluntly asked Bliss what he thought of the University of Texas program. Bliss responded by telling Penders the opportunity was great at Texas but at the same time, he warned him to be careful. He said first and foremost, get everything in writing. When Penders asked why, Bliss said Weltlich, a close friend and former assistant, who worked with him on Bob Knight's staff, had been promised a lot of things that never happened. Penders also inquired about the team. Bliss said Travis Mays was the only promising player on the squad and if Penders took the job, it would definitely be a rebuilding project. Before concluding their conversation, Bliss offered Penders one final tip on recruiting, telling him that in order to be successful he should plan on tapping the plentiful junior college market of Texas. With what Bliss had told him, including the unsolicited advice on recruiting, Penders knew the situation was right. He would be cautious when it came to getting things in writing, and he would rebuild this program as he had done at Tufts, Columbia, Fordham, and most recently, Rhode Island.

They arrived in Austin that night. On the mini-tour, Penders and his wife were shown the campus including the Erwin Center. "This is where you play and practice," one of the university officials said. Penders was impressed. "Wow! This is incredible!"

After seeing the remainder of the campus, including his future office in Bellmont Hall, Penders knew Texas was where he wanted to be. It was now official. Penders was the next head basketball coach and it would be announced the next day at a press conference. Later that evening, Penders called Chuckran and told him he was going to take the job at Texas. Chuckran told Penders he needed to talk with President Eddy first, before he officially accepted.

Eddy tried to talk Penders out of accepting the new position, but after he heard the numbers being offered by Texas, he could only wish Penders and his family the best.

On April 6, 1988, Thomas Vincent Penders was officially announced as the 22nd head basketball coach at the University of Texas.

Chapter Two

First Things First

Soon after being announced as new head coach, a voice from Texas basketball's past called to congratulate the new coach and like Bliss, warned him. It was the 20th coach at the University of Texas – Abe Lemons.

Lemons, who had coached at the university for six seasons including the NIT championship season of 1978, and who was the last coach to lead Texas to the NCAA tournament, told Penders that he learned during his tenure on the Forty Acres (name for the campus because its expanse covers 40 acres) not to be too trusting of Dodds. He warned Penders to get everything in writing.

"Hey, I got a contract," Penders responded.

Penders thought about his remarks, remembering the contract was still not an official document, but only a piece of paper Dodds had handwritten on in the Dallas hotel room which contained the terms of the contract and his signature. From that conversation, Penders knew he needed to get an official contract. This soon became a top priority.

In an effort to get the contract done quickly, Penders called on the services of Mitch Dukov, a financial consultant who had previously worked with the university on Bob Weltlich's contract. Penders thought Dukov's familiarity with the university would get the contract done in a relatively efficient manner. Unfortunately, he was wrong.

On Dukov's first trip to the university, he had all intentions of meeting with Dodds and converting the contract written on a piece of paper into an official, legally binding document. Dodds, however, referred Dukov and the contract issue to university attorney W.O. Shultz. Not a good start for Dukov, and it would only get worse.

In the meeting with Shultz, both sides came in with their own contracts. Dukov, on behalf of Penders, was willing to accept the university's version of the contract, if they would only add a clause on termination. Penders, as he had had written in previous contracts, insisted on the contract stating that he could be terminated from the university if "he knowingly and intentionally violated material provisions of NCAA rules or state laws." Something, according to Penders, that was considered a serious violation and he knowingly did. When approached about the clause, Shultz, with Dodds' original signed piece of paper in hand, gave Dukov an ultimatum – either Penders signed the university's contract, or he could go somewhere else. Dukov left the meeting in a state of shock with no official contract.

The final contract was not completed until later in the first season. Despite that, Penders did get paid according to the original terms of the contract Dodds had handwritten on the piece of paper.While Dukov tried to iron out the kinks of the contract, Penders' first order of business was assessing the program. As a part of the assessment, he wanted to get feedback from the players so he met individually with each player on the squad. When all the player meetings were completed, Penders recognized one common thing – frustration. Each player appeared to be beaten down following the

16-13 season in which they advanced to the second round of the NIT. Surprisingly, individual after individual expressed a positive attitude when the future of the program was discussed.

"There was excitement because it was something new coming in – having a coach with some enthusiasm," said Travis Mays, second all-time leading scorer at the University of Texas and a junior during Penders' first year. "Coach Penders came in saying that he was going to run and we all wanted to do that because we weren't drawing any fans, weren't winning any games. We just had a style of play that just wasn't fun to watch and wasn't fun to play."

Even with the positive attitude, there was still some uncertainty. Mays said the players knew they had to re-establish themselves under the new coach. "It was scary. Those two years under Bob (Weltlich) were thrown out the window. It was about asserting yourself over again."

In order to make the transition and adjustments to the new coaching staff easier, several individuals from inside the program including Darrell Royal and then-baseball coach Cliff Gustafson, as well as players such as Mays, suggested Penders should retain the services of Assistant Coach Eddie Oran. Oran was a favorite of the players because of his likeable demeanor on and off the court.

"They (the players) all had pretty good relationships with me," Oran said. "I think there were also some people in the community, both inside and outside the program, that voiced the opinion of give me a shot, or really take a close look. I think that really helped." Oran's connection with the players went deep because he was, in most cases, the coach who had recruited and got each player to come to Texas.

Mays said it was Oran who understood the players and what they were going through. "He was the one who would try to keep us positive and keep us going even though he couldn't go against the things that his boss (Weltlich) was saying. The players had a great relationship with him. A lot of players wanted him to stay because that would give us a little bit of a comfort zone. It would give us a buffer between the new coach and the players because he could tell the new coach what he thought about each and every one of us and he would be on point."

Penders was impressed. "I assured them that I was going to keep all the positive things (from the previous regime), like Eddie."

After Penders listened to each athlete provide his feedback on the program, Penders made a commitment. It was something the players hadn't heard since they had arrived at the university – they would make the NCAA tournament.

"I know that was the only thing he was putting in our minds. He was saying the NCAA is what we're shooting for. We're not shooting for the NIT. We're not shooting for any type of invitational tournament. We want the NCAA," Mays recalls Penders saying during his early days in Austin. "And that's what we wanted to hear. We were used to hearing if you don't do this or you don't do that, you're not going to go here. You're not going to make this."

In the subsequent months, Penders settled in, trying to get things organized for the upcoming season. He got his staff in place. He brought with him one assistant from Rhode Island in Jamie Ciampaglio, while his top assistant, Al Skinner, stayed behind and succeeded him as head coach. Penders kept Oran and Dave Miller of the previous

Texas coaching staff because they were familiar with the recruiting grounds of Texas and the South.

With his coaching staff set, Penders concentrated on generating excitement and enthusiasm for a program that had no national recognition and whose local fan base was severely lacking. Penders hoped to create a home-court atmosphere like other big-time college programs in the country. He wanted the arena filled each game with raucous fans, a necessary component in recruiting, but one he also believed could result in as much as 10 points a game. To do this, Penders went to the fans. First, he went to the students on campus, then to alumni.

Penders was regularly seen at meetings of alumni and booster groups throughout the state, promoting his new, fast-paced style of basketball. In those engagements, he described how the team would press and try to create turnovers, which in turn would produce a transition game and allow the team to score 100 points on any given night. He also christened the team with a new nickname – the "Runnin' Horns." The fans loved it and were genuinely excited about Texas basketball and the upcoming season. In a state and a school known for its football tradition, basketball was getting support and all this without the team even setting foot on the court. This excitement was something the school hadn't seen in years for basketball, and was quite welcomed by Dodds and the administration.

Initially, the university administration didn't have high expectations, either. Understandably, they didn't want a team like the majority of Weltlich's squads, which just managed to keep their heads above water with .500 records year in, year out. The main concern of administration was putting an entertaining team on the floor that could put fans in the seats, and win more games in the process. By no means did it expect Penders to take the team to the top in the early years, just out of the doldrums. They didn't say, "We want a top-10 program." They just said, "Please save us. We're drowning. We need somebody to lead us out of the wilderness."

Chapter Three

The First Season, 1988 – 1989

Before the first organized practices under the new head coach began, players, like the fans, approached the season with guarded enthusiasm. They had heard from Penders directly as well as seen the reports of their coach and his speeches to various groups around the state about this new style of basketball they would be playing. They heard the new nickname. To them, all of it was a welcome change, or at least they hoped.

"He was saying we were going to run after TV timeouts, we're going to run here and run there," said Travis Mays. "He was saying a whole bunch of stuff that was exciting us all and what we wanted to hear. It was a totally different approach than Bob's. It was just refreshing to hear the stuff like that. But still, we were saying, 'We're going to see if he's just saying that or are we going to have some fun when we play.'"

When the first practices began, Mays and the rest of his teammates recognized the difference. Running was definitely part of the game plan. "The practices were different. The practices were much more relaxed. We were used to going hard. He never had to crack the whip to make us go hard. If anything, he would try to throw some things into practice to make them more fun. We couldn't believe they were happening because we had never had anything like that.

"Tom told us early on we're not going to line up and do a whole lot of running (drills) because we're going to run enough in practice. That was refreshing and gave you energy and made you *want* to come to the gym instead of dreading it."

Although the players had a new, positive outlook toward the future, Penders wasn't as sure. "I didn't have real high hopes for the team because Travis (Mays) was the only guy back. But I believe in positive teaching, positive reinforcement and setting high goals."

As the season and first game got closer, the enthusiasm of the players began to grow. Subsequently, each began to show more promise on the court. The excitement, which had started with the fans and administration months earlier, had spread to the players at just the right time – right before the season. It was contagious. The Texas basketball train was rolling full steam ahead. Unfortunately for the train's conductor – Penders – his excitement in the new program took a hit before the team ever played a game.

It came shortly after the team began practices, when to Penders' surprise, the team never made it over to the Erwin Center, the facility he was shown on his first visit to Austin and where he was told "the team played and practiced." Instead, the team practiced only on rare occasions at the Erwin Center that first year and most of the time at Gregory Gymnasium, the home court gym for the Texas basketball team from 1931-1977. Gregory Gymnasium, which had a $26-million renovation in 1996-1997, was in 1988, according to Penders, "a place that should have been condemned."

The 57-year old building at the time was without air conditioning and had a floor in serious need of repair, or replacement. To make matters worse, Penders and his squad had a window of opportunity for each practice where the team had to come in, get in their practice, and get out, in order for others to use the dilapidated facility. "We only had it for two hours because the recreational groups were in there."

Although Penders expected more out of a school that was paying him $400,000 a year and was known for its big-time college athletics, there wasn't much he could do. He was brand new at the school. It wouldn't look good if he created an upheaval with the administration right out of the gate. Instead, he decided they would overcome the obstacle. Just deal with it the best he and the players could and make things work, was his thinking. Unbeknownst to him, this particular situation would rear its ugly head again, only in the coming years it would get worse.

After several scrimmages with a team of soldiers from Fort Hood and an exhibition team from Australia, the Horns opened the 1988-89 regular season a long way from home in Honolulu, Hawaii.

The Regular Season
The First Game

On November 25, 1988, Tom Penders made his debut as the University of Texas head basketball coach against the Pepperdine Waves in the first game of the Tip-Off Tournament in Hawaii. The debut was a success for Penders and his new team. In front of burnt-orange clad fans scattered sporadically throughout Blaisdell Arena, the Penders-led Longhorns defeated Pepperdine 82-79 on a last-minute steal by transfer player Joey Wright.

Two nights later against the host-team Hawaii, the Longhorns suffered their first loss under Penders. The Longhorns stumbled out of the blocks early but recovered by half-time for a 46-46 tie. In the second half the Horns built a nine-point lead, only to see it vanish down the stretch as the Rainbow Warriors defeated Texas 85-84 and sent the Longhorns back to the mainland with a 1-1 record.

Although Penders would have liked to return to Austin with two wins, he was not upset with the overall team performance. He was, however, concerned with the performance of his expected star player, Travis Mays. In the first two contests of the season the junior guard had scored a combined total of 21 points on seven of 25 shooting, and appeared to be playing scared.

"I got off to a really bad start because still, everything had been practiced but when the game situations come around and you've had two years of everything so structured, you still want to get out there and take a good shot," Mays said. "What ended up being a good shot later on (under Penders), would have never been good shots in Bob Weltlich's system."

Mays said he vividly remembers being approached by Penders about his struggles. "He said, 'Well son, I guess you want to sit over here beside me on the bench.' 'No, I want to play,' I answered. "He said, 'I can't have my top gun being shy with the ball. If you can't get that Bob Weltlich system out of your game, you're going to sit over here and watch the game beside me.' He wasn't going to have to tell me that twice," said Mays, who is now in his tenth year of professional basketball.

Despite the loss in Hawaii, the campus back in Austin was abuzz about the new basketball program. The Sam Houston State Bearkats were in town and it was the first chance to see Tom Penders and his up-tempo style of basketball in person.

UT came out sluggish as they had in their previous game against Hawaii. The fans that had expected to see the run-and-gun style were disappointed early on when the Longhorns posted a total of just three points six minutes into the contest. But Texas recovered, particularly in the second half, when Mays, fresh off his conversation with Penders, came to life. The junior guard, who remained in a funk in the first half converting just one of eight, hit seven out of 10 and scored 19 of his 21 points in the second half. The Bearkats hung tough, but Texas held on for an 87-79 victory.

Admittedly, the performance against Sam Houston wasn't worthy of sending a tape to the Basketball Hall of Fame, as Penders said after the game, but it was a win nonetheless. By all accounts, including the 7,000 plus in attendance, it was a successful home opener and a promising preview of things to come.

In the next contest, Texas fans witnessed something that hadn't occurred since 1982 as the Horns reached the 100-point plateau in a game against Northwestern State of Louisiana. The 5,560 in attendance at the Erwin Center watched as the Longhorns and Mays, who finished with a team-high 24 points, pulled out the 109-104 victory. The point total for the Horns marked the fifth-highest total ever at the school and the most since Abe Lemons coached the team to a 113-80 victory over SMU in 1980.

In four out of the next five games the 100-point mark wasn't such a thing of the past. Against Oral Roberts in Tulsa, Okla., the Horns, led by Mays' 24 and Wright's 23, set several new school records en route to a 119-91 victory. The 119-point total, which included a team-record 10 three-pointers, was the most ever scored on the road by a Longhorn squad and the second highest total ever. It also marked the first time since 1978 that a Texas team had scored 100 points in consecutive games.

The only sub-100 game during the five-game span occurred against Lehigh in the first round of the Longhorn Classic. Although the Longhorns didn't hit the 100-point mark, they were close. With 7,313 in attendance, the Horns scored 96 points against the Engineers in a 96-73 rout.

Texas returned to its 100-point ways in the championship game of the Longhorn Classic scoring 103 in a blowout over the Tennessee-Chattanooga Moccasins, 103-88. More than 6,600 in the Erwin Center watched as Travis Mays poured in 38 points and Lance Blanks added 19 for the team's fifth consecutive win.

Although the two games at home were nice, Penders knew the Longhorn Classic, which was created during Weltlich's tenure, was set up to add a couple of numbers to the win column. Even though Penders liked winning as much as the next coach, he was a firm believer in quality over quantity. If he had the opportunity to play a small, no-name team at home for an almost certain victory, or a top-10 team on the road and gain valuable television exposure and experience for his players, Penders, without hesitation, would do the latter.

"He was very interested in building a program as opposed to how many games you could buy and get wins down the road," said a former athletic department administrator who asked not to be identified. "He was willing to help to build the schedule and build the program. If you were going to get this basketball program to the level that everybody wanted, you were going to have to go play some of those people on the road. Tom was completely willing to play anybody, anytime, anywhere."

Since his predecessor had already set the schedule and there were wins for the taking at the Longhorn Classic, Penders and his squad were obliged to take them.

Following coronation as victors of the Longhorn Classic, Texas won back-to-back games scoring 100 points and winning in convincing fashion over Long Beach State and Southern Utah State. In the first game on the road in Long Beach, Calif., Texas, led by Heggs' 31 points and Mays' 26, cruised to a 117-86 victory over the 49ers and, in the process, extended its winning streak to six.

Back in the Erwin Center and in front of 8,456 fans, UT orchestrated another dominating win over lesser competition with a 117-78 defeat of the Southern Utah State Thunderbirds. With the win, the Longhorns' record stood at an impressive 8-1, and would be put to the test in the final two games before conference play.

Following the Christmas break and a 10-day hiatus, the Horns went north of the Red River to participate in the All-College Tournament in Oklahoma City.

Against the Oklahoma State Cowboys, Penders and the Longhorns were up to the challenge in front of a partisan sellout crowd of 14,005. The Horns pulled off a come-from-behind victory in dramatic fashion, 85-84. The win improved UT's record to 9-1 — a considerable improvement from the season before when the team was 5-5 after 10 games.

In the final game of 1988, the Longhorns hoped to bring in the New Year with a bang in the finals of the All-College Tournament against their rivals from north of the Red River, the sixth-ranked Oklahoma Sooners.

Unfortunately, it was Oklahoma who closed out 1988 with a bang as they outscored Texas in a blowout win, 124-95. Mays had a solid offensive performance with 34 points, but it wasn't enough as the Longhorns returned home with a 9-2 record heading into Southwest Conference action.

When the Arkansas Razorbacks came to town, a crowd of 12,647 fans converged on the Erwin Center to watch the top two teams in the SWC battle it out for conference supremacy. In a game that featured two push-it-up-the-floor teams, fans of the Burnt Orange and White were pleased with what they saw initially. Texas led by as many as 11 points in the first half of the fast-paced game.

But it wasn't enough as the Hogs prevailed with a 99-92 victory. With the loss, Texas dropped to 10-3, and 1-1 in the conference while Arkansas improved to 8-2 and 2-0 in SWC action.

Following the disappointing loss, the Horns traveled to Houston and Autry Court to take on the Rice Owls. Mays scored 32 points and set two SWC records with nine three-pointers and 17 attempts from behind the arc as the Longhorns won in a tight contest, 66-65.

Several days later Texas returned to Houston and Hofheinz Pavilion to face the Houston Cougars. Wright scored on the rebound of his own miss as time expired from the clock and Texas quieted the 6,698 fans in attendance with an exciting 88-86 win. With the last-second triumph, UT improved its record to 12-3 overall and 3-1 in SWC.

The Horns returned home to face Texas Tech in another SWC meeting just four days later in front of a raucous crowd of more than 13,000. Putting on an offensive display for the hometown crowd, Mays scored 35 points and Blanks added 26 as the Horns blew a 21-point lead late, but held on for the 90-86 victory and their 13th win of the season.

The Horns then headed to Nashville, home of the Vanderbilt Commodores, where a crowd of more than 15,000 packed Memorial Gymnasium to see if head coach C.M. Newton could earn his 500th career win.

Those in attendance, as well as many watching the regional television broadcast on CBS, got their first glimpse of Penders and the Runnin' Horns. The Commodores went on a late run in the first half that carried over into the second and UT never recovered. Despite 30 points from Travis Mays, fans of the black and gold went home happy as Newton earned his 500th win in convincing fashion with a 94-79 defeat of the Longhorns.

Texas stayed on the road but returned to conference play four nights later in front of a capacity crowd of 7,166 at Daniel-Meyer Coliseum in Fort Worth. It was the meeting of the first-place TCU Horned Frogs, with a 6-0 record in conference, and the second-place Longhorns, who were close behind at 4-1.

As the game started, everyone knew it was going to be a battle of styles. In the end, another strong performance from Lance Blanks and Travis Mays was more than enough as the Longhorns pulled off the minor upset on the road, 94-84.

Just past the midway point of the first season the Horns sat tied atop the SWC standings. Those administrators and others who weren't sure about Penders and his run-and-gun style were impressed not only by the number of wins, but by the number of fans. Even the players who had expected a turnaround were somewhat surprised by the overall success. Now, with Penders at the helm, the players were regularly getting congratulated as they walked to classes around campus.

Even Penders was somewhat surprised with the team's success, but continued to push his players, remembering his commitment before the season and knowing that the final destination – an NCAA Tournament berth – had never been given to a team halfway through the season.

With a tie for the lead in the conference, the Horns played host to their rivals from College Station in front of the first sellout crowd in three years. The buzz before the game was palpable as many of the 16,231 fans in attendance expected a blowout of Texas A&M, and why not? Texas had given SMU a shellacking just a few nights before and although the Mustangs' conference record (3-4) wasn't stellar, it was considerably better than the 1-6 mark brought in by the team from Aggieland.The Horns held off their rivals for a closer-than-expected 85-80 win. UT improved to 7-1 in the SWC and 16-4 overall.

On the road at Arkansas, Texas looked for a payback. After the 99-92 loss to the Razorbacks at the Erwin Center, the Horns wanted to exact revenge on the Hogs' home turf. It was also an opportunity for the Longhorns to prove they were capable of beating a highly-regarded team, which had yet to be done in the first year under Penders, and to gain the outright conference lead. The Razorbacks and head coach Nolan Richardson had other ideas. The Hogs turned away any thoughts of a Texas upset despite 30 points from Heggs, with a convincing 105-82 victory.

Trying to rebound from the tough loss in Fayetteville, the Texas players wanted to show the 9,269 fans in attendance at the Erwin Center and those watching on television that they were better than their performance against Arkansas. The Rice Owls and their 9-13 record overall appeared to be the perfect team to do just that. Building on a 23-point halftime lead the Horns defeated the Owls, 116-74.

The Horned Frogs of TCU were on the agenda for UT when they came to town for the regular season home finale. With 13,460 fans in attendance – the second-largest crowd of the season – the Horns wanted to end the season at home on a positive note for the appreciative and ever-growing fan base. Texas took control early and never looked back en route to a 107-82 victory.

The win was the tenth time Texas had reached the century mark during the season and added to their record. With two regular-season games remaining, Texas had scored a school-record 2,607 points for the season.

Texas finished up the regular season with two road games, the first of which was in Dallas against SMU. The Ponies, in their final home game of the season, came out a different team from the one Texas had embarrassed by 31 points a month earlier.

The Longhorns salvaged an 82-79 victory after a controversial call in the waning seconds. With the win, Texas temporarily had sole possession of first place with a 12-3 record in the SWC and a 22-6 record overall.

In the regular season finale with a four-game winning streak on the line, the Longhorns hoped to get a win on the road in College Station and earn a share of the regular season championship with Arkansas. It wasn't meant to be.

The Aggies were motivated on two counts, the first of which was that their hated rivals were in town. Second, a win could possibly save head coach Shelby Metcalf's job. A boisterous crowd of 7,462, or 38 short of capacity and about 5,000 more than the Aggies had averaged coming into the contest, showed up at G. Rollie White Coliseum.

What they saw, to their pleasure, was a dismal Texas shooting performance that allowed the Aggies to take a convincing 49-30 halftime lead and go on to an upset 106-89 victory.

Despite the poor finish, the UT men's basketball team and its fans had something to cheer about. A 22-7 regular season record was proof enough, but the prospects of getting a berth in the postseason, particularly the NCAA tournament, were more promising.

For his efforts, Mays was selected Southwest Conference Player of the Year just before the team headed to Dallas' Reunion Arena and the SWC Tournament.

The SWC Tournament

In the first game of the Southwest Conference Tournament, Texas had another battle on its hands against the SMU Mustangs. Still stinging from the controversial loss less than two weeks earlier, the Mustangs wanted revenge.

Revenge, however, didn't prove to be enough motivation against the more-talented Longhorn squad. It took overtime, but Texas won the game 93-91 with UT's final four points coming from Mays, who finished the game with 20. With the victory, Texas earned a berth in the second round against TCU.

In the second-round matchup, the Horns trailed the Horned Frogs by as many as 13 points in the first half. But Texas rallied late in the second half and tied the game to send it into overtime – the second extra session for the Horns in as many games. In overtime, Lance Blanks scored the first five points and Texas pulled away. The Horns, in front of capacity crowd of 16,240, were headed to the finals with a 93-89 win.

In the finals, the Longhorns faced a familiar foe, and one they had yet to beat under Penders – Nolan Richardson and the Arkansas Razorbacks.

The Hogs got off to a quick start in the first half as they opened up a 30-15 lead over the Longhorns in front of a capacity crowd at Reunion Arena, or Barnhill South as many referred to it because of the large gathering of Arkansas fans who always made the trip to Dallas. Those who made the trip weren't disappointed as the Hogs pulled away from Texas in the end with a 100-76 victory and were crowned SWC Tournament Champions.

The Horns, despite the disappointing loss, were still confident the NCAA Tournament Selection Committee would recognize that they were still deserving of an at-large bid to the Big Dance, and would reward them justly.

They were right.

For the first time since 1979, UT was in the NCAA Tournament and the commitment Penders made soon after taking the job had come true. There wasn't much time to celebrate. As a No. 11 seed, the Horns faced a tough ACC team in the sixth-seeded Georgia Tech Yellow Jackets. Penders wasn't bothered by the lower seed, and in fact, relished the opportunity to be the underdog. Not only would the expectations of Longhorn supporters not be as high – being content with just making the tournament – it would allow his team, as the case had been at his previous coaching stops, to surprise the opponent. Penders knew this team in particular was better than a No. 11 seed and they were setting out to prove it.

The NCAA Tournament

Against Georgia Tech in the first round of the Midwest Regional at Reunion Arena in Dallas, the Longhorns looked like a team prepared for battle. They jumped out to a 3-2 lead and never trailed. In the second half, Georgia Tech made several runs. Each time, the Horns responded. At the final buzzer, Texas had earned the 76-70 victory.

Following the game, members of the media reporting on the contest repeatedly remarked on how calm and relaxed the Longhorns played. Words like "unfazed" and "focused" were regularly used to describe the Horns and their first appearance in the Big Dance in 10 years.

Mays, who finished the game with a team-high 23 points, said the team's quality performance in the first-round game could be directly attributed to two things, the first of which was preparation by Penders and his staff. "We didn't change. What we did from day one, we did throughout. We started one way and that's how we finished. A lot of coaches will get to playoffs and start changing things. We didn't do that. We knew we were good."

He said the second reason for the solid performance against Georgia Tech was that the Longhorn players were motivated to prove wrong all those who doubted that Texas was a legitimate NCAA Tournament team. "We felt that we had to prove ourselves. We felt like the underdogs anywhere we went and we just wanted to prove ourselves so bad. Everybody figured that Georgia Tech was the better team and was supposed to beat Texas. We never thought that for a second. We couldn't wait to get the game on just to show the nation how good we were. That's what we wanted to do."

The players, fans, administration, athletic department and everyone else associated with the Burnt Orange were ecstatic. It was the first time since Leon Black guided the Horns in 1972 that a Longhorn basketball team had earned a victory in the NCAA Tournament. Penders was very pleased with the performance and happy to see those players, who had endured the previous basketball regime, finally receive acclaim for their efforts. He was also happy to see the team come together against the odds, destroying the claim that they were unable to beat a quality opponent, and doing so against a solid squad from Georgia Tech. But he also realized there was still a task at hand. You don't make it very far in the NCAA if you celebrate like you just won the national championship after every game. It was time to get back to work and prepare for another tough opponent in the Missouri Tigers, who were led by All-American Doug Smith.

Penders was somewhat familiar with the Tigers from the 1987-88 season, when Missouri was one of the three teams upset by his Rhode Island squad on its way to the Sweet 16. This year, the Tigers knew Penders and what his team was capable of. By no means were they overlooking Texas, as evidenced by their performance.

The sixth-ranked Tigers took the lead against the Horns early in the contest and never looked back. Despite being outsized, Texas trailed by only six with less than eight minutes remaining. But every time the Longhorns threatened, Missouri answered. When the game concluded, Texas came out on the short end of a 108-89 score. Smith lived up to his All-American billing, scoring 32 points.

Mays said the Horns weren't overconfident against Missouri after the big win over Georgia Tech in the opening round, but they weren't as sharp either. "We lost that edge of feeling we had something to prove, and we ran against a Missouri team that was good. If we would have had all the hunger that we had and the same willingness to prove something, we probably could have edged them."

Unfortunately, Missouri came out a hungrier team, and as a result was advancing to the Sweet 16. The fairy tale first season under Tom Penders and his team's run in the NCAA Tournament ended on a sour note, as is the case for 63 teams every year. Blanks, Mays and Wright combined for a 64-point effort, but it still wasn't enough. It was, however, something to build on for next season. Could Tom Penders possibly improve on his first season? Only time would tell.

The First Off-Season Longhorn Basketball Produces Windfall

Shortly after the conclusion of the first season under Penders, in which the team finished with a 25-9 record, went to the NCAA Tournament, and fan turnout was the largest gain in the nation from the previous years' attendance, the university received more good news related to the basketball program.

According to the assistant men's athletic director, Doug Messer, the school was expected to turn a profit of more than $220,000. Sure, the profit was a cause for excitement, but even more so considering the previous basketball season and the final year under Weltlich when the school had lost $62,000.

Messer said a large portion of the profit was a direct result from the NCAA Tournament appearance that earned the school $200,000. Other reasons for the profit were increased attendance, more television appearances, and donations from alumni – all things Penders was brought in to accomplish.

Penders Shuffles Assistant Coaches

Although things, for the most part, were positive during the first season, Penders had several issues he wanted to discuss with Dodds. He believed, even with the success of the program the first year, there was more that could be done to improve on that success and build toward the future. Recruiting was a priority. He wanted assistant coaches who could go out and find talent that wasn't already committed to the North Carolinas and Dukes of college basketball. He had good recruiters in place, but he wanted someone who knew and had access to the plentiful junior college ranks of Texas. He found that person in the piney woods of East Texas in Vic Trilli. To make the acquisition, Penders moved out Dave Miller, who took on a similar position at Arizona State.

Adding to the coaching mix, Penders also, on the recommendation of Dodds, hired Tom Douglass as a volunteer assistant. Douglass, who had played under Abe Lemons, returned to UT to get his degree and Dodds thought Douglass could provide the coaching staff with valuable assistance. Although the hiring, as the case is for most volunteer assistant positions, was insignificant at the time, it was Douglass' release a year later and his involvement with the program years later that would become significant.

In addition to hiring Trilli and Douglass, Penders had several other items on the agenda he wanted to put on the table before the team started its march into his second season. Among those, discussing the likelihood of getting a practice facility in the plans that would be devoted solely to the men's and women's basketball teams, and one that would include a locker room, film room and weight room.

Penders was concerned about a practice facility after the first season because his team was allowed to practice at the old Gregory Gym, only on a limited basis. And the times when it was available, the dilapidated facility itself was not conducive to quality workouts. The gym also didn't have a film room, so the players and coaches were limited to watching game film, which was taped with old video equipment (10-year-old camera), in the Erwin Center or in the basketball office.

"If there was a concert in there or something going on (in the Erwin Center), we didn't have use of our locker room and we had nowhere to show film to our players," Penders said. "We'd have a game coming up and we'd have no room. Instead, we had to get two or three players at a time and have them watch it in our office (in Bellmont Hall)."

This proved problematic because instead of the entire team watching the breakdown of the tape and learning from each other's mistakes, Penders and his staff were forced to make the same point repeatedly to the smaller individual groups.

While a practice facility was the top priority on his list, with the film room and new film equipment following close behind, Penders also wanted a facility that had a weight room that would allow the players to train during the off-season, and maintain their conditioning during the basketball season. In a related issue, Penders wanted to acquire the services of a full-time strength coach, a key ingredient that had not been present on a regular basis since his hiring. During the first season the basketball team shared a strength coach with the track and football teams.

With the somewhat limited resources available to the basketball program during that first season, Penders realized he had taken things for granted at Rhode Island where a strength coach was dedicated specifically to the basketball team and a film room was available at the team's discretion.

After Penders proposed the items to Dodds, he opted to wait and see what action, if any, Dodds would take on his proposal. In the meantime, the players and coaches would shuttle between Gregory Gym and other facilities scattered about town for practice. They would watch film in the Erwin Center locker room whenever it was available. And they would train in an old weight room at Gregory Gym with a coach who would be there whenever he wasn't helping track or football. By all accounts, not an ideal situation and undoubtedly, not what Penders had expected.

Report Alleges Assistants Provided Rides for Players

Two UT assistant basketball coaches, according to an anonymous complaint, allegedly committed a minor rules violation by providing rides for recruits.

The NCAA asked UT officials to investigate the complaint that volunteer assistant Tom Douglass and full-time assistant Eddie Oran provided rides to summer school at Austin Community College for Locksley Collie and Panama Myers. NCAA rules prohibit coaches and athletic department employees from giving rides to athletes and recruits.

After three weeks, UT Associate Athletic Director Butch Worley wrote up a report and determined that no violation had been committed and the coaches had not arranged for or provided rides for recruits during the summer. The NCAA was not satisfied with UT's findings and sent two investigators to conduct their own investigation. They spent an entire week interviewing players, coaches, UT staff and local merchants. No violations were uncovered. They left Austin and a year later cleared the coaches and closed the case.

Chapter Four

Eight is Great, 1989 - 1990

Going into the second year of action, Penders had a much better idea of what to expect from his team. He had a pretty good gauge from the previous year, where he witnessed, as Oran had originally predicted, the solid play of the two transfers – Blanks and Wright. Penders also saw Travis Mays was the "promising player" Dave Bliss had described before he took the job. Penders realized that all three, when working together, could be one of the best, if not the best backcourt trio in the country. The three were christened "BMW – the ultimate driving machine," before the season began. Expectations were already high for the three.

Adding to the mix were the big bodies of Myers and Collie from the JUCO ranks, another transfer player from Richmond in Hank Dudek, as well as former prep star Benford Williams regaining his eligibility after being a Proposition-48 casualty the year before. Penders realized the second year under his guidance could produce a solid season.

The Regular Season

In the season opener, UT picked up where it left off the season before. In front of a crowd of 8,344 – the largest home opener in 10 years – Texas racked up 116 points against UT-Arlington while the UT pressure defense limited the Mavericks to only 66 points in a staggering blowout. Up next on the schedule was the Longhorn Classic and an expected pair of victories.

The first game of the tournament for Texas played out like many other Classic games. The Horns toyed with the opponent early, then blew the game wide open late. Against the Manhattan Jaspers, Texas led by only seven at the break. However, in the second half the Horns got hot. When all the smoke cleared, Texas had run away from the Jaspers with a 108-63 win.

After the first two games in which the Horns had not been tested, Texas-San Antonio did not appear to be any more of a threat. The Longhorns and the partisan crowd of 7,723 got more than they bargained for as the Roadrunners surged to a seven-point lead early in the second half. But the Longhorns came storming back and eventually escaped with an 89-86 victory and the Longhorn Classic crown.

Texas next took on a tough Long Beach State 49ers team that had already defeated Purdue earlier in the season. The Longhorns led late in the first half, but the 49ers went on a 7-0 run to tie the game at the break. In the second half the game remained close. With Texas ahead by one and seconds remaining, Long Beach State's Lucious Harris hit a three-pointer at the buzzer to knock off the Longhorns, 89-87. It was Texas' first loss of the season and a heartbreaking one at that, for the team and the 8,051 fans in the Erwin Center.

Two nights later the Horns hoped to rebound from the tough loss against another quality opponent in the No. 24-ranked Florida Gators and future NBA player, center Dwayne Schintzius. The Horns held off a late Gator charge for the 105-94 victory.

Southwest Conference action was yet to get into full swing, but Texas had an early-season game on the schedule with SMU in Dallas. Mays came out hot for the Horns despite temperatures in Moody Coliseum hovering around 55 degrees due to a broken boiler on the SMU campus. The Longhorns prevailed with a 73-67 victory.

After the trip to Dallas, the Horns hit the road for another long trip, this time trekking to Stetson University in Florida. Although the game was somewhat of a homecoming for Mays, whose hometown of Ocala was 40 miles away, it was Wright who stole the show.

Against the Hatters, Wright more than made up for Blanks, who was suffering from food poisoning and Mays, who had a less-than-average performance. In the first half alone Wright scored 27 points for Texas including a two-minute stretch in which he scored 12 straight points for the Longhorns. In the second half, Wright's offensive production dropped off to an unimpressive 19 points, but it was more than enough for the Horns to win the game,102-82. Wright finished the game with 46 points. Mays finished with 17.

Texas and Wright took their road show to the Summit in Houston. In what soon became a trademark for Penders and his teams and was instrumental in rebuilding the program, the Horns took on a top-ranked, high-profiled LSU team.

According to one former athletic department official, Penders never backed down from the toughest of opponents and knew it would take going on the road for several years before the quality teams would return the favor and start making the trip to Austin.

"If we had the opportunity for a game that may not have been in 'his best interest' in terms of his bottom line record, he would still take it. We played LSU three times before we got them back to Austin. Nobody wanted to come to Austin and we couldn't buy them because there was no tradition."

In the first of the three meetings with the Tigers in the coming years, LSU was led by its 7-footers, Shaquille O' Neal and Stanley Roberts, as well as point guard Chris Jackson – all future NBAers.

The No. 11 Tigers and Longhorns put on an offensive display in front of 11,539 fans. Jackson, although the smallest of LSU's offensive weapons, definitely played the biggest against Texas. He finished the contest hitting 20 of 37 from the field on his way to a 51-point performance and had help from both O'Neal and Roberts, who combined for 42 points, 35 rebounds, and most impressively, 13 blocked shots. The trio of Tigers proved to be too much for the Horns as LSU improved to 7-1 with the 124-113 victory.

Returning to conference action and the Erwin Center, UT took on the Texas Tech Red Raiders. In front of a crowd of 10,721, Blanks and Mays continued their hot shooting as the two combined to score 34 in the first half on the way to a commanding 56-36 halftime lead. When it was all over, Texas had dismantled Texas Tech, 109-71, the largest victory margin ever in a Texas-Texas Tech game. The victory improved the Longhorns record to 8-2 overall and 2-0 in the SWC.

Two nights later the Baylor Bears came to town and the two Texas point guards came up big again. Blanks put on another offensive display as he went 14 of 21 from the field, including five of nine from behind the three-point line. Mays, who played the game with a sore left shoulder, added 30 points and the Longhorns earned the 109-89 victory.

In Fort Worth, the TCU Horned Frogs slowed the Horns. At the final buzzer, the Horns had escaped with an 83-80 win. With the victory, Texas improved to 10-2 overall and 4-0 in the conference – a half-game lead over Arkansas at 3-0 – as they headed into a battle with their foes from north of the Red River, No. 4 Oklahoma.

In what turned out to be another trademark of the Penders' years, Texas battled the Sooners in a nationally televised game; the first of five Texas games seen throughout the country that year. Although Penders knew the contest might be an uphill battle and could quite possibly result in a loss, he understood the importance of the large audience. He realized that among those watching could be potential recruits from around the country who had never before seen, much less heard of his Texas team and its style of play. This was just the type of visibility Penders wanted, and was one of the main factors in his hiring, according to one former athletic department official. "Tom had a lot of access to the media that we had not had at Texas. Coming from New York, his background was such that he had a lot of ties into the networks and ESPN."

The nation and 10,526 Sooner fans watched the up-and-down style of both teams as they pressed and pushed the ball up the court early and often. But Blanks, Mays and Wright, the trio which had teamed up all season for much of the Longhorns' offensive production, combined to shoot only 14 of 48 from the field and finished with 42 points – just 15 points more than Mays had averaged all season. The Sooners capitalized and prevailed easily,103-84. The defeat was tough on the psyche, but the Horns had to quickly regroup and prepare for the next contest, a home game against their other rival – Texas A&M.

Before an Erwin Center sellout crowd of 16,231, BMW was once again a driving force. Mays led the charge for Texas as he poured in 24 points including four of five from three-point land and nine of 11 overall in the first half. Mays added six more points in the second half for a game-high 30 and the Horns prevailed in a close one, 96-94. Overall, BMW was back on track scoring 64 points. With the win, Texas improved to 11-3 overall and 5-0 in conference.

Several days later, the Horns returned to action in front of another capacity crowd of 16,231 – the first consecutive sellouts since 1982. The game was an emotional one and not because Penders was facing his former school, Rhode Island. Instead, the crowd and Penders watched as Travis Mays, with 6:46 remaining in the game, surpassed Ron Baxter's decade-old record of 1,897 points to become the most prolific scorer in UT history. After Mays hit a 12-footer over two Rhode Island defenders to pass Baxter's mark, the game was temporarily stopped and Mays was appropriately honored with hugs from his teammates and a rousing ovation from the fans. The game ball was also presented to him.

Following the brief ceremony, Mays picked up where he left off, displaying the dedicated work ethic that had made him the all-time leading scorer. He finished the game with 29 points and Texas cruised to a 107-86 victory.

The Horns next played Texas Tech in Lubbock. Texas jumped to an early 20-9 lead and led 47-42 at the half on the strength of a 15-point performance from Wright. Texas finished the game shooting a season-high 56 percent and ran away from the Red Raiders and their fans with the 97-77 victory. The victory, which gave the Horns a 13-3 overall record and 6-0 record in SWC action, set up a showdown with Arkansas.

UT finished up their brief two-game road swing several nights later in hostile territory. Facing Arkansas, the Longhorns tried to achieve what seemed to be the impossible thus far in the era under Penders – defeating the Razorbacks. The hard-fought battle started ominously for Texas when not even midway through the first half, Mays went down with an injury to his finger on his shooting hand.

The Barnhill Arena faithful, already confident of defeating a Penders-led Texas team again, knew with the injury, victory for their beloved No. 6 Hogs was all but certain. The game remained tight until the end, but the Horns were never able to take the outright lead. Leading the way for Texas with 25 points apiece were Wright and the newest offensive weapon, Benford Williams. Williams scored his career high while pulling down 11 rebounds. Despite the two players' best efforts, the Razorbacks still managed to defeat Texas, 109-100.

Although no athlete, coach or fan will ever admit it, there are such things as moral victories, and Texas had just earned one. The loss was — yes — still a loss, but the Horns, even without their floor general and leading scorer, performed at a high level on the road against a tough, top-10 team. After successive losses against top-20 teams in Oklahoma, Louisiana State and Arkansas, the Longhorns felt they were due.

It was an uphill battle if there were any hopes of winning the SWC regular season title. If the Longhorns were to do so, they needed to get started in their rematch against Arkansas.

After losing their first four games under Penders to the Razorbacks by a total of 61 points or an average of slightly more than 15 points per game, the Horns were much more confident coming into the matchup against the Hogs. In the last contest, less than two weeks earlier, the unheralded Horns narrowly missed upsetting the Hogs on their home court, without their main scorer Mays, who was injured early in that game, but was suited up and ready to go in the rematch.

The confidence of the Texas players also stemmed from several motivating factors, the first of which was revenge. With four consecutive losses to their most competitive basketball rival, the Longhorns wanted redemption. One victory may not erase all the bad memories from the past including the last game, but it could definitely ease the pain. Second, with a victory, the squad would avert Penders losing back-to-back home games for the first time since his arrival on campus. And the third and final factor was pride. In their fifth nationally televised game of the season, none of which they had won, the players wanted to show the nation they were a top team. Although they had faced teams who were consistently ranked in the top 15 in the country, the Horns believed they should have won several of those games. In fact, as the heavy underdog in each of the games, the contests weren't decided until the latter stages. This game could be the breakthrough.

The game itself was expected to be an exciting, up-tempo scoring fest featuring the up-and-coming Longhorns and the elite Razorbacks, now up to No. 3 in the country. With a national television audience and a sellout crowd of 16,231 looking on, the game lived up to its billing. It would also go down in Texas-Arkansas sports lore as one of the most memorable games on the hardwood and not necessarily for what happened on the court.

Throughout the game, the two teams battled back and forth. The Razorbacks went into the locker room with a 44-40 halftime lead. In the second half, Texas looked like a team ready to get over the hump and prove that they did indeed belong. Down the stretch it looked like the fifth time would finally be the charm for Penders and his team.

With an 84-83 Texas lead and 14 seconds remaining, Arkansas' Lee Mayberry was called for an intentional foul on Lance Blanks. Obviously upset by the intentional foul call, Arkansas head coach Nolan Richardson had seen enough and casually left the bench area heading to the dressing room in what would be forever known as "the Strollin' Nolan incident." Blanks made both free throws and Texas led 86-83 and retained possession of the ball. The game, for all intents and purposes, appeared to be over.

On Texas' next offensive possession, Mays was fouled and headed to the line for a one-and-one. Essentially the proverbial "nail in the coffin." But Mays, a better-than-80 percent free-throw shooter, missed, to the dismay of the partisan crowd in attendance. Mays said later his injured hand affected the shot.

"I never had any confidence in my right hand up until the point where I got rid of all the tape and everything off of it. When I went to the line, I can remember almost hoping that I could make the free throws. That's never the way I stepped to the line. I stepped to the line normally saying I'm going to stick them."

Arkansas rebounded the Mays' miss and went back the other way. With time about to expire, Mayberry, the same player called for the intentional foul just seconds earlier, which seemingly ended any hopes of winning, shot a bomb from well beyond NBA three-point range and it fell. Overtime. The Texas fans, players and coaches couldn't believe it. Penders would be quite clear about his disbelief after the game.

In the overtime session, with Richardson back on the Arkansas bench, the Longhorns took an early lead but the Hogs, obviously rejuvenated after being brought back to life on Mayberry's prayer, proceeded to go on a 15-4 run to ice the game. When all was said and done, the No. 3 Hogs escaped the Erwin Center with a controversial 103-96 victory. With the stunning defeat, Texas dropped to 14-6 and 7-3 in the SWC.

Following the game, Penders took his case to the press saying a technical foul should have been called on Richardson for leaving the coach's box when he took the "stroll" to the dressing room. Texas Sports Information Director Bill Little said according to the game official Mike Tamco, Richardson did not receive a technical foul because he left the game during a dead-ball situation and was not trying to show up the officials. Penders responded that regardless if there was a stoppage of play or not, Richardson had earned himself a technical, which would have resulted in two more free throws for the Longhorns. After the fact, the NCAA determined later that Richardson should have received a technical foul.

Overcoming the hangover of the Arkansas loss, the Texas squad traveled to Waco with hopes of getting back on the winning track and ending their two-game losing streak.

Against Baylor and 9,172 fans at the Ferrell Center – the largest crowd since its construction two years earlier – Texas fell behind early. In the second half with less than 20 seconds left in the game, the Longhorns had a case of deja vu. Leading 94-91, Mays was fouled and headed to the line. This time however, the senior, who had re-injured his hyperextended finger in the game, sank both free throws to seal the victory over the Bears, 96-91. Texas improved to 15-6 overall and 8-3 in the conference.

UT returned home for its next contest against TCU, the first of two final home games before they embarked on a four-game trip that included a visit to Chicago and the DePaul Blue Demons. In front of 11,286 Mays battled through the pain of his injured finger.

The Longhorns almost blew a 20-point lead in the second half but held on to defeat the Horned Frogs, 85-77. Blanks, who finished with 22, and Mays, who scored a team-high 27, hit five free throws in the final minute to close out the win for Texas.

In the regular season home finale and final home game for Mays, Blanks, and seldom-used 7-footer George Muller, the Horns took on John Shumate's SMU Mustangs. A relatively small crowd of approximately 7,500 watched Mays close out his career at home with a 25-point performance that included six rebounds and five assists as Texas pulled off a 79-68 victory. Blanks didn't reach his season average of 20 points but did contribute 14 points, eight assists and four steals. With the victory, Texas improved to 17-6 and 10-3 in the SWC, one game behind Arkansas.

In College Station against the Aggies, the Longhorns had a tough contest against their rivals. The Texas trio of guards didn't have their best of games, but down the stretch Blanks scored a total of nine consecutive points in the final four minutes of the game to give the Longhorns a 79-73 defeat of the Aggies at G. Rollie White Coliseum. In addition to Blanks' heroics, Mays, still playing with an injured finger, accounted for 18 points that tied former Arkansas star Sidney Moncrief for third in SWC career scoring.

Following a much-needed 10-day hiatus, the Horns resumed action on the road at Autry Court in Houston against the Rice Owls. Mays' finger appeared to have healed during the days off as he scored 28 points and led Texas to an 86-84 victory. The win improved the Longhorns' record to 19-6 and 12-3 in SWC play.

After the victory in Houston, the Horns took their five-game winning streak to Illinois and the Rosemont Horizon Arena where they faced the DePaul Blue Demons in front of another national television audience. With no victories in their five previous televised contests including regional broadcasts, the Longhorns, who many considered to be on the NCAA Tournament bubble, wanted validation. This was the perfect situation.

Texas came out firing Blanks, as in Lance Blanks, who led all scorers with 30 points including a bank shot at the buzzer which gave Texas a 51-43 halftime lead. Blanks' hot performance of the day, which consisted of six of nine from three-point range, combined with Wright's 19 and Mays' 16 earned the Longhorns a much-deserved victory before the nationally televised audience, 89-79. The win, which was the sixth consecutive for the team, garnered respect for Penders and his program, which now had a 20-6 record.

The Horns' final regular season game wasn't any easier when they traveled to Hofheinz Pavilion to take on the Houston Cougars, who had an impressive record of their own at 23-6, and a 10-game winning streak coming into the game. With the largest crowd in Hofheinz history — 10,660 — the Cougars and Longhorns dueled to become the second seed in the upcoming SWC Tournament. In the end, it was the Cougars whose winning streak was extended to 11 with an 84-79 win over Texas. Texas finished up the regular season with a 20-7 record, 12-4 in the conference. With the loss, Texas was seeded third behind Arkansas and Houston.

The SWC Tournament

In the first game of the SWC Tournament, the Longhorns took on the Aggies. The first telltale sign of good things to come for Texas occurred against the Aggies when a new face stepped to the front when it mattered most. Guillermo "Panama" Myers, who had contributed statistically throughout the season in mainly the rebound category, played a major role in the Longhorns' opening-round victory, 92-84, over the Aggies. Myers contributed 15 points and pulled down 16 rebounds, both career highs in the win, while the usual scoring machine of BMW combined for 63 points including a game-high 27 from Blanks.

Myers' explosion onto the scene, both offensively and defensively, was a promising sign for Penders and his team and somewhat of a necessity if they expected to make a run in the NCAA Tournament. Penders knew the offense would be there in BMW, but he realized that other players would have to "step it up" substantially on both sides of the ball to have any chance in the postseason. With the win, the Horns next faced the Cougars.

If Texas had any intentions of ending their three-game losing streak to the Cougars, dating back to the previous season, they didn't show any signs of it early. Houston got off to the quick start and led by 15 points with eight minutes remaining in the first half. But Texas responded, due in large part to the effective long-range shooting of Mays and Wright, who each had 23 points in the game. It wasn't enough, though, as the Cougars held off the Horns for the 89-86 win. Another shot at Arkansas was lost, but who knew? If everything went as planned, the Texas team would get an invite to the NCAA Tournament and depending on how the brackets were seeded, they just might see the Razorbacks again.

Following the SWC Tournament, the Longhorns learned their fate for the postseason. For the first time in school history, the Horns, who had finished the season with a 21-8 record, were dancing in the NCAAs in consecutive years. And once again, it was against a team from Georgia. Last year, it was as the No. 11 seed against No. 6-seeded Georgia Tech. This year it was as a No. 10 seed against the University of Georgia Bulldogs, a No. 7 seed and regular-season winner of the tough Southeastern Conference.

Penders was pleased about the seeding. "I thought we'd be anywhere between an eight and a 10 seed. We have a No. 30 ranking *(AP)* and a No. 42 power rating *(USA Today)*."

Mays, in what turned out to be a prophetic statement, said he was also happy with the team's placement in the tournament. "I think we are in a real good bracket. If we play well, I see us in the Sweet 16."

The NCAA Tournament

In Indianapolis, in the first half of the first-round Midwest Regional contest against Georgia, Texas tried to offset a size difference in the front court by applying a full-court press. It worked as Texas jumped out to an early 19-7 lead. Mays led the way with 15 points despite picking up his third foul in the half. However, Georgia managed to fight its way back into the contest and led 41-40 at intermission.

With the motivation of receiving only honorable mention on various All-America teams, Mays came out in the second half with the intent of improving on his 15-point first-half performance.

After the contest, Penders said Mays' exhibition in the Indianapolis Hoosier Dome might have had some of the voters reconsidering their selections for the country's top players. "If that wasn't an All-American performance, I haven't seen one. Travis was down about not making All-American. I told him you can't do anything about it."

Mays said he had a chip on his shoulder before the Georgia game and he wanted to prove to those who didn't consider him for All-American status that he was worthy of such consideration. "It was my last hurrah and I was really pissed off because I thought I was one of the best players in the country that year. I'm on no one's All-American list at all," Mays would say later.

With Mays' performance and the Texas victory, the Longhorns advanced to the second round to face the Purdue Boilermakers, the No. 10-ranked team in the country and No. 2 seed in the Midwest Region.

In a contest where the Longhorns could have been intimidated by a highly-ranked team, its basketball history, including head coach Gene Keady, and literally, a home crowd of more than 37,000 in the Indianapolis Hoosier Dome, the Texas squad led by Blanks, Mays and Wright never wavered.

In the first half, the Longhorns tried to dictate the pace. They were unable to do so as indicated by the 35-33 score at intermission. In the second half, the Boilermakers got off to quick start and eventually had a nine-point lead with just less than 12 minutes remaining in the game. Then Texas rallied.

Led by the surprise production of sophomore reserve Benford Williams, who scored 10 of his 12 points in the final 12 minutes, the Longhorns managed to cut into the Purdue lead. With seven seconds left in the game, Texas had the ball and trailed 72-71. Mays was fouled and went to the line. After a timeout to ice Mays, the senior guard calmly drained both free throws and the Horns led 73-72.

What happened next will be forever remembered in Texas basketball lore.

On the in-bounds play, Purdue's 6-foot-3-inch guard Tony Jones took the pass and went the length of the court. After he slid past Texas guard Courtney Jeans, it appeared Jones had an alley to the basket. As Jones drove to the basket, UT senior Panama Myers committed to take on the much quicker guard. In an effort to avoid Myers and with just three ticks left on the clock, Jones released the ball, lofting it on a high trajectory. Before the ball reached its apex, Myers pounded it out of the air, almost pinning it against the glass. The ball fell to the floor and the Longhorns had held on to the 73-72 victory – what many called "the biggest win in Longhorn basketball history."

With the victory, Texas was now in the Sweet 16, and faced the Musketeers from Xavier, Ohio, who had upset Georgetown, 74-71 in their second-round matchup. The hard part was seemingly over. Texas had not only won its first-round contest against a higher-seeded team from Georgia, but it had also won its second-round game against a top-10 team in Purdue, and had done so in "hostile territory." Now they were headed back to Dallas and a venue that was much closer to home in Reunion Arena, which more than likely would draw more Texas fans because of its close proximity to Austin.

There was, however, one potential problem that could stand in the way of Texas reaching the Final Four for the first time since 1947. No, it wasn't even their next opponent. Instead, it was the team they could possibly face in the regional finals if both teams took care of business and won their respective games — a team they had lost to five consecutive times under Penders and twice in the previous season including a controversial loss in overtime. It was none other than their SWC nemesis from Fayetteville, the Arkansas Razorbacks.

First things first. It wasn't time to worry about Xavier or Arkansas for that matter; it was time to return home to Austin and relish the victory, albeit briefly. On the day after the win over Purdue, more than 100 fans began the celebration as they crowded into Robert Mueller Airport to greet their Sweet 16 bound team. Players and coaches alike were asked to sign autographs and even one fan delivered an orange and white Sweet 16 cake to Panama Myers, who had just celebrated his 22nd birthday.

Myers was quoted in the *Austin American-Statesman* about the outpouring of support. "This is great. It'll encourage me to push a little harder – not only me, but my teammates."

The *American-Statesman* also reported that Penders had spoken with the University of Florida about the school's vacant head coaching position.

The article said according to one report, "Penders has talked with Florida officials but canceled an interview in Gainesville, Fl., scheduled for Monday after the Longhorns defeated Purdue."

Jamie Ciampaglio would say later that before the Purdue game he had met with Texas Assistant Athletic Director Craig Helwig in Indianapolis at the Holiday Inn about the Florida job. Helwig asked what it would take to keep Penders and his coaching staff at Texas. "We don't want to lose you guys," Helwig told Ciampaglio.

Ciampaglio said he was confident if the Longhorns had lost to Purdue, Penders and the staff would have more than likely left for Florida. He said it wasn't because they didn't like their situation in Austin, but because it was so difficult to recruit players – even within the state – to come play basketball at UT. "We couldn't keep kids in Texas like Jimmy King and Ray Jackson (two members of Michigan's Fab Five who were from Texas.) In Florida there was good basketball."

When asked at the airport about the newspaper report, Penders said he wasn't going to discuss the issue. "I have no comment on that today. I'm just thinking about Xavier."

After all the hoopla and rumors of Penders' departure died down, the Horns got back to work and prepared for a Xavier team that was no fluke, as evidenced by their 28-4 record and a victory over the fifth-ranked Georgetown Hoyas that put them in the Midwest Regional semifinals.

Penders knew this game in particular was going to be difficult for his team. Not only did he have to guard against his players looking forward to a rematch against SWC archrival Arkansas, he also had to motivate a team that was in an ideal situation for an emotional letdown following the huge victory against Purdue. To make matters worse, Penders had to figure out a way to defend not one, but two 6-foot-10-inch players in the middle.

At Dallas' Reunion Arena, a capacity crowd watched as Xavier extended its 53-41 halftime lead to 57-41 early in the second half, and looked poised to advance to the regional finals. But as Longhorn fans had grown accustomed to throughout the season, the Texas players never quit. Blanks and Mays led a resurgent Texas offense in the second half and the Horns stormed back eventually blowing past the Musketeers for the 102-89 victory. Mays finished with a game-high 32 points as Texas was advancing to the Elite Eight.

With the victory, the worries of letdown and looking ahead were over. Arkansas was next. But in the interim, a little celebration was to be had by all.

Before the final buzzer sounded and victory was official, the University of Texas campus and many of its 50,000 students reveled in the fact that a Longhorn squad would be appearing in the round of eight for the first time since 1947, when the entire field was only eight teams.

Many fans caught up in the celebration had suffered through years of mediocrity, and sometimes, downright pathetic teams. Those fans who were relatively new to Texas basketball, including the present-day students, were equally as excited and displayed their fervor for their team by converging on Guadalupe Street, or "The Drag," for an impromptu midnight pep rally that lasted into the early morning hours. Guadalupe between Martin Luther King Jr. Boulevard and 25th Street was shut down because of the crowds spilling into the streets.

The scene was much the same across the city where large student populations were located. In apartment communities in South Austin, which were predominantly occupied by students, fans of the team were jumping into pools fully clothed, yelling, screaming, flashing the "Hook 'Em Horns" sign, and singing the "Eyes of Texas." It was a scene unfamiliar to the city of Austin and the University of Texas for this time of the year. Normally, these types of celebrations were reserved for football-related activities including big wins over A&M or when Earl Campbell won the Heisman Trophy, not for the University of Texas basketball team.

Two nights later, a packed house at Reunion Arena looked on as the Longhorns and Razorbacks took to the court. The atmosphere was electric. Never before had the two teams met in a basketball contest with so much at stake. Sure, football meetings in the past had determined national championships, but never before had the hardwoods provided for such excitement between the two storied rivals.

From the opening tip, fans in Reunion and those watching on television were on the edge of their seats as the Razorbacks jumped out to the early lead as a direct result of their full-court pressure defense described by head coach Nolan Richardson as "forty minutes of hell."

Hell is exactly what the Horns went through the entire first half and much of the second as they found themselves down by 16 points with 12 minutes remaining in the game. Texas had to make another miraculous comeback to advance. The Horns made a valiant attempt, but in the end came up short, losing to the Hogs, 88-85. With the win, Arkansas was headed to the Final Four in Denver.

For the Longhorns and their faithful fans, the Cinderella season was over, but the slipper had fit for three games. Texas finished with a 24-9 record and a No. 12 ranking in the ESPN/*USA Today* final poll.

The Off-Season
Fans Praise Basketball Team for Its Efforts

With an estimated crowd of 2,300 in attendance at the Erwin Center the next day, the basketball team was commended for its efforts in the "magical" basketball season.

Among those offering praise included Austin Mayor Lee Cooke, who did so on behalf of the city.

Penders received a loud ovation when he took the microphone, and he thanked the crowd and his team for the wonderful season. "This year was a very special year. A lot of people counted us out in the middle of the season," he told the audience. He said when the players felt they weren't given a chance to succeed, they took it upon themselves to disprove their doubters. "I think we developed an 'us against the world' attitude," he said. "This team proved to everyone in the country it's one of the top eight in the country." A thunderous applause sounded in agreement.

Penders Agrees to New Contract

For its appearance in the NCAA Tournament, which consisted of four games, Texas earned approximately $550,000 – a considerable increase from the 1988-89 season.

Soon after the Horns exited from the tournament, Penders and his assistants received a hike in their salaries. Penders' base salary increased from $92,650 to $105,000 and the overall package increased to seven years at more than $400,000 a year. (The contract wasn't officially completed and signed until after the 1991 season, and only after five revisions.) Assistant coaches Eddie Oran and Jamie Ciampaglio also received base salary increases from $43,110 to $60,000.

Dodds said he wanted to get Penders' new deal done before the coach headed to the Final Four in Denver, so he wouldn't be approached and tempted by other schools, as Dodds had done with Penders two years earlier in Kansas City. "I know what happens at those tournaments," Dodds said. "I've been there myself."

Two weeks after agreeing to a new contract in principle with the university, Penders received additional good news. University of Texas alumnus Jim Bob Moffett gave $1 million to the school's athletic department that established an endowment, which elevated Penders' recently increased base salary of $105,000 a year by an additional $60,000.

The endowment was the first such program at UT.

Penders Receives One-Game Suspension

After publicly criticizing Southwest Conference officials much of the 1989-90 season, Penders received a one-game suspension from SWC Commissioner Fred Jacoby.

Penders and his assistant Ciampaglio were placed on probation for the entire 1990-91 season and any addition criticism could result in single or multi-game suspensions.

Two weeks after the suspension, the SWC's five-member compliance committee denied Penders' appeal to the league. He would have to sit out the 1991 SWC opener at home against Texas A&M.

Penders Releases Volunteer Assistant Coach

During the summer, Penders released volunteer assistant coach Tom Douglass after former football coach and UT legend Darrell Royal told Penders that Douglass was involved in activities that could not only embarrass the program, but possibly lead to an NCAA investigation.

Penders said with that knowledge he had no choice but give Douglass his walking papers. He said when he confronted Douglass about the situation initially, the former UT player denied any wrongdoing. However, when Penders told Douglass who had informed him about the potential problem, Douglass admitted his involvement and agreed to leave the program.

Chapter Five

Farewell Arkansas, 1990 – 1991

Heading into the third season, Penders was more than pleased with his situation in Austin, and justifiably so. After two seasons at Texas and a record of 49-18 including two consecutive appearances in the NCAA Tournament and a near miss at the Final Four last season that had earned the school more than $500,000, Penders and his assistants had received new contracts and healthy pay raises.

In addition to the pay increases, the coaching staff received an operational benefit for the program in new video equipment. This, at the time, was a much-needed improvement over the antiquated equipment, which had been used in Penders' first couple of years, as well as many years prior to his arrival. The new equipment was a considerable upgrade and was expected to make the job of viewing game film much easier.

In addition to earning the respect and support of UT administration officials as evidenced by the new contracts and new equipment, Penders and his team had earned the respect of the pollsters. The Longhorns opened the season at No. 22 in the AP poll.

Penders thought expectations including the rankings in the polls were more than likely too high, especially after such a drastic change in team makeup with the loss of two key backcourt leaders, Mays and Blanks, who were now in the NBA as first-round draft picks.

"We're probably overrated. I don't know where we should be after losing two starters to the NBA, but it's a tribute to our program to make the rankings," he said.

Penders hoped the loss of the two stars might be offset by two additions, albeit at different positions, in the form of Dexter Cambridge, a forward and the third Lon Morris player to follow Trilli to Texas, and Albert Burditt, a top homegrown prospect from Austin's Lanier High School. Also coming in was Teyon McCoy, a quick guard who had transferred from Maryland.

If making adjustments to the new players and team chemistry wasn't enough, Penders had prepared an extremely tough schedule for his squad, which included the likes of Florida, Oklahoma, LSU, Arizona State, Michigan and DePaul. Although the schedule was designed to make his team better through competition with quality opponents, he knew it might also limit the team's win total and quite possibly, a chance at a third consecutive bid to the NCAA Tournament.

The Regular Season

The Horns opened the 1990-91 campaign in the Sunshine State against the Florida Gators. The game was close throughout and came down to the last few seconds. Texas led 75-74 and was staring at a season-opening loss when Florida's Craig Brown was sent to the line with four seconds remaining. Brown inexplicably missed both free throws and Texas held on for the 76-74 victory. The victory improved Penders' record to 3-0 in season openers at Texas and 23-0 when UT held the opponent to fewer than 80 points.

Before opening at home, the Longhorns continued their tour of the Southeast with a stop in Baton Rouge to take on the LSU Tigers. The 20th-ranked Tigers, led by big man Shaquille O'Neal, jumped ahead of the Horns early and pulled away for a convincing 101-87 win.

At home for the first time, the schedule didn't get any easier as the Horns hosted the 16th-ranked Oklahoma Sooners. If 26 points and 18 rebounds from LSU's Shaquille O'Neal weren't enough, the No. 23 Longhorns were shown for the second time in as many games how they lacked the presence of a big man in the middle. This time it was Oklahoma's 6-foot-8-inch Jeff Webster who lit up Texas for 35 points. Despite the inability to stop Webster, Texas had a balanced offensive attack of its own and stayed close for the duration. But it wasn't enough as the Sooners managed to hand Texas a 96-88 defeat. The loss, which was watched by 15,031 fans, dropped UT to 1-2 on the young season and marked the first time in 10 years that a Longhorn squad had lost the home opener.

In the first round of the Longhorn Classic against Loyola-Maryland, Dexter Cambridge, who had managed to score just three points in Texas' previous contest against Oklahoma, finally showed the promise that had earned him All-American honors in junior college. Cambridge scored 25 points on 9 of 10 shooting from the field, including three of three from behind the three-point line in just 18 minutes of playing time as the No. 23 Longhorns blasted the Greyhounds, 112-68. In the Longhorn Classic championship game against Texas-Pan American, UT rolled to the title with a 116-70 win.

After a 10-day break for final exams, the 23rd-ranked Horns went on the road and faced a tough Gauchos squad from California-Santa Barbara in front of a raucous road crowd and a national television audience on ESPN. As might be expected, the layoff was a factor and UT came out rusty. At the end of regulation the game was tied at 73. In the extra session, Joey Wright scored seven of Texas' 14 points and the Longhorns escaped with an 87-84 victory. With the victory, the Horns improved to 4-2 on the season.

Next came the Kuppenheimer Classic at the Omni in Atlanta, Ga. The No. 23 Horns fell to the 17th ranked Bulldogs, 79-71.

After the loss to Georgia, the Horns made a stop back in Austin for several days of practice before heading out west to the Arizona State Classic. In the first-round contest Texas faced Michigan. Texas held on long enough for a 76-74 win and earned a berth in the championship. Leading the way for UT was Locksley Collie with a team-high 16 points.

In the championship game Texas battled against the host-team Arizona State Sun Devils. The Horns trailed by only one at the half, 36-35. In the second half ASU increased its lead to double digits and the Sun Devils went on to the 89-82 victory and were crowned champions of the tournament. The Horns fell to 5-4.

Back in the Erwin Center for the Southwest Conference opener against Texas A&M, the Longhorns were without Penders who was serving his conference-imposed one-game suspension for criticizing SWC officials the previous season. Serving in his absence was Longhorn assistant coach, Jamie Ciampaglio.

The Longhorns appeared motivated not only by their coach's absence, but also by the fact they were playing their rivals from College Station. At the break, Texas was ahead 37-26. In the second half, it was much the same for the Longhorns. The 11,347 in attendance watched as the Longhorns won going away, 93-67. With the victory, UT improved to 6-4 on the season and 1-0 in the conference while the Aggies dropped to 4-7 and 0-1 in SWC action.

Against Baylor, who made the I-35 trip down from Waco, Texas, struggled early. In the second half, the Horns offense kicked into high gear including an 18-2 run to begin the half. The offensive push in the second half was the difference as a crowd of 13,181 watched Texas waltz to a 94-77 victory.

Before a record-crowd of 9,486 rowdy fans at Barnhill Arena, Texas had another struggle against the second-ranked Arkansas Razorbacks. Early in the game the Longhorns appeared unfazed by the Hogs, the crowd, and the cameras covering the nationally televised game on ESPN. At the half, Arkansas led 51-46. In the second half, the Hogs proved why they were ranked No. 2 in the nation as they extended their lead to double digits. In the waning minutes, Arkansas held off a late Texas charge to earn a 101-89 win.

The loss marked the seventh time in as many tries that Penders had lost to his counterpart Nolan Richardson and Arkansas. It also dropped Texas to 7-5 on the season and 2-1 in the SWC. Arkansas improved to 14-1 and became the early leader in the SWC race with a 3-0 record.

After two road games against the most hostile of crowds, the Erwin Center and a home crowd was a welcome sight for Penders and the Longhorns. A crowd of almost 16,000 – 15,743 to be exact – greeted the Horns and their 8-5 record as they took on the Houston Cougars in front of yet another national television audience. Unfortunately, the large audience, both in attendance and at home, saw the Texas squad come out cold, much like it had done in recent games. But also like previous games, Texas rebounded after the break and overcame the Cougars with a 90-84 victory. It was the first time in three years Texas had beaten Houston at home.

After overcoming one demon – the inability to beat the Houston Cougars at home – the Longhorns wanted to prove, once again before a national television audience, that they could beat another demon – a Blue Demon.

Unlike recent performances where the Texas offense failed to show up until the second half, if at all, the Longhorns, to the delight of the more than 13,400 in attendance, came out hitting long-range shots early and often against DePaul, as Texas defeated the Blue Demons, 90-80. With the win, Texas improved to 10-5 on the season.

With Joey Wright confined to the bench with an injured hamstring, Penders looked to other sources of offensive production against the Red Raiders on the South Plains of West Texas. Courtney Jeans more than made up for Wright's absence as he had a solid performance converting on 9 of 12 from the field for a total of 22 points, as the Horns cruised to the 83-65 victory, their fourth consecutive.

Several days later and in front of the largest Erwin Center crowd of the season – 15,775 – Wright returned to action for the Longhorns against the TCU Horned Frogs in a game that looked to be an even matchup. TCU came in with an overall record of 12-4 and 4-2 in conference play, while Texas was 11-5 and 5-1 in the SWC.

Looks can be deceiving. The final score: Texas 90, TCU 49. UT had won its fifth straight.

Against the SMU Mustangs, Dexter Cambridge displayed his offensive potential. The former JUCO All-American caught fire against the Ponies. Cambridge posted 15 points in the first half alone including 13 consecutive points late in the half. In the second half he added 11 more on his way to a career-high 26 and a 96-80 Texas victory. With its sixth consecutive win, Texas improved to 13-5 overall and was in sole possession of second place in the SWC with a 7-1 record, one game behind Arkansas at 8-0.

The Longhorns headed to College Station with the hopes of continuing their winning ways in the first of three conference road games.They were not disappointed. The Horns, led by Joey Wright and Locksley Collie, won all three games, improving their overall record to 16-5 and 10-1 in the Southwest Conference.

With March Madness looming around the corner, Texas and third-ranked Arkansas hooked up for the last time in the SWC regular season in a classic contest that had the atmosphere of an NCAA Tournament game.

The Erwin Center was sold out with 16,231 boisterous fans. This contest, which was seen by a national television audience, had all the makings of a battle royale. For Penders and Texas, it was an opportunity for the coach to get his first win in eight tries against Richardson and the Hogs and a chance for his team to prove they could compete against the upper echelon of teams, which Arkansas was clearly considered. It also was a chance for redemption after last year's game. For Arkansas, it was an opportunity to get a victory on the home court of one of their biggest rivals throughout the years. Nothing would be sweeter than sending home the UT fans disappointed with yet another loss in their final appearance in Austin as a member of the SWC.

In the first half it looked as if the Razorbacks might get their way when they headed to the locker room with a 55-45 halftime lead. The second half was much different. Trailing by 14 points just three minutes into the second half, the Longhorns staged a comeback of huge proportions.

With less than 10 minutes remaining in the game, the comeback was complete when Texas took its first lead of the second half on a pair of free throws by Locksley Collie. But could UT hold on for that elusive victory? At the six-minute mark the Longhorns had extended their lead to eight, 84-76, but the crowd wasn't convinced. They remembered last year's incredible comeback in which the reliable Travis Mays missed the front end of a one-and-one that could have iced the game. They remembered watching Arkansas' Lee Mayberry drain an improbable three-point bomb from almost 30 feet out to send the game into overtime. They remembered the Longhorns lost, 103-96. Until the clock registered zeros with Texas ahead, the sellout crowd couldn't be certain.

Texas never wavered. When the final buzzer sounded, the Longhorns had finally beaten the Razorbacks for the first time in Penders' three years as coach, 99-86.

With the win Texas had reached the 20-win plateau three consecutive years for the first time in school history. The victory improved the Horns' overall record to 20-7 and they finished the SWC regular season in second place with a 13-3 record. For Arkansas, the loss was their first in SWC play and only their third loss in 31 games on the season for an impressive 28-3 record.

The SWC Tournament

In the first round of the Southwest Conference Tournament in Dallas' Reunion Arena, the Longhorns, ranked 23rd in the nation after the win over Arkansas, faced the Baylor Bears.

Neither the Longhorns' recent victory nor its ranking impressed the Bears.

Baylor battled Texas through the entire first half and midway through the second. But with 10 minutes remaining, the Longhorns went on a 19-8 run and established control of the contest. The Bears had several mini-runs, but it wasn't enough as the Longhorns preserved a hard-fought first-round victory, 88-78.

In the second-round matchup against the SMU Mustangs, Texas established itself early. The No. 23 Horns jumped out to the early 12-3 advantage and never looked back. At halftime the lead was eight, 36-28. Texas maintained its distance in the second half and defeated the Ponies for an 82-74 victory.

With the win Texas improved to 22-7 for the season and advanced to the SWC Tournament Finals. Only one team stood in the way of Texas winning its first-ever tournament title, and it was a very familiar team, one that Texas had defeated just five days earlier in convincing fashion – Arkansas.

After defeating the Razorbacks, Texas came into the tournament finals with a considerable amount of confidence. Early on it showed.

Wright guided the Longhorns to a five-point lead midway through the half. But Arkansas answered in a big way near the end of the first half and for the duration of the second half. In the end, the Hogs prevailed with the 120-89 victory. With Arkansas bolting for the Southeastern Conference the next season, the Hogs win capped off a season in which they earned both the SWC tournament and the SWC regular season titles.

For its tournament effort, Arkansas had four players on the all-tournament team including Lee Mayberry, Todd Day, Arlyn Bowers and Oliver Miller. The only non-Arkansas player was Texas' Joey Wright.

The NCAA Tournament

At the University of Dayton Arena in Dayton, Ohio, the Horns faced a small, but quick St. Peter's team that came in with an impressive 24-6 record.

From the opening tip it was obvious that Penders, as he seemed to do before every NCAA Tournament game, had the Texas players relaxed and ready for battle. After a slow-paced, low-scoring first half in which Wright and Collie were surrounded each time they touched the ball, Texas led 32-30. The Longhorns had enough firepower in the second half to advance to the second round with a 73-65 victory. Next up was St. John's.

In hindsight, the Longhorns should have known March 17 wouldn't be their lucky night against the St. John's Redmen (now known as the Red Storm). After all, it was a day named after a saint – St. Patrick – and they faced an opponent, whose school was named after a saint – St. John's – the second such school in as many games.

The luck of the Irish and a considerable amount of skill were on the side of St. John's in the first half, as the Redmen jumped out to a 45-36 halftime lead. St. John's sent the Horns packing with an 84-76 defeat.

The 1990-1991 season was complete and Texas finished with a 23-9 record and a No. 23 ranking. Wright, who capped off his career with a spectacular 32-point performance, finished as the third-leading scorer in UT history (at that time) with a total of 1,819 points in just a three-year span.

Last, but certainly not least, Penders had taken the Horns to an unprecedented third consecutive NCAA tournament. Returning to the NCAA a fourth straight year would be much more difficult for Penders with the loss of five seniors from his eight-player rotation including JoeyWright, Courtney Jeans, Teyon McCoy, Panama Myers and Locksley Collie.

The Off-Season
Penders Seeks Administrative Replacement

Although Penders would find out later he had little influence in the final decision; his first order of business following the 1990-91 season was to help find a replacement for Assistant Men's Athletic Director for Development Craig Helwig.

Helwig, who came to Texas from Kansas State with Dodds in 1982 and originally interviewed Penders for the basketball head coaching position, unexpectedly resigned in early February. Penders was troubled by Helwig's sudden departure because Penders' "conduit," as he described it, to the administration was effectively gone.

Penders said Helwig was the basketball program's weekly voice with senior administration and he was instrumental in getting things accomplished for the program. Penders said it was Helwig who had pushed for and got the new high-tech video equipment prior to the 1990-91 season. Helwig also learned about future promotions from the administration, and kept Penders apprised of what was coming down the pike. Along those same lines, Helwig set up and accompanied Penders on trips to speak with alumni organizations

On another level, Penders said Helwig helped the team on road trips with items such as the itinerary, which included making sure the team was at the proper hotel. Penders said coaches don't like handling those types of things and when someone like Helwig is around, the coaches' jobs are that much easier. Essentially, Helwig was the behind-the-scenes guy that made everything run smoothly for the basketball program.

Penders said the main reason Helwig was helpful in so many areas was due to his knowledge of athletics and particularly, basketball. Helwig said he was never officially declared the liaison for basketball, but he worked with the program on a regular basis. "I worked with a lot of different sports, but I certainly worked with basketball and was close to that program."

Helwig's official job duties as assistant AD included fundraising and establishing the Longhorn Foundation for men's athletics. From that, the Foundation raised enough money to finance a $1 million endowment to supplement the head basketball coach's salary and a $1.5 million supplement for the head football coach's salary.

In what turned out to be an eerie case of foreshadowing, Helwig left Texas to serve as vice president of the Southwest region for Host Communications, which had the radio and television rights to many collegiate athletic programs, including the University of Texas.

In the interim until a replacement was named, former Longhorn quarterback and assistant director for development, Robert Brewer, was in charge.

In late April, Brewer was officially given the title of assistant athletic director for development and was in charge of raising funds through the Longhorn Foundation – essentially, Helwig's replacement. However, two months later, it became apparent that Brewer's new job title was not equivalent to Helwig's previous position and authority when a new associate athletic director position was created.

Suitors Inquire About Penders

Less than two months after Penders and the Longhorns bowed out of the NCAA Tournament, Penders' name, as had happened the previous year, surfaced on lists across the country as a potential candidate for several openings. This year, however, it was of a more serious nature as one of the team's showing considerable interest was the New York Knicks.

On May 11, DeLoss Dodds told the *Austin American-Statesman* that the Knicks had been given permission to talk with Penders about the club's vacant head coaching position. "They said they have about four or five people they are talking to," Dodds said. "This (Texas) is a great job. Tom's happy to be here, and we're happy to have him. But if you have good coaches, you are going to get contacted about them."

Penders would say later this type of language from Dodds became more common after each season. He said not only did Dodds never discourage Penders from listening to other teams and their offers regarding head coaching vacancies, but Dodds more than once encouraged Penders to look into other positions. Penders said in particular, following both the 1991 and 1997 seasons Dodds told him in order for his contract to be renegotiated, Penders needed to "appear" as if he might be interested in a vacancy and might leave the University of Texas. This way, as Dodds described it, Dodds would have more leverage with university officials in renegotiating Penders' deal.

"When people would call and ask for permission, Dodds would say, 'I think you ought to talk to these people because I think it will help me get you a couple years on your contract,'" Penders said, recalling conversations with Dodds, which he said occurred on several occasions.

Penders, familiar with the critics in the Austin sports media who often said he personally put his name in the running, said he never did such a thing. "I've never made a phone call for a job. It was always somebody calling me or calling DeLoss and asking for permission to talk to me. That's what they do for Rick Majerus and everybody else. It's common. If nobody is calling about your coach, that means he either is bad, about to be fired and nobody wants him, or he's got such an unbelievable job and security (such as Duke's Mike Krzyzewski), he can't even possibly think about leaving."

In addition, Penders said during his tenure at Texas he never once asked Dodds to increase the money on his contract, but instead asked for a contract extension because he was more interested in job security, longevity at Texas, and using his contract as a recruiting tool.

He said it is a customary practice in college athletics for coaches to get contract extensions whenever their contracts get to four years or less. The reason — when a coach is sitting in the home of a potential recruit, he can tell the player that he will still be the coach in four years when the player graduates or exhausts his eligibility. "If the school is interested in their programs being successful, they want to extend the contracts of the coaches for recruiting purposes," Penders said. "Every recruit wants to know from the coach and the AD what the contract status of the coach is. It's common."

In most cases it's the coach who approaches the AD about a new contract. However, it is not uncommon for an AD to recognize he has a successful athletic program and initiate contract talks when the coach's contract nears the four-year time frame. Penders said, on occasion, when a team has had a poor season the year before or is not performing up to expectations and it's near the four-year time frame, the athletic director might not be as generous when approached by a coach about an extension. "If they (coaches) are struggling and not producing, they might ask for it but they're told, 'Come back next year. Right now I can't do it. You're struggling.'"

For Penders, this was clearly not the case. The team was thriving and generating both interest and money for the university. It had made the NCAA Tournament three consecutive years. And finally, recruiting was going as expected. Simply put, all the teams expressing interest throughout Penders' career called for one reason – they wanted a proven coach who could win.

New York Knicks Court Penders

On Wednesday May 15, the *Austin American-Statesman* reported that Penders was scheduled to meet with the Knicks that Friday, May 17. It happened sooner than was reported. In fact, as Austinites were reading the Wednesday sports section of the paper that described the scheduled meeting, Penders was on a plane to Chicago where he met with Knicks President Dave Checketts and Vice President Ernie Grunfeld.

Although almost two dozen names had been mentioned as possible replacements for departing Knicks coach John MacLeod, Penders was the last of the four candidates actually interviewed by the Knicks. The other three candidates included former Chicago Bulls coach Doug Collins; Knicks assistant coach and former NBA player Paul Silas; and Pat Riley, former Lakers coach who guided his team to four NBA titles in nine seasons and was a commentator for NBC. Riley was reported to be the heavy favorite for the job, but speculation was swirling that Riley was considering withdrawing his name from consideration.

With the other three candidates and their respective NBA pedigrees, Penders appeared to be the odd man out with no NBA coaching experience. No one really knew if, and how serious the Knicks were about Penders.

In the first meeting in Chicago, Penders told the two Knicks representatives that he was happy at Texas and it would take a deal of large proportions for him to even consider leaving. Finances weren't a concern for Checketts and Grunfeld, as evidenced by their interest in Riley, who, according to several reports, would command a salary in excess of $1 million to return to the sidelines.

The meeting lasted several hours and Penders described it later as "pretty serious and in-depth." He said the two gentlemen were most interested in how he would get the Knicks back on the winning track. They asked questions such as: "How would you rebuild the franchise? What do you think we would need to get to the championship level?" Penders said he was also given an idea of what and who he would be working with when he was shown the team roster, player salaries, and the remaining years on each player's contract.

Before Penders returned to Austin on Thursday morning, the two parties met several more times to discuss the position, once again, in general terms. When Penders left

Chicago, he had no idea where he ranked in terms of becoming the next head coach of the Knicks. "I have no feel for that," he told the *American-Statesman*. "They're playing conservative with that, and I didn't ask."

In the next few days, Penders didn't hear from the Knicks organization. The opening with the team was never of much concern to him because he had too many other things on his plate including the Southwest Conference spring meetings in Vail, Colo.

It was from Colorado that Penders made one phone call, which helped make his decision on the Knicks if they were to offer him the job. It was a call to UT President William "Bill" Cunningham on behalf of his boss, DeLoss Dodds. With Dodds' wife Mary Ann in the room, Penders called and told Cunningham if Dodds received a five-year extension on his contract, which expired the following year, Penders would take his name out of consideration for the Knicks position.

With such a successful basketball program under Penders, who was hired by Dodds, it was conceivably a "no-brainer" for Cunningham. However, the football program and head coach David McWilliams – another Dodds' hire – had a 26-20 record in his first four seasons. With football king at the University of Texas, many critics, which is the tendency when things go bad, were very outspoken about Dodds. Despite that, Cunningham assured Penders he would get Dodds the five-year extension. The conversation concluded. Penders was staying at Texas.

Back in Austin and several days later, Penders received a phone call at his home. It was Ernie Grunfeld. Grunfeld told Penders that Pat Riley was their first choice for the position, but if he declined, as had been speculated in numerous reports, Penders was their next choice.

"Would you still be interested?" Grunfeld asked Penders.

After the conversation earlier in the week with Cunningham, Penders was firm with his decision. He informed Grunfeld he was staying in Austin. Grunfeld was surprised that Penders, a college coach, would turn down an opportunity to coach in the NBA, and of all places, New York, not to mention the potential increase in salary. Grunfeld — not necessarily in agreement — respected Penders' decision.

Before the conversation ended, Grunfeld had one last request of Penders. He asked him not to go public with his decision. Presumably, this request was made because, at the time, it wasn't clear whether or not Riley would take the job. If Riley declined after Penders had taken his name out of consideration, Grunfeld, Checketts, and the Knicks organization would have had major egg on their face with their two top choices rejecting them. The New York media would have had a field day.

Penders told Grunfeld he would not publicly make an announcement.

On Friday, May 31, after weeks of discussions regarding the salary, Pat Riley was named head coach of the New York Knicks. In the end, all parties came out feeling good. The Knicks and their fans got their man and the University of Texas retained the services of their popular coach.

UT Creates New Associate Director Position

In June, a committee made up of members from the university athletic community including Penders and then-football coach David McWilliams, were responsible for locating potential candidates to fill the newly created associate athletic director for external services. The new position was developed to oversee fundraising as well as marketing, advertising and sports information. The job was of a broader scope and more along the lines of what Craig Helwig did while at the university, not what Brewer was currently doing as Helwig's replacement.

At the end of June, Dodds announced Larry Franks, a former bank president and All-Southwest Conference basketball player at Texas in 1965, as the new associate AD.

Following Dodds' announcement, Penders was both surprised and concerned about the selection. The surprise came because as a member of the search committee to find Helwig's replacement, all those on the committee had reviewed a number of candidates up for the position and narrowed it down to three finalists. From that list, Dodds would make the final selection. The three finalists were James Saxton, Jack Cowens and James Street.

"They were all former UT football players but guys that I knew. David (McWilliams) and I were both real comfortable with them and thought (they) would be good for UT fundraising. Then all of the sudden Larry Franks was hired and he wasn't even on the list. DeLoss told me I was just going to love him because he played basketball at UT."

Penders' concern was that the job, which was responsible for four very important areas in university athletics, had been given to a person no one knew anything about – with the exception of Dodds – other than he was a former UT basketball player. All those on the committee were equally concerned and questioned why they had even been part of the committee if their recommendations for the new associate AD were to be ignored by Dodds. Unfortunately, the decision was irreversible.

Despite his uneasy feelings, Penders tried to remain open-minded on the selection of Franks. However, his doubts on the former banking executive and his ability as associate athletic director were heightened months later when one of Franks' first items of business led to an extensive NCAA investigation of the basketball program.

Report Says UT Officials Misused Phone Card

According to a report in the *Dallas Morning News*, an investigation was underway to determine if any basketball players had a role in the apparent theft of an 800 number for remote access to long-distance service.

The newspaper reported that use of the phone credit card assigned to assistant coach Eddie Oran had resulted in a November bill of $1,318. The January bill increased to $4,273 and by February, the total had increased to a staggering $12,382.

Penders said the bill, which included 5,625 calls for 56,637 minutes of long-distance time, was "as thick as phone book," and he, as well as university officials, knew something wasn't right. "It was obvious something funny had happened."

Penders also said he had warned the players of the consequences of using an authorized access number at a team meeting after the bill had been received. "We told them that strange things had happened with a phone bill and if anybody had used an 800 number, they had better come forward because they could be held responsible and prosecuted."

Theft of long-distance phone access codes is a federal offense and NCAA rules violations could result if it was proven that athletic personnel supplied the code to student-athletes.

Butch Worley, UT's assistant athletic director for administration, said the NCAA hadn't been notified. "Based on what I know right now, I don't see it as a student-athlete problem. If there is an NCAA problem, that's an athletic department matter and we'll make that determination."

UT Denies Ciampaglio Deal for Camp

In June, the university rejected Texas assistant basketball coach Jamie Ciampaglio's bid to buy a 52-percent interest in a summer basketball camp after UT officials determined it to be too great a responsibility for the school.

Ciampaglio had hoped to purchase the Five-Star Summer Camp, which has three sites in Virginia and Pennsylvania. He had been a camper and counselor for 15 years.

A loophole in NCAA legislation made the purchase legal, but a Wake Forest assistant coach gave up controlling interest in the camp because of pressure from other Atlantic Coast Conference Schools.

Dodds said he was concerned with the purchase because of an NCAA rule that went into effect that summer that prohibited Division I coaches from serving as instructors or counselors at privately owned, non-institutional camps in an effort to reduce recruiting advantages.

"It's not illegal, but we'd be responsible for every college coach who worked the camp," Dodds said. "If they did one thing wrong, the University of Texas would take the hit."

Ciampaglio said he didn't believe that was the reason he was turned down. "Dodds wouldn't let me buy the Five-Star Basketball Camp, which was completely legal, because the NCAA (told him) it's legal if he does it, but if he does it, we're going to come in and look at every single piece of paper in your athletic department."

He said Dodds and the university didn't want that.

II. The Middle Years

Chapter Six

Double Trouble on the Forty Acres, 1991 – 1992

With the 1991-1992 season less than two months away, Penders was gearing up to begin his fourth season at the helm of the University of Texas basketball program. Unfortunately, his attention which normally focused on the upcoming practices as well as recruiting for the following season, was redirected as two of Penders' assistant coaches came under investigation for two completely separate incidents.

UT's Ciampaglio Subject of Investigation

The first investigation began in September after Athletic Director DeLoss Dodds, Dr. John Butler, a member of the athletics council, and two others in the men's athletic department received an anonymous, two-page typed letter that alleged an "assistant coach in charge of basketball finances" had been pocketing players' meal money.

Although the letter never mentioned a specific name, it was obviously referring to Assistant Coach Jamie Ciampaglio who was responsible for doling out meal money for the basketball players. It alleged that Ciampaglio, who had served in the same capacity under Penders at Rhode Island, was signing for $15 per player for home games, but only giving the players $10. It also said that the assistant did not provide players with the correct amount of meal money allotted to them by the NCAA for the Midwest Regional in Dayton, Ohio, the previous season. As a result, the meal-money controversy led to confrontations between the players with the assistant and severe morale problems at the NCAA tournament.

After Dodds informed Penders about the letter, Penders called Ciampaglio, who was in San Francisco. Ciampaglio, concerned about the situation, cut his plans short in California and caught a plane back to Austin the next day.

Upon arrival in Austin, Ciampaglio met with Penders in his office.

"What's there to this?" Penders asked his assistant.

"There's nothing to this," Ciampaglio responded.

"Well, why's everyone going on about this?" Penders questioned.

"There's nothing to this Tom. It was in September. I was doing what I think was..."

"Get the players together and explain to them what you did," Penders interrupted.

Ciampaglio said after his meeting with Penders, he and the staff met with all the players in the basketball office.

"I went to the chalkboard and put up on the board how I handled and distributed the meal money, and how it went out. And tried to explain to them what had occurred," Ciampaglio said, recalling the meeting. He said that was the last time he discussed the situation with any members of the team. "That's where it ended with the players."

In the next few weeks the situation grew quiet. However, it was by no means over. In fact, the reason for the silence around Bellmont Hall and the athletic department was because the issue had been turned over from Dodds and company to the university's internal audit department.

The internal audit department, as part of its investigation, interviewed Ciampaglio and asked him for a statement. Ciampaglio said he explained what had occurred. "I showed how I did things and what exactly I did, and why I did what I did," he said. "Basically, how I went about taking the money and distributing it at certain times and places."

Ciampaglio said after that meeting, he realized the situation was getting more serious by the minute and he expressed his concern, first to his wife, then to Penders.

"Tom, I think I need a lawyer," he said. "I think there's a problem here and I think it's being handled as a criminal investigation or some type of investigation. What do you think I should do?"

"Don't worry about it. It will all be taken care of. It will all be blown off," Penders responded.

Although Ciampaglio hoped Penders was right, he couldn't be sure. Ciampaglio said as he continued to talk about the situation, an uneasy feeling persisted. He believed he needed an attorney and approached Penders again.

Penders, at that point, referred Ciampaglio to Austin attorney Abraham Kazen. Ciampaglio said Penders told him Kazen would try and get everything straightened out.

Soon after, Ciampaglio called and made an appointment with Kazen.

In their first meeting, Ciampaglio said he explained to Kazen everything that had occurred. After he heard the whole story, Kazen instructed his new client not to speak with anyone else.

Ciampaglio said after following the original plan for several days and not speaking to anyone about the situation, Kazen opted for a change in strategy. Instead of sitting quietly on the sidelines as he had done, Kazen wanted Ciampaglio to be proactive. He wanted him to meet with reporters and personally explain exactly what had happened with the meal money and how it was distributed. Ciampaglio complied.

Within days, Ciampaglio said several reporters from the *Austin American-Statesman* were in his office, listening as he explained – in detail – what happened with the handling of meal money for the men's basketball program.

On November 14, 1991 – just six days before the season opener against the Washington Huskies – the headline in the sports section read "Ciampaglio Admits Holding Back Meal Money."

In the article Ciampaglio conceded he had not given the meal money according to proper school procedures, but he said he eventually always gave the players the exact amount allowed. During the past two years, he said he saved a portion of the money owed the players for postgame meals at home and distributed it out on road trips, partly as a motivational tool and partly as a way to cope with higher road expenses.

He said initially, when the anonymous letter was written, he considered hiring a private investigator to determine the source of the letter. "Somebody thinks I'm stealing. Why on God's green earth would I jeopardize everything for a couple of dollars? There's no legitimacy to anything in the letter," he said.

Ciampaglio said he kept the extra meal money in an envelope wrapped in aluminum foil in his freezer because he was so scared the money would be stolen before the next road game. "It was a fund, and whenever it ran out, it ran out," he said. "A player might say, 'Coach, I only got $10,' and I'd say 'Guys, this is all I got.'"

The coach said when he first started in 1988, players were allowed only $10 to make up for the dinner meal they missed at the dorm as a result of a home game. This changed to $15 in 1989. Ciampaglio said he would save the extra.

He said at the 1991 NCAA Tournament, where the anonymous letter alleged a controversy arose between players and an assistant, Ciampaglio said each player was entitled to $300 for the six-day trip, or $50 per day ($25 for dinner, $15 for lunch and $10 for breakfast). The school, however, paid for the breakfast as a daily team meal, so players were not given the extra $10.

Ciampaglio said he gave the players $40 each the first day, then $100 before the team played St. Peter's, $40 the third day, and $120 the day the Longhorns took on St. John's. He said he thought dividing the meal money helped motivate the players for games in the single-elimination tournament, and he told the players they would receive parts of their meal money as they continued winning.

He said although the internal audit was continuing, a member of the Texas business or ticket office would be traveling with the team and handle the payments, a practice that was used by the football team because the payments sometimes involved up to 90 players for road games.

In the article Penders said he stood behind his assistant and believed someone outside the program planted the letter to hurt his team's recruiting, which had started several days before.

"I think it's a lot of garbage," Penders said. "I have total trust in Jamie. He's a guy of great integrity. A lot of the things in the letter are inaccurate. Our guess is the kids got every dime they were supposed to. If an assistant coach of mine ever shortchanged a player, I'd fire him. But I have full confidence Jamie did what he's supposed to."

While Ciampaglio's admission was the talk of the local sports scene, behind the scenes on the University of Texas campus, the matter had been turned over from the university's internal audit department to the university police department.

Ciampaglio, who had been on the sidelines for the first two games of the season — two wins over Washington and Princeton — said he soon learned responsibility for the investigation had switched hands again when he and his attorney were summoned to appear at the university police department.

He said at police headquarters he was interviewed by an officer who regularly traveled with the basketball team to out-of-town contests and served as somewhat of a protector of Penders, his staff and the players. Ciampaglio said the officer asked him to provide a written statement, which he did, and asked him to answer several questions.

After the question-answer session was complete, Ciampaglio and Kazen left. Kazen returned to his office and Ciampaglio returned to the team as they planned to depart for New York City and the Preseason NIT Tournament.

In the next several weeks talks of the investigation were again quiet as university police continued to probe the matter. It wasn't until mid-December that Ciampaglio learned the matter had switched hands, yet again, when he was called in to answer another round of questions. This time, the questions came from a representative of the Public Integrity Unit of the Travis County District Attorney's office, or a branch of the DA's office that investigates and prosecutes cases dealing with misapplication of state funds.

Different week, different office in charge.

Ciampaglio, Kazen, and acting chief of the Public Integrity Unit, Claire Dawson-Brown and an assistant were present at the meeting. Ciampaglio explained to her the situation. "I went through the same thing with her that I went through with everybody," Ciampaglio recalls.

"I told her exactly what I did and what happened."

"Listen, ma'am, someone's got to explain to me why I would, for any reason, someone who has a bright career in front of them, is going to throw it all away for $10,000 to $12,000. We're not talking $100,000. We're talking $5 a player after a game. Instead of giving them $15, they got $10."

"Why would I throw it all away for $5 a player for 12 home basketball games, that's $400, $500, $600," Ciampaglio said, almost pleading and with the hopes she would understand even he recognized it wouldn't be worth the risk.

"You've got to be kidding me. I don't smoke. I don't drink. I don't gamble. I've got a wife, one child, pregnant with the second. I don't have credit card debts. I am a coach. What am I going to throw it all away for? What was I doing? Why would I do that for this miniscule amount of money?" Ciampaglio asked, trying to convey his point.

After the meeting with Dawson-Brown, Ciampaglio said he began asking himself questions about the situation. "Who would benefit the most? What would be the reason for getting rid of Jamie? What were the consequences of getting rid of Jamie?"

Ciampaglio said he figured if he could answer those questions, he might uncover who was behind the anonymous letter. He wouldn't have any answers until the season was finished and his name once again appeared in the headlines.

Assistant Trilli Finds Trouble

While Ciampaglio was dealing with his crisis, another Texas assistant, Vic Trilli, was having a crisis of his own.

In October, Trilli, who was going into his second year at Texas, approached Penders regarding his financial situation. Penders said Trilli told him that the combination of his son's lengthy stay in the hospital and his part-time status as coach had put his family in a financial bind and they needed some kind of financial assistance. Penders told Trilli he would be unable to help him personally. NCAA rules not only prohibit giving money to assistants, but loaning money as well. Penders advised Trilli that he should speak with Robert Brewer, the new assistant athletic director for development.

After an initial meeting with Brewer, in which Brewer told Trilli to calculate all his debts and credits owed to him personally, Trilli again approached Penders about the situation.

"I told him, 'Vic, be up front and put down all things you owe and all things that you have coming to you,'" Penders would say later recalling the conversation. Penders said the idea was for Trilli to get all his present finances down on paper so the university might assist him in locating a banker or somebody in the Longhorn Foundation to get him a loan from a bank.

Following the meeting with Penders, Trilli met with Brewer again. In that meeting, Trilli presented a work sheet with all his debts and all the credits owed to him personally. One of the credits owed was $2,000 from Locksley Collie, a former player who had completed his eligibility the year before. Although it was not discovered until much later, Collie owed Trilli $2,000 after Trilli had loaned him his credit card that summer to use as collateral on an engagement ring for his girlfriend, Cinietra Henderson, a standout on Jody Conradt's Lady Longhorns squad.

Immediately following the meeting, Brewer, according to various athletic sources, suspected Trilli had incurred the debt by paying players. Concerned by the $2,000 owed to Trilli, Brewer went to Larry Franks, the new associate athletic director. Brewer told Franks he wasn't sure about the situation, but he believed this was something Franks should oversee as his supervisor. Franks, who had been at the position for several months, took the issue straight to Dodds, never once calling Trilli or Penders to explore the situation further. Penders said he was told later by an athletic department official that Franks told Dodds "he had proof Trilli had loaned money to a player."

Surprisingly, as Franks had done, Dodds never called Trilli to question him about the matter, or Penders to ask him if he knew anything about it. Instead, Dodds and the university reported it to the NCAA. Penders was finally made aware of the situation two weeks later when Dodds called him into his office.

In that meeting, Dodds began by telling Penders the NCAA had been notified that Vic Trilli had given money to a player.

"What are you talking about?" Penders asked, stunned by Dodds' statement. "He's in debt and doesn't have any money, that's impossible. Have you had Vic in here? Have you talked to him?" Penders asked his athletic director.

"No," Dodds answered emphatically. "We've called the NCAA and they told us not to talk to Vic and tell him anything; not to alert him. You cannot tell Vic either," Dodds continued. "I'm telling you because you're the head coach. The NCAA doesn't want me to tell you this, but I've got to tell you so you're not surprised when the NCAA comes in."

"I think you ought to bring Vic in here and ask him because I think this is garbage. What did he do?" Penders questioned. Before Dodds answered, Penders continued. "No. 1, there are only two kids in this program that have cars. My son has an old beat up piece of junk, and Benford Williams has an old piece of junk. These guys aren't walking around with gold on, and I doubt if any of them have sports jackets," he said.

"The NCAA is going to come in and figure that out," Dodds told Penders.

The conference ended and Penders wasn't pleased. Penders would say later that he was dismayed the way the whole situation was handled. "They (Dodds and Franks) weren't specific when they called the NCAA. They didn't say this was a former player or whatever. They just told them 'Come in and look at us.' "

"I couldn't believe they were doing that. I've worked at other NCAA schools and if there's a possible NCAA violation, the AD will ask the coaches or the compliance person will ask questions such as: What's going on here? Did you loan money to somebody? Do you have proof of records? Can I look at your records?" Penders said. "If there's nothing there, there's nothing even to report. I thought it was a strange way to operate. I wasn't thrilled with the way Dodds handled that because he ultimately is the athletic director, not Larry Franks."

After the meeting with Dodds, Penders met with assistant coach Eddie Oran to discuss the upcoming investigation. When Penders told Oran how Trilli had allegedly loaned money to a player, Oran scoffed at the thought. "That's ridiculous Tom," Oran said. "He's in debt and he's got four kids. Don't even worry about it."

In the next few weeks, before the NCAA's arrival, Penders never mentioned to Trilli the pending investigation regarding the loan. "I didn't tell Vic because I gave him (Dodds) my word I wouldn't," Penders said.

When the NCAA arrived, each player was interviewed separately in an office on the ninth floor of Bellmont Hall. Present at each session were two members of the university compliance staff and a member of the NCAA, who asked each player a series of questions. Penders said as a rule, a lawyer is present when these questions are being asked in an investigation, but one was not present for these interviews. As the investigation neared its end, the NCAA had found no evidence of any wrongdoing regarding Trilli and the loan to Collie. However, the NCAA had several more players to interview, including Dexter Cambridge.

Cambridge, who was about to enter his senior season as a Longhorn, answered the initial questions with relative ease. Then, the NCAA representative asked Cambridge several questions that would affect Cambridge, the basketball program, and the university for the next several months.

"Did you ever have a car?" the official asked.

"Yes," the senior-to-be answered.

At that point, Associate Athletic Director Butch Worley told the NCAA official that Cambridge needed an attorney. The meeting was then stopped and scheduled for the next day. Worley also told W.O. Shultz, the assistant general counsel to the university, that Cambridge needed an independent attorney for the NCAA investigation.

During the second session between Cambridge and the NCAA official, no independent counsel was present despite Worley's request. Instead, a UT lawyer was the only counsel present.

The line of questions resumed regarding Cambridge's purchase of the car.

"How did you buy it?" the NCAA official asked.

"I paid for it," Cambridge responded.

"Where did you get the money?" the official asked continuing on the lead from Cambridge's previous answer.

"When I graduated from Lon Morris, my sponsor gave me a graduation present and I bought a car with it," Cambridge answered innocently, not realizing the significance of what he had just said.

Although Cambridge was simply being honest with his answer, he had completely opened up a whole new avenue for NCAA investigators to explore. They did.

NCAA representatives then listened as Cambridge volunteered information regarding the graduation present. He explained how he received $7,000 in 1990 from Keith Heingartner, a former assistant coach at Lon Morris Junior College in Jacksonville, Texas, where Cambridge went to school his freshman and sophomore year.

Cambridge said he had worked for Heingartner, a businessman who owned a temporary services company that employs many of the students who attend the two colleges in Jacksonville, and the two became good friends. When he left, Heingartner gave him the $7,000 check for graduation of which he used $5,000 for a down payment on a Toyota Supra that was later repossessed.

That was more than enough information for NCAA investigators. Although Cambridge had explained how he and Heingartner were good friends, the NCAA did not necessarily believe that was the case. They deemed that the money was given not out of friendship, but as an inducement to play basketball. On November 20, the day Texas opened the season at home against the Washington Huskies, the NCAA ruled Cambridge ineligible for violating his amateur status by taking the money.

However, Cambridge's attorney, Ralph A. Rash, acted quickly following the ruling and obtained a temporary restraining order in state district court from State District Judge Jon Wisser that allowed Cambridge to play for 10 days and prevented the university from following the NCAA's instructions to suspend him. In the order, Cambridge denied any wrongdoing and asserted that the university violated his constitutional rights by denying him due process without a hearing. Cambridge's attorney also sought a temporary injunction against the school and Wisser set a date for a December 3 hearing on the matter.

The Regular Season

With the restraining order granted, Cambridge opened the season with a 29-point performance against the Washington Huskies as the Longhorns routed the visitors 104-83 in the first round of the Big Apple National Invitation Tournament game.

Cambridge, seemingly unaffected by his off-the-court situation, tallied the 29 in just 28 minutes of action as 13,502 watched him convert 13 of 16 from the field. With the win, which improved Texas' record to 17-0 in three years under Penders when the team scored 100 or more points in the Erwin Center, the Longhorns earned a second-round berth at home against Princeton. Despite the lack of offensive production, resulting directly from Princeton's slow-it-down style of basketball, the Horns managed to prevail by a 57-46 margin and advanced to the NIT semifinals in New York City.

Before the Horns headed off to the Big Apple, the *American-Statesman* reported that Cambridge would be unable to appeal his eligibility with the NCAA until he asked the state district judge to lift the temporary restraining order.

Dodds said in the article that the restraining order was a stumbling block in the NCAA's appeals process. "That's what the NCAA is telling us. That's their strategy."

Cambridge was placed in an awkward situation. If he agreed to have the order lifted, the NCAA Eligibility Committee could rule against his appeal and his college career would be over. The NCAA could also opt to suspend him for a portion of the season; something UT officials were hopeful of since the school had self-reported the violation.

Whatever the decision, Cambridge decided it wouldn't be Ralph Rash and Dan Laney to defend him in the case. Cambridge opted for attorney Phil Maxwell. "Dexter was uncomfortable because the school helped him find us," Rash said.

With Austin and investigations behind them, the Texas players welcomed the opportunity of playing in the semifinals of the Big Apple NIT Tournament in New York City. However, before the first game against Georgia Tech tipped off, university officials back in Austin and UT fans across the nation were in shock as Cambridge and his situation were thrust into the national spotlight. It wasn't actually Cambridge's situation that was disconcerting, but what might be the end result. According to a report by ESPN's Dick Vitale on the pre-game show, Penders might leave the Longhorns after the season because of the way university officials had handled the Cambridge situation.

Following two disappointing losses, to Georgia Tech and the Pittsburgh Panthers, the Horns returned to Austin to regroup and prepare for the Eighth Annual Longhorn Classic. Cambridge returned with the team, but he wasn't sure if he would ever return to the court with his teammates as the ruling on his eligibility was to occur in a matter of days.

However, before that ruling was made, the NCAA and the university filed a petition that moved the case from State District Court to U.S. District Court. Robert Roller, an attorney with the NCAA, said the case was removed from state district court because the organization believed due process was a federal issue. NCAA spokesman James Marchiony added that the NCAA usually tried to litigate in federal court. "The NCAA spans 50 states and over 800 schools. It's a national organization, not a regional one," Marchiony said.

With the case in a new court, the original ruling scheduled for December 3 was delayed and rescheduled for December 6. U.S. District Judge Walter Smith of Waco moved the date back three days to determine if the University of Texas case belonged in his court. In the meantime, he extended the temporary restraining order.

After several days, Smith set a hearing date for a week later in Austin to receive evidence on the lawsuit. However, he did not extend the restraining order a second time and Cambridge was ruled ineligible until the hearing was held. Until the issue was resolved, Cambridge would be allowed to practice, but not allowed to participate in games.

That night the Longhorns took the court against North Texas in the first round of the Longhorn Classic without their leading scorer. Texas eventually wore down the Eagles and pulled away for a 124-107 victory. Leading the way offensively for Texas, in Cambridge's absence, was the team's only other senior – Benford Williams.

In the championship game of the final Longhorn Classic, Benford Williams stepped up his effort once again and led the Longhorns to an 85-58 victory over the San Diego State Aztecs. With the win, Texas improved to 4-2 on the young season and won the Classic for the seventh time in its eight-year history.

Although the tournament was a success for UT as far as putting victories in the win column were concerned, the tournament never drew any big-name schools — a necessity when trying to build a tough non-conference schedule that can increase the likelihood of a berth to the NCAA Tournament in March.

Penders said when he originally arrived in Austin he tried to get some big-name teams to come to Austin for the Classic by sending out invitations to the top 100 college basketball teams in the country. Not one responded. In addition to a lack of interest from other schools, he said the interest from the university also began to wane in the latter years.

"It was too much work. A lot of people really did try to help but they didn't have the power or decision-making power to make a lot of the things happen," he said. "They (administration) didn't want to deal with anything until football was over, which is normally January. Also, it's hard to draw good teams unless you pay them good money or get one of the games on television. We were going to the Arizona State Classics and all these other tournaments and getting big money. Sometimes even television exposure. I remember playing Michigan at the Arizona State tournament. Our people weren't willing to do that. We didn't have any budget for that."

Penders said when he realized they couldn't draw the top teams they decided to go to plan B, which consisted of bringing in teams from Austin and the surrounding area. "At the end we found that the only way to keep it going was to get teams like UT-San Antonio and teams that might bring local fans. We made it part of the season ticket package so fans could actually attend a couple more home games."

Following the final Classic and before the Horns faced the Oklahoma Sooners, the Longhorns received some bad news. The NCAA had revoked Cambridge's entire season of eligibility for what they classified as a rules violation that affected his amateur status.

With the ruling, Cambridge still had two options – either of which might allow his return to the team. First, if he was successful in his lawsuit to obtain a preliminary injunction, which was scheduled for hearing in a couple of days, he could return most likely for the remainder of the season because the case would not be completed until after the season.

The second avenue for a potential return to the lineup would be by way of a successful appeal with the NCAA Eligibility Committee. UT officials had argued for leniency in the case because Cambridge did not realize he had committed a violation and because the school had cooperated with NCAA procedure by self-reporting the violation. Butch Worley, the Texas associate athletic director, said the five-member appeals committee would not hear the case for at least a week.

Either way, Cambridge had to sit out a third game as his teammates took on Oklahoma in Norman. In the contest, which was televised nationally on ESPN, the Horns trailed by only six at half, 51-45, to the 17th-ranked Sooners. In the end, Oklahoma defeated Texas soundly, 106-91.

Several days later, the first of two options for Cambridge's possible return to the Texas sideline was eliminated. The NCAA Eligibility Committee upheld the decision that Cambridge was ineligible for violating his amateur status and would not return to action. The ruling, according to NCAA spokesman James Marchiony, was based on two factors. "It was a combination of the amount of money and the fact that the money was a direct result of athletic performance."

Cambridge and the Horns were down to their last strike. The ball was now in someone else's court, more specifically, the U.S. District Court in Austin and Judge Walter Smith of Waco, who planned on ruling on the case in a couple of days.

Two days later it was official – Cambridge was finished as a member of the University of Texas basketball team as Smith denied Cambridge's request for an injunction. Smith wrote in his opinion: "While it is always unfortunate when a young athlete is declared ineligible ... decisions regarding violations of NCAA rules are best determined within the framework of its procedures."

Penders said he thought the penalty was much too harsh and his superiors, UT President William Cunningham and Dodds agreed. "We have appealed, and we will continue to vigorously pursue that appeal on Dexter's behalf," Cunningham said.

With the decision final, Cambridge's attorney, Maxwell, said he would appeal the decision to the 5th Circuit Court of Appeals in New Orleans. Maxwell said Cambridge also had one appeal with the NCAA remaining in which Cambridge would appear before the NCAA Subcommittee on Eligibility in early January at the NCAA Convention.

While all the legal maneuvering continued following the decision, the players had to officially plan for the future sans Dexter Cambridge. There wasn't much time to think about it as the future began that night with the eighth-ranked Connecticut Huskies in town.

Connecticut showed no pity for the Horns and the loss of their star player in front of the 14,309 gathered in the Erwin Center. Despite a 31-point performance from Benford Williams, the loss marked the worst defeat at home for a Texas squad in four seasons under Penders, 94-77. After the day's losses, both on the court and in court, December 14, 1991, was a day members of the University of Texas community — staff and supporters — wanted to soon forget.

Cambridge, himself, wanted to put the incident behind him as he left the U.S. to return home to his family in the Bahamas. Before he left, Cambridge said he was considering his options, but wasn't too positive about returning. "I can only say that this has been an ordeal, and perhaps it is time to say enough is enough," Cambridge said in a statement issued by the University of Texas sports information department before he left for the school's five-week Christmas break. "I have certainly been, and am, disappointed and not very encouraged with my chances at this time with another NCAA appeal that involves the same people and organization," the statement said.

Following the loss at home to Connecticut, the Horns schedule didn't get any easier as the California-Santa Barbara Gauchos came to town before the Christmas break. Texas wasn't in a gift-giving mood, as evidenced by only eight turnovers in front of a crowd of 11,971. The Horns were back on track with a 90-77 victory. With the win, Texas improved to 5-4 on the season and avoided the first three-game losing streak at home since Penders arrived in 1988.

In the first round of the Sun Carnival Classic in El Paso the Horns handed Clemson its first loss of the season, 95-87. With the victory, Texas improved to 6-4 and earned a berth in the finals against the host team, Texas-El Paso.

In the first half, UTEP outdueled the Longhorns and led at the break, 49-35. In the second half, UTEP had extended its lead to 29 points with less than 10 minutes remaining and appeared on its way to victory. The Longhorns and B.J. Tyler had other ideas. Tyler scored 18 of his game-high 27 points in the second half as Texas stormed back to within one point with less than a minute left in the contest. All the effort fell just short as the Horns missed two opportunities to tie the game late. UTEP held on for the 92-88 victory and their 21st title in 31 years of the Sun Carnival Classic.

In the first game of 1992, there was no let-up in the Texas schedule. The Horns traveled to New Orleans to take on the LSU Tigers in front of a huge crowd at the Louisiana Superdome. A crowd of 42,211 — the largest ever to watch a Texas basketball team — looked on as the Tigers pulled off a thrilling 84-83 victory in the final minute. Texas had a chance to win the game with less than 10 seconds, but LSU's big man, Shaquille O'Neal, blocked the shot. The loss dropped the Longhorns to 6-6 for the season.

In their second attempt to secure a win in 1992, the Horns found success against Murray State. The Racers, led by Popeye Jones, were no match for Texas and its offensive firepower. Five players scored in double figures for the Horns as they breezed to a 93-75 victory.

Following the win over Murray State, Texas prepared to open the Southwest Conference season at home against the Houston Cougars. However, before SWC action got underway, Dexter Cambridge's name reappeared once again. This time the news was somewhat positive.

At the NCAA Convention in Anaheim, Cali., Cambridge, his attorney Phil Maxwell, as well as university officials including DeLoss Dodds and President Bill Cunningham spent more than an hour in talks with the NCAA Subcommittee on Eligibility Appeals. The NCAA officials listened as university representatives and Maxwell presented an affidavit that detailed how $2,400 of the $7,000 Cambridge received was for work performed. With this new information, UT officials appealed that the one-year suspension be reduced. To further the case, UT officials and Maxwell cited an earlier case in which a female basketball player received $4,600 for appearing on the *American Gladiators* television show and was suspended for only half a season.

Following the meeting, Dodds said he was pleased with the overall tone of the session. "I appreciate the committee's willingness to work with us. You have to be encouraged. I think the appeal went real well."

According to Janet Justus, head of the subcommittee and NCAA director of eligibility, UT officials had raised an interesting point – one that might result in Cambridge returning to the basketball court. "If more information that would support the affidavit can be provided, about more hours, work performed ... if there is new information, it could result in a different decision."

With that, the subcommittee planned to send the case back to the eligibility committee to restart the appeals process.

Penders said President Cunningham's attendance at the meeting was significant for several reasons. Not only did Cunningham's presence add credibility to Cambridge's case with the NCAA, but it also showed Penders that the president at one of the largest universities in the world was willing to take time out of his busy schedule to fight for something he truly believed in.

"Bill Cunningham, to his credit, fought it," Penders recalls back to the controversy. "He flew out to California and really got upset with the NCAA because he felt it had nothing to do with Texas and it was a gift from a guy who he knew in junior college."

Back on the court, the Horns opened the SWC season against Houston before 12,343 Erwin Center fans and a national television audience. The contest was nip-and-tuck throughout. In the second half, three unlikely players, reserves Michael Richardson,

Tony Watson and Gerrald Houston combined during a seven-minute span to score 15 consecutive points that kept Texas in the game and eventually gave it the lead — one it would never relinquish. Houston made a run at the close of the game but the Longhorns fought it off and escaped with an 86-75 win.

Two days later the Horns played host to the visiting team from Lubbock. In another close contest, UT outlasted the Red Raiders with a balanced attack from its two main scoring guards. Rencher and Tyler combined to score 55 points in the contest as Texas earned an 88-83 victory.

Following the two conference wins, Texas tried improving to 3-0 in conference against its rival in College Station. The Aggies, who came into the game with a 3-9 record, took advantage of poor Texas shooting early on and led in a low-scoring contest at the half, 37-34. In the second half, Texas rallied behind its two offensive leaders Rencher and Williams, and finished with a tough 76-73 win at G. Rollie White Coliseum.

Riding a four-game winning streak and sitting tied atop the SWC standings, the Longhorns were confident as they headed into a showdown with TCU in Fort Worth. However, before the Horns made the trip to north Texas, the NCAA ruled on the Cambridge matter.

No — eligibility would not be restored and the original ruling was upheld. Just what Penders and Texas officials didn't want to hear, and didn't expect to hear after providing NCAA officials with new information regarding the money Cambridge had received.

Acting chairman of the three-person committee, Max Williams, said the new information did not sufficiently corroborate that $2,400 of the $7,000 Cambridge received was for back wages earned from Keith Heingartner's temporary employment business. Williams, who was a faculty athletics representative at the University of Mississippi, said that "even if the committee could have accepted that the new information corroborated that $2,400 worth of wages was performed, then it would have rendered the same decision."

UT officials were confused. The NCAA had not only suspended the student-athlete after the school had self-reported the violation, but now the NCAA had upheld the season-long suspension after repeated pleas of leniency from the school due to the inadvertent nature of the violation, and after new information was provided at the subcommittee's request. Despite that, Cambridge and the university held out hope on one last appeal with the subcommittee, which was to be held in the coming weeks.

In a statement Dodds said, "I am very discouraged, for Dexter, and for the university, as well as with the process ... I am hopeful that the subcommittee will carefully review the facts that they asked us to provide. Based on my experience with that group, I am confident that they will do so."

With the Cambridge situation on the back burner – for now – the Longhorns visited the Horned Frogs for a battle of SWC supremacy. TCU held off the Horns for the 80-76 victory. The win moved TCU into first place with a 3-0 record in the SWC while Texas had its four-game winning streak snapped and dropped to 10-7 overall, 3-1 in the conference.

After the TCU loss Texas tried to get back on the winning track in conference play versus the SMU Mustangs. Rencher led the Horns scoring a team-high 28 points in a 106-91 defeat of the Ponies. With the victory, Texas improved to 11-7 overall and moved into first place in the SWC with a 4-1 record.

Following the SMU win, Dexter Cambridge's name returned as the sports topic around Austin. "Will he or won't he return?" was the predominant question asked by Longhorn fans as the NCAA prepared to make its ruling on Cambridge's final appeal.

In a conference call that lasted more than five hours, the five-member NCAA Council Subcommittee on Eligibility Appeals ruled that the 6-foot-7-inch forward could return to action for Texas as they reduced his one-year suspension to a half-season. The subcommittee was convinced by Cambridge's representatives that $2,400 of the $7,000 was for back wages Heingartner owed Cambridge for work performed at his temporary employment company.

All those in the Cambridge camp, including Cambridge himself, were somewhat surprised, but nonetheless very happy with the decision. "I couldn't believe it," he said. "To tell you the truth, I didn't think I had a chance ... I want to thank everyone for believing in me."

Cambridge now had a second chance with the Longhorns. There was, however, one catch. He had to raise the $4,600 before he could play again. When asked about raising the money, Cambridge couldn't help but laugh. "I don't want to talk about money anymore. I'll get it."

Janet Justus, NCAA director of eligibility, said Cambridge was permitted to receive a student loan to pay off the remaining money.

Penders said although the Cambridge situation was officially resolved, the whole ordeal left a bad taste in his mouth. He said it could have been completely avoided if Dodds or Franks had asked Trilli or Penders about the loan when the original suspicions arose, instead of taking the matter directly to the NCAA. Penders said as a result of the Trilli/Cambridge situation, the university changed its policy and began conducting internal investigations before going to the NCAA.

With the final ruling, the Longhorns would have returning to the lineup a player who had averaged 23.5 points and 12.5 rebounds before the suspension. Although the same production wasn't expected initially, both fans and players expected an improvement in Texas basketball. "We were just starting to jell without him," Rencher said. "We can't do anything but get better with him."

The first opportunity for the Longhorns to show they were a better team with Cambridge would have to wait until Cambridge served his half-season or 16-game suspension. This wouldn't occur until the Horns visited Rhode Island in early February. In the meantime, the still Cambridge-less Horns headed to Waco for a contest with the Baylor Bears.

Texas left with an 84-68 loss and a record of 11-8 overall and 4-2 in conference. The return of Cambridge and his offensive production were, needless to say, eagerly anticipated.

Following the tough conference loss in Waco, the Longhorns returned to the Erwin Center for the first of several mid-season, non-conference games. Against the Virginia Commonwealth Rams, the Longhorns erased the memories of recent subpar shooting performances as the team shot better than 50 percent from the field en route to a 105-94 victory.

Two days later both Penders and Cambridge made grand returns. Cambridge returned from his half-season long suspension while Penders returned to face his former Rhode Island team.

With hordes of media following both stories, the Longhorns and Cambridge were an even match for the Rams (14-3) until early in the second half. Just two minutes into the half, Cambridge picked up his third and fourth fouls and had to sit. When Cambridge departed, Rhode Island promptly outscored Texas 11-4 and never looked back. They went on to a 92-79 victory and spoiled the returns of both coach and player.

After the two non-conference games, Texas returned to SWC action against the Rice Owls. It also marked the first time Longhorn fans had an opportunity to see Cambridge since his last game in November. Cambridge received a warm ovation when he was the last of the Texas players introduced in pre-game introductions.

Cambridge gave the 11,867 fans more to cheer about early in the game when he scored the first 10 points for Texas on his way to a 15-point first-half performance. In an effort to shut down Cambridge in the second half, Rice collapsed down on defense and limited him to only four points. Rencher, however, filled in capably as he led UT with 24 points, including the winning free throw with seven seconds that gave Texas the 88-87 victory. Texas, which shot better than 48 percent for the night, improved to 13-9 overall and 5-2 in the SWC, one half-game behind TCU in the standings.

In their next game, the Longhorns visited the Houston Cougars at Hofheinz Pavilion. With 8,931 fans and a regional television audience looking on, the Horns had upset on their minds against the 16-4 Cougars. To pull it off, Penders called for relentless pressure defense. It worked. The Longhorns won convincingly, 87-72. The win moved the Longhorns into a first-place tie with TCU.

In Lubbock, the Longhorns had a chance to take sole possession of first place in the conference with a win over Texas Tech. Early on, the Texas offense sputtered as the team managed to hit only two of its first 16 shots, which resulted in a nine-point deficit in the first half. However, the Longhorns bounced back late in the half on the strength of a 14-point first-half performance from Rencher. In the second half Rencher went on to score a total of 26 points, to lead all scorers and lead the Longhorns to a 93-90 victory.

UT returned to SWC play in a crucial game with TCU. With a win, Texas would have the outright lead in the conference standings with only four conference games remaining, while a loss would move the Longhorns into a tie with Houston for second. With so much riding on the line, the intensity of play was high in the first half. At the break, Texas led 47-42.

In the second half the Longhorns had their best offensive half of the season in front of the largest home crowd of the season. After the offensive spurt, the Longhorns led 80-60 and coasted in for a 99-77 win. The victory extended the Texas winning streak to five and gave it sole possession of first place in the SWC with an 8-2 record.

Alone atop the SWC standings, the Texas team was clearly marked with a bull's eye and the other SWC teams were ready to take aim. Up first, in Dallas, the SMU Mustangs.

The Longhorns found a rhythm early in the first half against the Mustangs as they scored 15 points off 12 SMU turnovers. As the half closed out, Texas converted 11 of its last 14 shots and headed into the locker room with a 48-37 lead. In the second half the Ponies battled back from the 11-point halftime deficit and with less than six minutes remaining in the contest, SMU held a five-point lead. But Texas countered and with 28 seconds left, the game was tied. After Dexter Cambridge was fouled away from the ball, the senior calmly sank a pair of free throws for two of his career-high 31 points and the Longhorns snuck out of Moody Coliseum with an 88-86 victory. The winning streak was at six.

In the final non-conference contest of the regular season, Texas played host to the Golden Eagles of Oral Roberts University. Unfortunately for the Golden Eagles, the hosts weren't so gracious. The Longhorns shot better than 57 percent for the game including 61.5 percent in the second half and scored 128 points in the 128-108 scoring frenzy.

The Erwin Center crowd of 11,972 watched the Horns earn their seventh consecutive victory and were witness to something never seen before at Texas, as three players – Rencher, Cambridge and Tyler – each exceeded 30 points. Even the prolific trio of Lance Blanks, Travis Mays and Joey Wright had never accomplished the feat. Rencher led the way with 34 points while Tyler added a career-high 33 and Cambridge equaled his career-high set in the previous game against SMU with 31. The combined total of 98 points from the three players was staggering. The overall point total of 128 for the team was equally impressive and the second highest ever by a Longhorn team.

The win, which improved the Longhorns' record to 19-9 on the season, marked the 30th time Texas had exceeded 100 points in 127 games under Penders. It also improved the team's overall home record to 20-0 when it reached the century mark. Before Penders arrived, Texas had scored 100 or more points 28 times in 1,840 games.

Back in conference, Texas hosted the Baylor Bears and the players had payback on their minds. Following an 84-68 defeat earlier in the season in Waco, and some harsh post-game comments from the Bears, the Longhorns wanted to redeem themselves in a big way.

After the first half, in which Texas went on an 18-6 run, the message was sent in the form of a 41-29 halftime lead. But the Longhorns weren't finished. In the second half, Texas went on a 22-2 scoring streak that put the contest out of reach. When the humiliation was over, the Longhorns had won their eighth consecutive victory by a 97-67 margin. The win improved the Horns record to 20-9 overall and 10-2 in SWC action. It also marked the fourth consecutive year Texas had reached the 20-win plateau.

In Houston, the Horns tried to make it win no. 21 with a victory over the Rice Owls. For much of the contest, with neither team establishing dominance over the other, it appeared the game would come down to the final seconds as it had in recent games between the two teams. But Rice went on a 16-3 run just past the midway point of the second half and Texas never recovered. The winning streak ended at eight as the Horns lost 103-97. With the loss, Texas fell to 20-10 and 10-3 in the conference and into a first-place tie with Houston.

The Longhorns hosted Texas A&M in the regular season home finale and final home game in the careers of seniors Dexter Cambridge and Benford Williams. A crowd of 14,272 watched Texas put away the Aggies early. When it was finished, including the 22-point performance from Cambridge, UT had won 86-63 and earned a share of the

SWC regular season title with Houston, who also finished 11-3 in SWC play. It was the first regular season SWC title for Texas since the 1986 season. The Longhorns, which finished with their best home record since 1978 at 14-1, received the No. 1 seed in the tournament by way of defeating Houston both times during the regular season. Their first opponent in the SWC tournament was the same Aggie team they had just defeated and was seeded No. 8.

The SWC Tournament

In the opening round of the SWC Tournament, the top-seeded Horns were tested by the No. 8-seeded Aggies. In fact, at halftime they trailed A&M by eight, 42-34. The halftime break proved to be most beneficial for the Horns and detrimental to their counterparts from College Station. Junior Michael Richardson led the resurgent Longhorns to a come-from-behind, 88-69 victory. With the win, Texas advanced to the second round where they would face the Red Raiders.

In the second-round contest against Texas Tech, the Horns enjoyed a 97-87 win, which earned them a berth in the tournament championship game against Houston.

In the SWC Tournament Championship, the matchup was perfect. The two teams that had battled to identical 11-3 records in regular-season conference action and tied as co-champions were matched up in the finals. Texas appeared to be the favorite after it had defeated Houston by a combined 26 points in the two previous meetings. But the Cougars, despite a double-overtime semifinal game against TCU, weren't convinced Texas was the better team. The Cougars, which had committed 49 turnovers in the two earlier contests against Texas, committed only 12 in the championship, and it proved to be the difference as Houston won in surprisingly easy fashion, 91-72. The loss prevented Texas from earning its first-ever SWC tournament title and dropped its record to 23-11 on the season.

Following the game, the Horns received a berth in the NCAA Tournament for the fourth consecutive year. Texas received a No. 8 seed in the East Regional and would face the No. 9-seeded Iowa Hawkeyes in the first round.

The NCAA Tournament

At Greensboro Coliseum in North Carolina, the Horns battled against the No. 9-seeded Hawkeyes of the Big 10. A crowd of 15,800 definitely got their money's worth as the two evenly matched teams struggled to establish dominance over the other. At the half, Iowa had one of the game's biggest leads at 49-42.

As exciting as the first half was, it paled in comparison to the second half. Both teams came out of the break firing and hitting, on all cylinders. Any time one team scored consecutive buckets, the other team answered. When the game concluded, it came down to percentages. Texas made 13 of 31 or 42 percent from three-point range for the game — impressive numbers by any standards. However, Iowa, not to be outdone, converted a mind-boggling 71 percent in the second half. That alone was enough for the Hawkeyes to advance to the second round with a hard-fought 98-92 victory. With the loss, Texas exited the NCAA Tournament in the first round for the first time since Penders' arrival in 1988. The Horns finished the season with a 23-12 record.

Chapter Seven

The Ciampaglio Investigation – Part II

After the first-round loss in the NCAA Tournament, Penders was immediately looking to the future and next season. More specifically, he was ready to put behind him the previous season of NCAA investigations and all kinds of allegations. But before Penders could say "Ciampaglio," his assistant coach's name was back in the headlines of the *Austin American-Statesman* sports section.

In the April 12 story titled, "Players: Coach Withheld Money, UT's Ciampaglio Blamed for Missing Thousands," Ciampaglio was accused by several players of withholding thousands of dollars in university funds intended for team meals on road trips and after home games. The article quoted anonymous current and former players who said Ciampaglio had taken money from them during the 1989-90 and 1990-91 seasons, and they did not know where the money went. Ciampaglio, back in November when the story originally broke, admitted to withholding meal money but asserted that each player eventually received the correct amount of money.

The article cited several hundred pages of travel expense reports obtained under the state's open records law. The records, according to the story, indicated that Ciampaglio checked out $70,227 in cash during the past two years, and of that, $3,670 was in meal money for home games that could not be accounted for based on players' estimates of $5 per player that was withheld from them.

The story quoted players and school officials who said team members' signatures were forged by someone more than two dozen times on the travel expense reports that players were supposed to sign after they had received the money. "We were signing blank meal sheets," said one team member. "He'd have a couple around to sign. He'd get the players to sign, but if the player wasn't there, he'd get somebody to sign it."

What proved to be most interesting about the first of many *American-Statesman* articles on the continuing saga was that it quoted a variety of players who had experienced problems with Ciampaglio and his handling of the meal money. The article said: "After receiving an anonymous tip last fall, the *Austin American-Statesman* has found more than a half-dozen current and former players who say Ciampaglio shorted them $5 apiece per meal at home..." However, the first story on the situation back in November of 1991 stated just the opposite. It said, "None of the current or former Texas players contacted by the *Austin American-Statesman* over the last month knew of any wrongdoing by Ciampaglio."

Several days later, the April 14 edition of the paper included another story contradictory to what it had originally reported during the first go-round of the Ciampaglio meal-money controversy. The article, titled "Ciampaglio's Handling of Funds May Have Violated NCAA Rules," said Ciampaglio might have violated two NCAA rules in the way he handled the team's meal money from 1989-91 according to an NCAA official.

The story said according to Dan Dutcher, NCAA director of legislative services, the assistant coach might have violated the unethical conduct rule in the way he allegedly handled meal money for the 1991 NCAA subregional and he might have also broken the organization's rule for meal-allowance limitations by giving the players less money at home and giving them more on the road.

"I would think if there were potential violations existing, the enforcement staff definitely would be interested," Dutcher said.

The article also said Chuck Smrt, NCAA director of enforcement, declined to say if Texas or Ciampaglio could receive any sanctions if allegations against Ciampaglio were proven true.

Texas Athletic Director DeLoss Dodds was also quoted in the story and said he was satisfied the school had broken no NCAA rules. "I don't think there's an NCAA issue. But we always look at that side."

Dodds' quote and Smrt's lack of a quote were along the lines of what the *American-Statesman* reported in its original story in November of 1991. In that story, it stated that "None of the allegations involve potential NCAA violations."

Had the *American-Statesman* changed its story or learned of new information? And if it were the latter, where was the information coming from?

Ciampaglio said he basically knew the source of the information. "Somebody on the inside of the University of Texas was giving my information away and things started popping up in the Statesman." Ciampaglio said a perfect case in point was in a story that appeared the next day – April 15. The article, titled "Assistants Charged Personal Calls to Texas," said that Ciampaglio and assistant Eddie Oran had charged more than $5,000 worth of personal long-distance telephone calls to the university over three years according to documents viewed by the *Austin American-Statesman* and interviews with school officials.

The story said Oran had paid back his $2,200 phone bill while Ciampaglio had started to work out a payment plan to reimburse the school for the $3,000 worth of calls. It said "Telephone records obtained by the *Austin American-Statesman* show that at least $2,500 in calls were placed to Ciampaglio's in-laws in Mattapoinsett, Mass; his father in Morristown, N.J., and Westerly, R.I.; and his brother in Rockaway, Hope and Chester N.J."

"Who told them to go look at my phone records?" Ciampaglio asked, referring back to the article. "The next article; all of the sudden my Barton Creek bills appear in the paper." Ciampaglio was referring to another article that appeared on May 6, three weeks after the phone bill article. However, before that story broke, two other stories concerning the matter were printed.

In the April 26 edition of the paper, an article titled "Coaches' Statements Worry Players, Longhorns: Investigation Might Prompt Penders to Leave" described how three basketball players said Penders had told them he would leave as head coach if Ciampaglio was forced out by the current investigation.

The article quoted several players who had "interpreted" statements from Penders to mean that he wanted the players to recant sworn, notarized statements they had previously given to investigators describing how Ciampaglio withheld thousands of dollars in meal money.

According to the article, two players said that during a team meeting held less than two weeks earlier on April 14, Ciampaglio told them that a number of their former teammates had agreed not to cooperate with the investigation being conducted by the district attorney's office. The players said they had no plans of changing their stories.

Ciampaglio would say later that soon after the April 26 article ran he was subpoenaed to appear before the grand jury for tampering with the players during the team meeting. He said the charges were totally unfounded. "The meeting was in the basketball office. Eddie (Oran) was there and the players and managers were there. I called the meeting after the season was over and we discussed weightlifting, schoolwork, next year's schedule, and plans for the summer."

Ciampaglio said apparently someone who was in the meeting saw it differently and notified the district attorney's office. "Somebody from that meeting said Coach Ciampaglio called the meeting and they called the DA. Then the DA subpoenaed me in front of the grand jury."

Ciampaglio said when he appeared before the grand jury, he even asked why he was being subpoenaed. He was told it was as a result of his holding a meeting to tamper with witnesses. "I told them to call Eddie about what occurred at that meeting. Not once did the investigation come up (in the team meeting)."

Penders was also quoted in the April 26 article and said that he never told the team he would leave because of the investigation. "No way, no way," he said. "What I did say was, 'I'll tell you this, if you're not going to be up front with me, I can't coach you. However, if one of you feels this way (that Ciampaglio was shorting them money), I'll back you. I'll go to the wall for you."

In the article, according to the players, it wasn't the first time Penders had suggested he might leave the university over the Ciampaglio matter. The players said at a meeting earlier in the year Penders told them he would leave if Ciampaglio was forced out because of the investigation. "He said if anything happened to Jamie, or Jamie goes to jail or gets fired or whatever, then he's going to leave, too," a player recalled Penders saying.

Numerous other quotes were in the article from the unidentified players. The story said the players had requested anonymity because they said they feared threats would be made toward them personally if their names were known. "If somebody gave their names, then yeah, definitely, we'd get threats," a player said.

Several days later, in an effort to clear up the claims of players who said Penders told them he would leave over the Ciampaglio matter, Penders held a press conference against the requests of the DA's office who had asked that Penders and all his coaches and players remain silent on the issue.

In a three-page statement, Penders acknowledged the district attorney' s request about his players and coaches making no further comment. He also denied he ever told the players he would leave.

"The first paragraph (of the *American-Statesman* story) implied that three unnamed players said I told the players I would leave the University of Texas if Jamie Ciampaglio was forced out by an ongoing investigation," the statement said. "This statement is false. I never said I would leave Texas if Jamie Ciampaglio resigned, was forced out or was found guilty from the investigation."

"The second paragraph (of the story) implies that I told the players to recant sworn, notarized statements that involved the investigation. This allegation is ludicrous and completely false. I have never seen any sworn statements by any of the players or managers. The only thing I have ever told the players regarding the investigation is to be truthful and to cooperate fully with anyone who is authorized to question them."

After Penders' press conference, the name Ciampaglio was absent from the sport section headlines for more than a week. On May 6, Ciampaglio's name once again became, as he described it, the "flavor of the month." The latest headline read "Coach Billed UT for Golf That Wasn't Played."

In the story, the *American-Statesman* reported that according to documents obtained through the Texas Open Records Act, Ciampaglio was reimbursed $295 for rounds of golf for four ACC officials at Barton Creek Country Club. A spokeswoman who had worked for 11 years scheduling officials in the Atlantic Coast Conference said she had never heard of the names.

When discussing the article seven years later, Ciampaglio said the names were completely fictitious and even laughed about it. But he said he still questions how the paper obtained the specifics on items such as the Barton Creek bill.

"How's the paper getting all that information? They said they went through the Texas Open Records Act. If they were given all my receipts turned in from the time I came to UT, there would be boxes and boxes of receipts. All of the sudden they pull out this Barton Creek bill. Somebody had to help them find it."

Ciampaglio admitted that he should have handled the situation differently when it occurred back in 1992, but he maintained that he did nothing out of the ordinary when it came to writing up expense reports for extra money.

"It's part of the business. Everybody needed extra cash to do little things with. To entertain a coach a little bit extra and take him to a nice restaurant. We're talking $50, $60, $70. We're not talking $100,000."

He said another method of acquiring "extra cash" occurred at alumni functions where assistant coaches from the various athletic programs tried to accrue as many receipts as possible in almost a game-like atmosphere. "It used to be a free-for-all to see who could get receipts, and that's part of the business."

Ciampaglio said that in other instances when an assistant needed some extra money, the coach would ask his fellow assistants for their extra receipts. "Coaches would ask other coaches if they might have a receipt from a restaurant such as the Marriott in Houston (for example). 'OK, guys, who is in Houston that I can say I took out to dinner?' "

"Don't tell me I was the only one doing it," Ciampaglio said.

Ciampaglio said someone from the university was singling him out because they wanted him removed from the program. The means to achieve that end was either through directly leaking the information to the newspaper staff, or pointing them in the right direction on where to find the information. "After they release my phone records, then they start going through my expense reports checking every receipt. Checking to see if they were done properly. Checking to see if they were written up properly, were they turned in properly, were they from a legitimate restaurant. They started killing me."

Ciampaglio said after the Barton Creek bill story, UT officials were informed that another article – with him as the subject – was scheduled to run in the next few days. Although the previous articles were, admittedly, negative publicity for the school, the athletic department, and more specifically, the basketball program, the next scheduled story would be even more embarrassing. He said the article was going to describe how Ciampaglio visited certain "male entertainment" establishments.

Ciampaglio said it was not a common practice, but on certain occasions he entertained coaches at the Colorado Bar and Grill — a topless bar in Houston. He said the *American-Statesman* staff had somehow learned of his visits to the establishment, sought out his receipts, acquired them, and then planned on using the information in the next story. Ciampaglio said the newspaper staff's ability to pinpoint his receipts from the bar was interesting, if not suspicious, because receipts from this establishment, and others like it don't include the real name of the establishment on the ticket. Instead, they use a fictitious name such as "Joe and Sally's Bar."

"They know all corporations and companies when they turn their receipts in from places don't want to see the name of a topless bar," Ciampaglio said. The receipt for the Colorado Bar and Grill was no different.

In other words, someone had to research the names on his receipts to find out exactly what the fictitious name was for the Colorado Bar and Grill. Ciampaglio said when he learned that the Colorado Bar and Grill story was going to run, he quickly narrowed down his choices on who was tipping off the *American-Statesman*. It was only a select few. He said Penders never knew anything about it.

Before the unflattering story ever made it to print, UT President William Cunningham acted. Cunningham called Dodds, who then called Ciampaglio's attorney, Abraham Kazen. Dodds told Kazen the university was tired of seeing articles on Ciampaglio in the paper. He said they were going to fire him.

On the night of May 6, Ciampaglio said he received a call from Kazen who told him that he needed to meet with him immediately. Around 9 p.m., Ciampaglio arrived at Kazen's office. Kazen explained to Ciampaglio how the university was growing increasingly impatient with the articles in the paper. "The university is releasing you," Kazen told his client.

Ciampaglio was in shock. He started crying hysterically. He said all he could think at that point was that his life was shattered. After regaining his composure, he called his mom, dad and several friends to tell them about his situation. All those he spoke with tried to encourage him. One of his close friends gave him some advice. He told him if he was going to get fired or resign, make sure he did one thing – get something out of it. "Get your name saved," the friend told Ciampaglio. At that point, Ciampaglio wasn't sure if it was too late.

The next day, the story on Ciampaglio's visits to the Colorado Bar and Grill never made the paper. Behind the scenes, Kazen worked with university officials to allow Ciampaglio to resign rather than be fired. "They agreed to let me resign and they said I could call a news conference and resign so that at least it looked like I wasn't fired and I resigned from the University of Texas. And I can go about my business."

To work out the details of Ciampaglio's resignation, a meeting was held at Dodds' office. Those attending included Dodds, university counsel Patricia Ohlendorf, Kazen, Penders and Ciampaglio. In the meeting Ciampaglio agreed to repay the university for the missing university funds in a lump sum payment. To accomplish this, he signed a piece of paper that returned all the money he would have received for vacation pay, as well as any other funds due him that he had earned during his tenure at Texas. All totaled the amount equaled between $13,000-14,000.

After all the transactions had been agreed upon and signed, Ciampaglio said he had to write a check for $54 to make up the remaining balance owed by him to the university. He said seeing the money owed him disappear before his eyes was too much. "I broke down in tears in Dodds' office. I excused myself to go in Dodds' bathroom and broke down crying again."

After regaining his composure, Ciampaglio returned to the meeting and expressed how he wanted to get everything done. Finally, all the details were hammered out. It was agreed that if Ciampaglio resigned and paid back the money, which he had already agreed to do, several university officials including President Cunningham would pick up the phone and call the DA on his behalf, explaining that as far as they were concerned, the Ciampaglio issue was a done deal. It was also agreed that he would hold a press conference the next day explaining that he was leaving the university.

After the meeting, Ciampaglio went home and began writing his resignation speech. He said initially the tone was apologetic, but around 3 a.m., he had a change of heart. "I said bullshit to this. I've got too much pride to stand up there in front of everybody and say I'm sorry for what happened, and that I'm a bad boy and I made mistake; thank you to the university."

On May 8, Ciampaglio resigned. His resignation statement read:

I have at this time submitted my resignation, effective immediately, to DeLoss Dodds, athletic director at the University of Texas. This resignation is by no means an admission on my part of any wrongdoing. The mistakes I made were not made with any thought of achieving personal gain. Any settlement that has occurred with the University is in the best interest of both myself and my family. At this time, my main concern is for my family.

I would like to take this time to thank my wife, Andrea, my family, and my lawyer, Mr. Kazen, for their support during this whole affair. Also, my thanks go out to fellow assistants, Vic Trilli, Melvin Haralson, and especially Eddie Oran, who have made my coming to Texas an enjoyable transition. As far as Coach Penders is concerned, it was our goal to build the University of Texas basketball program into one of the most respected programs in this country. I feel the program here at Texas is by far better off now than when I first arrived. For Coach Penders, words will never express my gratitude for all his help.

Most importantly, my thanks go out to all the players I have had the privilege of coaching these past four seasons. I hold no animosity toward anyone for anything that has been allegedly reported in our local papers. It has always been my feeling that the players were being manipulated and controlled by the press. The respect the players have shown me for the past four years is something that I will remember for a long time. It has been a complete joy watching them compete and I wish them much success and the best of luck.

To the media, I respect the professional way in which most of you have handled your job. However, there are a few, in the print media especially, who have been on a witch hunt from day one. For those few, I hope you are satisfied and that now you will be able to win another award for investigative reporting.

My wife, I am happy to say, is three months pregnant and we both request for our well being, and the well being of our unborn child, to be left alone. Enough is enough. Abraham Lincoln once said, and I quote:

"If I were to try to read, much less answer, all the attacks made on me, this shop might as well be closed for any other business.

"I do the very best I know how – the very best I can; and I hope to keep on doing so to the end.

"If the end brings me out all right, what is said against me won't amount to anything.

"If the end brings me out wrong, ten angels swearing I was right would make no difference."

I have been beaten, bruised, and battered. However, I have not been defeated. I am proud of what I have accomplished so far and I will bounce back.

They can take my job away, but they cannot take away my abilities. I am good at what I do and I look forward to being back in coaching in some capacity in the near future.

Thank you, Jamie Ciampaglio

In an oral statement, Ciampaglio made one last comment: "On a final note, all of you take a picture, look at my face and remember the name. Someday all of you are going to wish I was back here at the University of Texas."

After the statement, he did not take any questions.

His animosity toward certain members of media was obvious. However, one line in his resignation statement turned out to be prophetic. "For those few, I hope you are satisfied and that now you will be able to win another award for investigative reporting."

In 1993, *American-Statesman* writers Kirk Bohls and Suzanne Halliburton received three honors for their investigative reporting on the matter.

Ciampaglio didn't win any awards or points, for that matter, with Cunningham for what he said in his resignation statement. In response, Cunningham called off the deal in which he was supposed to put in a good word with the DA's office. Ciampaglio said because he didn't have it in writing, Cunningham didn't have to hold up his end of the bargain. Ciampaglio was on his own.

On May 23, Ciampaglio pleaded guilty to a single count of tampering with governmental records – a third-degree felony – and was sentenced to five years probation.

In a plea bargain agreement with the DA's office, if Ciampaglio fulfilled the terms of the deferred-adjudication probation, the charges against him would be dismissed. He also received 160 hours of community service.

Robert Smith, assistant district attorney who prosecuted the case, told the *American-Statesman* his office would not pursue any more charges against Ciampaglio, including allegations that he withheld thousands of dollars in meal money. "He's lost his job. He's paid back a lot of money. And he's walking around on felony probation. I think that's appropriate enough."

Despite what Ciampaglio thought about Cunningham's disdain for the remarks in his resignation statement, it was apparent someone from the university spoke to the DA's office on his behalf. It was finally over. Ciampaglio was the "flavor of the month" no more.

Trilli Receives Promotion

Five months after Ciampaglio resigned from the University of Texas, Assistant Coach Vic Trilli was promoted as Ciampaglio's replacement.

The lengthy vacancy period was a result of school officials waiting for the NCAA to conclude its investigation of the basketball program, which had started in November of 1991. Although the investigation was still incomplete, UT officials had to name a new assistant since the fall semester had started, and they were confident Trilli and the school would be exonerated.

Chapter Eight

Injuries and Suspensions, 1992-1993

With the year of off-the-court distractions including NCAA investigations, resignations, and allegations officially behind them, Penders and his Texas team looked to the future.

On the court, the Longhorns and their fans both anticipated a promising season. Following a fourth consecutive year of 20 wins and subsequent appearances in the NCAA Tournament, expectations were high. Even with the departure of last year's leading scorer Dexter Cambridge, the Horns looked to be offensive with production coming from players such as B.J. Tyler, Terrence Rencher and Mike Richardson – all part of the three-guard offense. Tyler and Rencher appeared to be the obvious choices for "go-to" guys as the two combined to average 37 points a game in 1992. Tyler was questionable heading into the season with a stress fracture in his foot, but was expected to return at full strength before the first game. The Longhorns also hoped to get some offense from a couple of freshmen in 6-foot-10-inch Sheldon Quarles and 6-1 Al Coleman.

The Regular Season

Texas got the season off to a positive start with a 136-97 blowout over Oral Roberts on the road in Tulsa. Following the high-scoring affair in Tulsa, the Longhorns had to make a considerable adjustment in playing against the Princeton Tigers and a completely different style of basketball. They adjusted well. Texas was led by its only senior, Mike Richardson, to a 63-53 victory in the first round of the Diet Pepsi Tournament of Champions in Charlotte, North Carolina. With the win, Texas earned the right to play the North Carolina Tar Heels in the championship game.

Against Dean Smith's Carolina team, the Longhorns were no match. The Tar Heels showed why they were the seventh-ranked team in the country and several notches above the Horns and where they wanted to be as a team, as UNC won the game in easy fashion, 104-68.

Two weeks later the Horns resumed action on the road in Utah. Before an ESPN audience and a crowd of almost 13,000, the Longhorns put in another solid effort, but had another lackluster shooting performance converting 37 percent from the field. The team's overall inability to hit the shots eventually ended with an 87-76 defeat at the hands of the Utes and a 2-2 record early in the season.

It may have taken the familiar surroundings, but the Longhorns got back on the winning track several days later. The Longhorns struggled again from the field hitting just 39 percent, but outlasted the Lumberjacks from Stephen F. Austin, 83-70.

The day after Christmas, the Longhorns were not in a giving mood. Instead, Illinois was. The Fighting Illini, which came into the game with a 7-2 record, was forced into committing 25 turnovers by the stingy Texas defense and the Longhorns prevailed, 89-72. More than 14,000 watched as Texas turned up the defense, and finally awoke on offense. Texas improved to 4-2.

In the first round of the All-College Tournament in Oklahoma City, Rencher broke out of a recent shooting slump and several other Longhorns found the offensive stroke as Texas won 104-96 over Weber State. Rencher scored a team-high 30 points and Richardson and Albert Burditt scored 21 apiece. Another number, however, was more significant. The victory, which earned UT a berth in the championship game, also marked the 100th win for Penders at Texas against 41 losses. His overall career record improved to 370-250.

Following the 100th win for Penders at Texas, the Horns battled the No. 15 Oklahoma Sooners in their next contest in an attempt to garner their coach victory No. 101. The Sooners failed to cooperate with a strong inside game from several players, and prevailed 85-76 in the championship game of the All-College Tournament.

Before the Southwest Conference opener against Rice, the Longhorns were dealt a serious blow. Junior B.J. Tyler suffered a broken bone in his right foot after landing awkwardly in practice. The bone was the same one which had suffered a stress fracture before the season. By all indications, Tyler and his 16.9 points and 6.8 assists per game were lost for the season.

In the SWC opener against the Rice Owls, Tyler's absence was obvious to his teammates and the 11,297 fans in the Erwin Center. Without Tyler and his offensive leadership in the lineup, the Longhorns trailed by 21 points early in the second half. It was only after the ejection of Penders following a second technical foul that the Horns played inspired basketball and battled back, only to come up on the short end of a 92-87 score. The Horns' 17-game SWC home-winning streak was snapped.

After the loss to Rice, Penders did something he hadn't done in five years – he closed practice. Penders had said earlier in the season he had no reason to scrap his fast-paced offense, but with the loss of Tyler, it was apparent there was considerable retooling going on behind closed doors.

Against SMU in the second game of conference play, the Longhorns came out with a new look including a different starting lineup, a new defense, and a more patient offense. The results, however, were much the same. Southern Methodist pulled out a 102-92 victory. More than 11,000 fans gathered in the Erwin Center and watched as the Horns dropped to .500 at 5-5 on the season and 0-2 in the conference.

The troubles for the Longhorns continued several nights later at Hofheinz Pavilion in Houston. An ESPN audience and 6,762 fans witnessed the Horns, which trailed at the half 40-30, lose their fourth consecutive game, 81-67. Texas dropped to 5-6 on the season and 0-3 in the conference. It was the team's worst start in the conference since 1983-84 when Bob Weltlich's team started with four losses in SWC play.

Against the Baylor Bears in Austin, the Horns looked to regroup and bring their four-game losing skid to a halt. With a little over a minute left, the Longhorns were close to accomplishing their goal as they clung to an 86-83 lead. But Baylor scored two buckets down the stretch including the game-winning shot with two seconds and the Horns, before a crowd of 12,271, fell again, 87-86. The defeat extended the Horns' overall losing streak to five — the team's longest since 1984, and dropped them to 5-7 and 0-4 in the SWC.

With a five-game losing streak in progress, the Longhorn players and coaches looked for any positives to build on — anything to reverse their recent misfortune. However, before things got better, they got much worse. The Longhorns suffered the loss of two more key players when star center Albert Burditt was ruled academically ineligible and leading scorer Terrence Rencher was suspended indefinitely for academic inadequacies.

Burditt, who was already on scholastic probation, failed to meet university standards for grade-point average and his final appeal was denied. He was expected to return the next fall with one year of eligibility remaining. Rencher, who was averaging 19.6 points per game, was suspended because, according to Penders, he was taking too long to finish an incomplete fall course and doing the bare minimum in his other three courses. Penders said the suspension was expected to last at least a couple of weeks. "Terrence has been slow in taking care of business. I've warned him. He cut some classes in the fall, and I disciplined him (with extra running.) In 21 years of coaching, I'd never lost a kid academically for a semester. Albert is the first one, and I don't ever want it to happen again."

To make matters worse, the Horns also lost the services of sophomore forward Al Segova who suffered a knee injury. The knee was not examined because the swelling had not receded, but it was feared the injury might be career-threatening.

With three starters out, Penders and the remaining eight scholarship players and two walk-ons traveled to Kentucky to take on the Murray State Racers in another attempt to end the losing streak. In the first half, it didn't look good as the Horns trailed by as many as 15 points. But in the second half Texas stormed back. When the final buzzer sounded, the Horns had pulled off a thrilling come-from-behind victory, 79-74, and the losing streak was officially over.

With their overall losing streak snapped, the Horns hoped to end their four-game conference losing skid when they played host to Texas Tech. In front of 11,379 in the Erwin Center, the Longhorns emphatically put an end to their conference losing streak with a 92-74 victory over the Red Raiders.

If two consecutive wins and the first win in conference play weren't enough to get the players and fans excited, reinstatement of Terrence Rencher was. Rencher returned to the team after academic counselor Curt Fludd told Penders that Rencher had been meeting his academic requirements.

In Rencher's return to action, the Horns were unable to stop the inside play of the Rice Owls and center Brent Scott. Scott scored 27 points and grabbed 14 rebounds as the Owls pulled away for a 101-83 victory.

Continuing in SWC play, the Longhorns visited Fort Worth and the TCU Horned Frogs in a battle of cellar dwellers – UT at 1-5 and TCU at 0-5. In the end, it came down to free throws. The Longhorns hit 58 percent from the line for the game while TCU – a 55.8 percent free-throw shooting team and worst in the conference coming into the game – hit 22 of its last 27 to put away the Horns for the 83-77 triumph.

In a respite from conference play, the Horns took on Dale Brown and the LSU Tigers.The Longhorns played an inspired game after falling behind early 18-0, but it wasn't enough in the end as the Tigers came away with a hard-fought 84-81 victory in front of 8,815 at the HemisFair Arena in San Antonio.

Back in the SWC, Texas needed no inspiration in its next game when the Aggies came to town. An Erwin Center crowd of 11,024 watched as the Texas defense clamped down in the final five minutes of the game and held Texas A&M without a field goal. During that same time, the Longhorns, which had failed from the free throw line in their previous conference game against TCU, converted from the line including 9 of 11 in the final two minutes to secure the 82-78 win. The win snapped the Horns' three-game losing streak and improved their record to 8-10 overall, 2-6 in SWC.

With the victory over A&M, the Texas players were positive heading into a game at Georgia. That positive energy could also be attributed to the return of B.J. Tyler to practice, albeit in a limited capacity. Tyler, who had been out since early January, participated in some full-court drills, but was not allowed to participate in full scrimmages.

In Georgia, the Horns were given yet another dose of reality. Tyler may have been practicing, but he wasn't on the court in game situations where he was desperately needed. Despite Tyler's absence and a 13-point deficit in the second half, the Horns mounted a comeback late and actually took the lead, but a scoring drought in the final two minutes prevented Texas from earning its ninth victory of the year. Instead, the Bulldogs walked away with a 78-70 win.

Back at home against Virginia Commonwealth, the Longhorns struggled offensively throughout the game. The shooting performance, which was second worst for the season behind only the 28.6 percent against North Carolina, concluded with Texas finishing on the short end of a 66-60 score.

Trying to avoid a third straight loss, the Longhorns ventured up the road to Waco for a date with the Baylor Bears. With a crowd just over 6,000 strong, Terrence Rencher had his best performance of the year scoring 27 points and the Longhorns pulled off the upset, 88-73.

Two nights later, the Horns continued in College Station with the second game of their three-game conference road swing. The lack of Texas offense allowed the Aggies to run away with a 77-57 win. The 57-point total, 22 of which came from Rencher, equaled the team's lowest in five seasons under Penders.

In Lubbock, the Horns looked to begin a strong final push in the last three regular-season games in an effort to gain momentum heading into the SWC Tournament. If they had any hopes of making the postseason, they had to win the tournament and receive an automatic bid to the NCAA. Nothing else would extend the streak of four consecutive appearances in the postseason. While the hopes may have been somewhat unrealistic, they became more realistic with the return of B.J. Tyler.

Tyler returned to the lineup against Tech for his first game action in almost two months. Despite the layoff, the junior guard returned in grand style scoring a season-high 32 points against the Red Raiders. Unfortunately, Tyler's effort wasn't enough as Tech pulled off the win, 105-103, with a last-second buzzer beater.

Texas returned home to face the tough Houston Cougars and their 17-6 record. 8,000 plus fans in the Erwin Center watched as Houston capitalized with an 86-79 victory.

In the regular season home finale, the Horns and TCU battled again for the SWC basement bragging rights, or rather, the team who wasn't at the bottom of the conference standings. Texas proved to be the better of the bad teams pulling off a 102-84 victory. With the win, Texas improved to 10-15 and 4-9 in SWC action.

In Dallas at Moody Coliseum, Texas faced the first-place SMU Mustangs in the regular season finale. SMU dominated the game from the start and in the end came away with a 96-80 victory to earn the SWC regular season title. Texas finished at 10-16 overall and 4-10 in the SWC. They received the seventh seed and would face Rice in the first round of the SWC Tournament.

The SWC Tournament

With nothing to lose, the Horns opened SWC Tournament play a relaxed team against No. 2-seeded Rice. It showed in the early going as the Longhorns built a 19-point lead over the Owls in the first half. In the second half, Rice, which had already beaten Texas twice during the regular season, mounted a charge. But it wasn't enough as Texas held on for the upset victory, 81-76. The victory propelled the Horns into a second-round matchup with the No. 3 seed, Houston.

If losing B.J. Tyler once early in the season wasn't enough, the Longhorns learned they had lost him a second time before their second-round contest against Houston. The Southwest Conference ruled that Tyler was ineligible before the second round of action. The conference released a one-sentence statement regarding Tyler's status that said: "B.J. Tyler of the University of Texas has been found in violation of Southwest Conference eligibility rules and has been declared ineligible."

An assistant director of the SWC said players were randomly given drug tests after tournament games, but would not say whether Tyler had failed a drug test.

Against Houston, once again Texas had nothing to lose and played that way in the first half. Houston held off the Horns in the end for the 58-50 victory.

With SWC action – both regular season and tournament – over, the Longhorns in years past prepared for the NCAA; not this year. Instead, they prepared for next year. The 1992-93 season was definitely a season to forget as the Longhorns finished with an 11-17 record – by far the worst since Penders had arrived five years earlier.

The Off-Season
Tyler Enters Lucas Program

Just three months before the Longhorns began the 1993-94 season, star point guard B.J. Tyler withdrew from school and entered the John Lucas Center — a substance-abuse treatment center in Houston.

With his withdrawal for the fall semester, Tyler would not be eligible until mid-December.

Tyler released a statement through the school. "My reason is not cocaine abuse, alcohol abuse, etc., but instead to rid myself of a minor problem that could prevent me from reaching my potential as an athlete and more importantly as a man ... I would like this to be looked at as a development process, not a correction process. In other words, a new beginning, not an end."

Penders said he was happy with Tyler's decision to work with Lucas and his well-respected program. "I think this is going to be good for B.J. in the long run. I think he is doing a wise and mature thing ... I've talked to John Lucas, and I'm excited about John's interest."

Burditt Returns

With the loss of Tyler until mid-December at the earliest, the news wasn't all bad for Penders and the program when it was announced several days later that Albert Burditt had enrolled for the fall semester. Although this was good news, the staff was still cautious about Burditt's future.

"We want to make sure he makes progress. If he takes care of everything he is supposed to, he will be fine," Curt Fludd, assistant athletic director for academic services, was quoted as saying in the *American-Statesman*.

Penders said he wanted to make sure Burditt didn't fall back into bad academic standing and would be closely monitored. "Right now he seems determined to do the work, but I want to make sure he does. I don't want him doing what he did in the past. If he goes to class and studies, he will play. But he will have to prove himself every day."

Burditt, who averaged 14.9 points, 14.1 rebounds and 4.2 blocked shots before being ruled ineligible, would not be cleared to play for the fall semester, and therefore, would miss the first four games of the season.

Tyler Making Progress

Just a month after entering the John Lucas Center, Tom Penders said B.J. Tyler had made sufficient progress in dealing with a "behavioral problem."

"John (Lucas) said B.J. doesn't have a substance abuse problem," Penders told the *American-Statesman*. "He has a behavioral problem. Part of it is he's learning to deal with setbacks."

Penders said Tyler was undergoing treatment for depression that he began suffering from after he broke his foot in practice early in the 1992-93 season.

Although Penders was prohibited from commenting on the results of a drug test, which reportedly resulted in Tyler's suspension from the SWC Tournament before Texas' second-round contest with Houston, sources close to the school and the conference told the *American-Statesman* that Tyler had tested positive for marijuana.

Chapter Nine

Winning Ways Return, 1993-1994

Following the 11-17 season marred by injuries and a variety of suspensions, the Horns and Penders were ready to improve and show they were a much better team in the 1993-94 campaign. With Rencher and the expected return of Burditt and Tyler early in the season, as well as the addition of newcomers such as freshman Reggie Freeman from New York, transfer players Roderick Anderson from Angelina Junior College, Rich McIver from Michigan, and Tremaine Wingfield from Louisville, Penders was confident 1993-94 would be considerably better.

The Regular Season

The much-improved team Penders thought he had before the season failed to show up in the first contest on the road against LSU. In Baton Rouge, the Longhorns, who were without the services of guard B.J. Tyler for at least the first four games, were never able to get on track offensively. With the lack of offensive production from Texas, the Tigers took advantage and easily won the opener by an 86-66 margin.

Two nights later the Horns had another road test in Lincoln, Nebraska, against the Cornhuskers. This time however, Texas came into the game much more focused offensively, and converted better than 50 percent of its shots for the game. In the waning seconds with Texas ahead, junior Lamont Hill made two key steals that sealed Nebraska's fate and a Longhorn victory, 78-75. Rencher led the Horns in scoring with 35 points, two shy of his career high. The win by UT ended Nebraska's 30-game home winning streak against non-conference opponents.

Continuing on the road, Texas visited Nacogdoches and the Stephen F. Austin Lumberjacks. The Texas starters played uninspired throughout much of the contest and at one point early in the second half, Penders had seen enough. Instead of waiting to see if his starters would break out of the daze, he benched them all. The reserves provided enough spark down the stretch and the Horns managed to pull off a sluggish 78-66 win.

In the home opener, the Horns looked to improve on their recent lackadaisical performances and treat the Erwin Center faithful to a victory over the Florida Gators. Unfortunately for those 12,170 in attendance, the Gators weren't too accommodating. Florida made eight consecutive free throws in the final three minutes of the game to cap off a 76-68 defeat of the Horns. After four games, Texas was 2-2. Not time for panic just yet, but concern, yes. Penders hoped B.J. Tyler, who had missed the first four games because he had not attended school in the fall semester, and his return from treatment at the John Lucas Center in Houston would spark the team. If this were the case, it had to happen in the Horns next game against another tough opponent – the 16th ranked Connecticut Huskies in Connecticut.

Against the Huskies and Penders' alma mater, Tyler showed why he had been sorely missed those first four games of the season. Before a crowd of 8,241 in Gampel Pavilion and an ESPN national television audience, the senior point guard returned to action and posted 16 points and made five steals in the game. Despite Tyler's performance and a team-high 20 points from Burditt, the Longhorns were unable to overcome a 23-point second-half deficit, losing the game, 96-86.

Following the loss at Connecticut, Penders made a statement to his team and in particular, junior Terrence Rencher. He benched him. Penders said freshman Reggie Freeman would replace Rencher who had hit 13 of his last 50 shots including two of 21 from three-point range.

With the early-season schedule that included four road games against competition such as LSU and Connecticut resulting in a 2-3 record, Penders knew it wasn't going to get any easier as his team had its next three games on the road at the Maui Invitational in Hawaii.

Just being in Hawaii was nice for the players and the coaches, but Texas' first game was by no means a vacation as the Horns faced fifth-ranked Kentucky. Against the Wildcats in the Lahaina Civic Center, the Longhorns were overmatched, and Kentucky ran away with an 86-61 victory.

In Texas' next contest at the Maui Invitational, the Longhorns took on the Tennessee Tech Golden Eagles. Rencher, who had been re-inserted back into the starting lineup before the game, scored 33 points including 14 of 20 shooting from the field, pulled down eight rebounds, and made six assists as the Longhorns improved to 3-4 on the season with a solid 97-85 win.

In their final game in Hawaii against Notre Dame, the Horns had one of, if not the best, all-around performances of the season. When it was finished, Texas had earned fifth place in the eight-team tournament with an 89-72 win. Texas returned to the mainland with a 4-4 record.

With a crowd of almost 12,000 in the Erwin Center, the Longhorns appeared reinvigorated from their trip to Hawaii, if not a little tanner. Against Oklahoma, the Horns overcame a four-point deficit in the second half on the strength of a 20-3 run and pulled away from the Sooners for an 87-75 victory. Tyler, who appeared in his first home game since last season, led Texas with 24 points. The win over Oklahoma was the first time in 10 games Texas had come out victorious over their Red River rivals and the first time ever under Penders.

Two nights later Texas hosted the Utah Utes in a game that began on December 29, 1993, and almost ended in 1994 with a 93-91 victory.

After the dramatic finish at home, the Longhorns went on the road to face the 22nd-ranked Fighting Illini. Illinois, which came into the game with a 6-2 record, had more than a week to prepare for Texas. In front of 16,129 in Assembly Hall, the preparation paid off as the Illini held off a late Longhorn rally for the 83-78 victory.

The Longhorns remained on the road in their next contest, although it was much closer to home at HemisFair Arena in San Antonio against Texas-San Antonio. More than 6,000 watched the Horns go on a 31-7 scoring streak in the first half to essentially put away the Roadrunners before the intermission. In the second half Texas cruised to a 91-69 win.

On the road again, Texas traveled to the not-so-friendly confines of G. Rollie White Coliseum in College Station for its Southwest Conference opener. In the end, the Horns ran out of time and the Aggies prevailed, 85-84.

Back in the Erwin Center against the SMU Mustangs, the Horns hoped to forget about the tough loss that had occurred just days before in College Station. The difference in the two games was Texas had time to recover against the Ponies, and they did. The 10,264 fans were pleased to see the Longhorns bounce back and mount an offensive charge of their own. When all was said and done, Texas had a hard-earned 91-79 defeat of the Ponies.

In Waco, the Horns continued SWC play against the Baylor Bears. If previous games in Waco between the two teams were any indication, this was going to be a battle. Texas won in impressive fashion, 110-85 over the Bears. A crowd of 9,376 in the Ferrell Center saw the Horns improve their record to 9-6 and 2-1 in the conference.

In a break from conference action, the Longhorns played host to the Georgia Bulldogs. Texas, which led by as many as 35 points early in the second half, was almost too gracious as the host team as they allowed the Bulldogs back into the game. With 2:34, the Horns' lead was down to seven. But Texas, in front of a partisan crowd of 10,235, regrouped late and held on long enough for a 107-96 victory. Texas had a four-game winning streak and a record of 11-6.

The Longhorns returned to conference action on the road at Hofheinz Pavilion in Houston. It was a successful return to say the least. Texas, which led by 25 at the break, continued to pound the Cougars in the second half for the 110-78 win, its fifth consecutive. The only negative of the game occurred late in the contest when B.J. Tyler fell awkwardly to the floor, suffering a broken bone in his left, non-shooting hand.

Against the Rice Owls and without Tyler, whose broken hand had him listed as day-to-day, the Texas offense was still able to build a 17-point lead early in the second half. But like several games early in the season for UT, the lead slipped away and had all but evaporated. With seven minutes remaining in the game, Rice trailed by only three. At that point, clinging to a tenuous three-point lead, the Texas offense managed to regroup and ran off the next 11 points to put the game away. At game's end, Texas had defeated Rice 85-70 for its sixth consecutive victory.

With TCU in town, Texas had to play without the services of star point guard B.J. Tyler for a second consecutive game. In his absence, Roderick Anderson was asked to step up. The former junior college All-American, who started the season slow due to injuries, stepped up in a big way as the Horns rolled over the Horned Frogs, 95-73.

In Dallas at Moody Coliseum, the Horns tried to win their eighth in a row against a struggling SMU team. Texas got off to the quick start and was ahead 19-6. With the 13-point lead and 13 minutes remaining in the half, the Horns received a considerable boost when B.J. Tyler took off his warmups and entered the game. The Texas portion of the 4,378 in attendance gave Tyler a standing ovation. He finished the game scoring 18 points including three of six from three-point range in just 19 minutes of playing time, and the Horns embarrassed the Mustangs 94-66. Texas improved to 15-6 and 7-1 as they headed into a showdown with Texas A&M.

Back home in the Erwin Center, the Horns took on the Aggies in a battle for first place in the SWC. The Aggies were due a payback after they handed the Horns their only conference loss, and their last defeat — nine games ago and a month earlier — in the waning seconds. In this game, Texas used runs of 10-1 to end the first half and 16-0 in the second half to dispose of the Aggies rather easily, 85-68.

Atop the SWC standings, the Horns hoped to stay there by defeating the Baylor Bears in the Erwin Center. A crowd of 11,384 watched as Tyler averaged better than a point a minute – 27 points in 24 minutes – and the Horns racked up 113 total points in a 113-91 rout of the Bears. With the win, Texas improved to 17-6 overall and 9-1 in the SWC. The win streak had reached double digits at 10 and equaled the longest winning streak for Texas since Penders arrived in 1988.

In Lubbock, the Red Raiders, who had suffered an embarrassing 108-79 defeat less than a month earlier in Austin, wanted revenge. After regulation play was complete, Tech had not exacted that revenge, but the Horns hadn't escaped with another victory, either. Instead, the game headed to overtime. After one overtime, the game was still undecided. Texas was faced with its second double-overtime contest in 15 games. This time however, unlike the game against Utah, the Horns came up short. Tech outlasted Texas, 128-125 in the highest-scoring game in SWC history. The winning streak was over. UT dropped to 17-7 for the season and 9-2 in SWC play, a half-game behind A&M and its 9-1 record.

Trying to start another winning streak, Texas returned home to take on a non-conference opponent in Lamar. Against the Cardinals, the Horns found a new inside weapon in junior Rich McIver, who had, without question, his best performance of the season. McIver, who had transferred from Michigan before the season, had yet to prove himself on the court and because of that, was limited by Penders in his playing time. But before the game, Penders challenged the 6-foot-9-inch player, and he responded. McIver finished the game with 22 points, doubling his previous career-high, and 11 rebounds, a tie for career best, as the Longhorns cruised to a 105-75 victory.

After the brief non-conference hiatus, Texas returned to SWC action at home against the Houston Cougars. The Horns dispatched of the Cougars almost as easily as they had their previous opponent Lamar, winning by a comfortable 88-70 margin in front of 10,502 Erwin Center fans. Texas improved to 19-7 and 10-2 in the conference.

In the final home game of the season, Penders wanted his seniors to leave the Erwin Center one final time as victors. They did, in a big way. UT destroyed the Golden Eagles by a staggering 37 points, 106-69. The win improved Texas to 20-7 on the season and marked the fifth time in Penders' six years that the team had reached 20 wins. The team also finished the season at home with a 12-1 record.

At Autry Court in Houston, Texas looked to clinch at least a tie for the league's regular season title with a win over the Rice Owls. The Longhorns struggled early but found offense late in the half and held a 38-33 lead at the break. In the second half, Texas, led by Tyler, who finished with 27, played steady basketball, and Rice never challenged for the lead. With that combination, Texas left Houston 78-70 victors. The win improved the Longhorns' record to 21-7 overall and 11-2 in conference. It also earned them a share of the SWC regular season title.

In the final game of the regular season, Texas had several motivating factors. The first, of course, was earning the first outright SWC championship for Texas basketball since 1974. The second was defeating a TCU team in Fort Worth for the first time in four tries.

The Longhorns had no problem achieving both goals in front of 4,145 at Daniel-Meyer Coliseum. Penders, who knew before the game that A&M had lost and Texas was already the regular-season champion, used all 14 of his players in the game and all of them scored. When all the scoring was finished, the Horns had won the game in a blowout, 111-78. It was Penders second SWC title in six years. Anderson had 18 points and Burditt added 17 in the winning effort. The victory — Texas' fifth consecutive and 15th in 17 games — improved the Longhorns' record to 22-7 and 12-2 in the SWC and earned them a No. 1 seed in the SWC Tournament.

Before postseason action began, two of Texas' four seniors received high praise for their efforts on the season. Albert Burditt was voted defender of the year in the Southwest Conference by SWC coaches as the 6-foot-8-inch senior ranked second in the league with 2.2 blocks per game and sixth with 1.9 steals. He also averaged 8.6 rebounds and 15.4 points.

B.J. Tyler, despite missing the first four games of the season, was named Southwest Conference Player of the Year, also in balloting done by SWC coaches. Tyler finished the season averaging 23.3 points, 6.3 assists, and 3.1 steals per game. He also averaged four three-pointers per game. Tyler also received honorable mention on the U.S. Basketball Writers Association All-America team.

Joining Tyler on the SWC first team was Burditt.

The SWC Tournament

In the opener of the SWC Tournament, the 25th-ranked Longhorns picked up where they finished the regular season. After defeating TCU by 33 points just five days earlier on the road in Fort Worth, the Longhorns moved east to resume the whipping of the Horned Frogs. In Dallas' Reunion Arena and in front of 9,835 fans, the Horns won their sixth consecutive game, soundly defeating TCU again, 96-75. After receiving the honor as top player in the conference, Tyler proved to any of those who may have doubted, posting 21 points in the winning effort. Up next for Texas was a matchup against the Rice Owls.

Against Rice in the second round of the SWC Tournament, Texas jumped out to an early 15-point lead less than five minutes into the game. From there, the Horns extended their lead to 27 before the first half had concluded. Rice battled back in the second half, but never got closer than eight points and the Longhorns advanced to the tournament championship game with a 101-89 win. The victory improved Texas' record to 24-7 on the season and extended its winning streak to seven. It also earned Penders his 400th career victory in 23 years as a head coach. His record improved to 400-272, including a mark of 130-63 in six years at Texas.

With a crowd of 11,164 in Reunion Arena and a national television audience watching on ESPN, Texas played Texas A&M in the rubber match of the season. The Aggies were no match for the Longhorns in their third meeting of the season and Texas cruised easily to an 87-62 victory.

Although it was always important to defeat the Aggies, the game had considerably more significance for Texas. For one, it marked the first time in the tournament's 18-year history that Texas had won it. Second, and most importantly, the Horns had earned a berth in the NCAA Tournament and didn't have to wait and see if they were an at-large selection by the NCAA Tournament Committee. They already knew they were in; it was just a matter of what position, against what team, where, and when.

When the selections came out, Penders and his players were pleased. Texas was rewarded for its 25-7 season with a No. 6 seed and would face the 11th-seeded Western Kentucky Hilltoppers, who had a 20-10 record.

The NCAA Tournament

In the first-round Midwest Regional matchup against Western Kentucky in Wichita, Kan., the Longhorns came out flat. Were they looking forward to a second-round matchup against the Michigan Wolverines and the remaining four players out of the "Fab Five?" No one knew. The only thing certain, Texas was not playing like the Texas team that had gone 25-7 on the season.

After the halftime intermission, Texas looked like the Horns of old as the team stormed back on the strength of senior big man Albert Burditt and junior point guard Roderick Anderson. The Horns advanced to the second round with a 91-77 victory. Next up – Michigan.

Versus the Wolverines in the second round, Tyler had to break out of his brief shooting slump in order for Texas to have any chance at success. Unfortunately for Tyler and the Longhorns, the senior point guard fared no better against the 11th ranked and third-seeded Wolverines in the second-round game. Tyler missed 10 of 11 shots from three-point range and shot six of 24 overall. Despite the poor shooting performance, Tyler managed to score 22 points and the Longhorns had a chance to win the game late. But Texas missed multiple free throws in the final five minutes and Michigan made nine consecutive free throws during the final minute and six seconds to defeat the Longhorns, 84-79. Texas finished the season with a 26-8 record, which tied the school record for most wins in a season.

In the final *Associated Press* poll, the Longhorns finished No. 20, and in the final ESPN/*USA Today* coaches poll, the Horns finished No. 24.

The Off-Season
Penders to the French Quarter?

Several months after leading the Longhorns to a 26-8 season that ended with a second-round loss in the NCAA Tournament to Michigan, the *Austin American-Statesman* reported that Penders might be a possible candidate for the head coaching position at the University of New Orleans.

Penders told the paper he was not interested in leaving Texas and was only talking with UNO Athletic Director Ron Maestri in an advisory capacity. "I have talked to their AD, but it's just an advisory thing. Three people called me and asked me to recommend them. That's how the conversations started."

However, the paper reported that one school source said Penders was very interested in the position because he was unhappy at Texas for several reasons. First was a disagreement over his contract situation. And second was his disbelief, still two years later, on the way the school handled the Dexter Cambridge situation.

Penders, who had four years left on a seven-year contract that paid him an estimated $400,000 per year, denied he was upset about the Cambridge situation and said he was happy at Texas.

Penders, UT Discuss Contract Extension

In another report by the *Austin American-Statesman*, Penders maintained he was not interested in the New Orleans position, but did admit he had had discussions with Dodds since March about a possible contract extension. Penders said Dodds had told him he wanted him to stay at Texas after he had been contacted in some manner by three different schools soon after Texas reached the NCAA Tournament for the fifth time in his six years.

"DeLoss said, 'We want you to stay,'" Penders told the paper. "I don't have any big concerns. I just think it's time to talk about extending the contract. Recruits want to know if you have security."

Dodds told the paper he had already discussed a contract extension with UT President Robert Berdahl and Ed Sharpe, special consultant to Chancellor William Cunningham.

"I think we can do this fairly quickly, as far as taking something to Tom," Dodds told the paper. "I'd say we'll know where we are within days. Then we have to go to the president and regents. That takes time. Tom just wants security."

Chapter Ten

Losses Are Few and Far Between, 1994-1995

Penders wasn't sure what to expect for the 1994-95 season. One poll had his team ranked 19th, another 46th. Following the departure of SWC Player of the Year B.J. Tyler and his 22.8 points per game, Penders hoped to find a nice complement to his remaining backcourt players in Terrence Rencher and Roderick Anderson. Among the possible replacements were newcomers Brandy Perryman and Cal Varner. In addition to the loss of Tyler, Penders had to replace SWC Defensive Player of the Year Albert Burditt, who averaged 15.7 points, 8.6 rebounds, 2.2 blocks per game, and more importantly, a big catlike presence in the middle. Possible candidates included Sonny Alvarado and Nate Gilmore.

While Penders was unsure of who would fill the voids left by Tyler and Burditt, he knew he had a strong nucleus of players returning. In addition to Rencher, who averaged 15.7 points and 5.4 rebounds, and Anderson, who averaged 12.3 points and 5.2 assists per game, sophomore forward Reggie Freeman looked to receive a considerable increase in playing time, as did part-time starters Rich McIver and Tremaine Wingfield in the front court.

No matter who played, one thing was certain – the speed at which they played would be fast. Penders wouldn't have it any other way.

The Regular Season

Texas couldn't have opened its season with a more difficult contest. On the road in Chapel Hill against legendary coach Dean Smith and the No. 2-ranked North Carolina Tar Heels, not to mention a home crowd of 21,572 eagerly awaiting the start of their team's season. No chance for the Longhorns, right?

That's what many, including some in the Dean E. Smith Center, thought before the Texas-North Carolina game started. By the time the game had finished, those who doubted that Texas' chances at victory were slim to none, were believers. The Longhorns opened the season with a loss, but it was an impressive loss at that. The Tar Heels overcame the Horns late in the game for a hard-fought 96-92 victory. Although Texas came up on the short end of the score, it was a promising sign of things to come.

In the home opener against Lamar the Horns completely dominated the Cardinals. Sophomore Reggie Freeman had a career-best performance offensively as he hit 10 of 14 shots from the field and totaled 24 points for the game. Anderson scored 20 and Rencher added 17 as Texas evened its record at 1-1 with a 97-54 blowout. It was Lamar's second-worst defeat in school history.

After a nine-day layoff, 12,514 filled the Erwin Center and watched as the Horns got off to a fast start against their neighbors from San Marcos, the Southwest Texas State Bobcats, and led at the half, 51-18. The Longhorns easily dispatched the Bobcats, 105-60. The Horns record stood at 2-1 and they extended their Erwin Center winning streak to 14 before they hit the road and headed to Florida to take on a top-10 team in the Gators.

In Gainesville, the Texas players were confident they could pull off the upset of the No. 6-ranked Gators. After all, the No. 2 team in the country only narrowly defeated them to start the season. Florida was not impressed by the Longhorns' near-miss at North Carolina as it went on to win its 15th consecutive game at home with a 91-73 victory.

The Longhorns opened the new year against No. 19 Nebraska. The Horns, which had lost 13 consecutive games to top 25 teams, dating back to March of 1991, hoped to reverse their recent misfortune against quality, ranked opponents. In front of 13,477 fans in the Erwin Center, Rencher led the charge for UT with a game-high 25 points and the Longhorns defeated the ranked Cornhuskers in a blowout, 102-74. With the win, Texas improved to 6-2 for the season.

Following the convincing win over Nebraska, the Horns had another test, this time against the LSU Tigers. The Tigers, which unlike Texas had defeated the 13th-ranked Florida Gators just days before, came into Austin confident. With the first sellout of the season looking on, UT proved they were the better team down the stretch defeating Dale Brown and his Tigers, 80-71. With the victory, Texas headed into Southwest Conference action with a five-game winning streak.

In Fort Worth at Daniel-Meyer Coliseum, a sellout crowd of 7,166 watched as the Longhorns took on a familiar foe. Not the team, but their new head coach Billy Tubbs. Tubbs, who had been passed over for the Texas job when it was awarded to Penders, continued his domination of Texas as the Horned Frogs snapped Texas' winning streak, handing the Horns a 102-98 defeat.

After the loss at TCU, Penders decided to change things up in an effort to find a better mix of team chemistry. With that, Carl Simpson replaced Rich McIver at center, and Carlton Dixon replaced Reggie Freeman at small forward.

With a crowd of 14,105 in the Erwin Center and many more watching on ESPN, the shakeup earlier in the week appeared to have worked. Six players scored in double figures for Texas as the Longhorns ran roughshod over the Aggies with the 115-82 victory, their 17th consecutive at home.

In Dallas in the first meeting of the season against SMU, the Horns hoped to get off to a good start in their first of three consecutive road games. There wasn't much doubt after the opening tip. The Longhorns coasted in for a lopsided 100-59 victory. The win improved Texas' overall record to 9-3 and 2-1 in the conference.

With Billy Tubbs now in the Southwest Conference at TCU, Penders and his Longhorns traveled to Oklahoma for a look at new first-year head coach Kelvin Sampson and the Sooners. It was a look they wanted to soon forget. Texas, which held a 13-point lead in the first half, fell to Oklahoma in Norman by a 100-75 margin. Almost 11,000 fans and an ABC regional audience watched Oklahoma beat Texas for the 10th time in the last 11 meetings. The loss dropped Texas to 9-4.

Returning to conference play, Texas battled the Baylor Bears in Waco. The Longhorns, always tested by the Bears in the Ferrell Center, were outscored by a 10-4 margin in the game's final four minutes including a last-second shot that evened the score at 89 at the end of regulation. In the overtime session the Horns overcame one of their biggest problems all season – free throws – and pulled out the 107-100 road win. Texas improved to 10-4 overall and 3-1 in the Southwest Conference.

After the overtime contest against Baylor, Texas returned to the Erwin Center to host the DePaul Blue Demons. With the 12,176 in attendance and an ESPN audience watching, the Longhorns mounted a monumental comeback in the second half. With eight minutes remaining and trailing by 14, the Longhorns rallied. As time expired, the game was tied at 76. Overtime. In the overtime session, neither team pulled away and the game was tied at 86 when the buzzer sounded. Second overtime. To start the second extra session, Brandy Perryman hit a three-point basket that gave UT its first lead of the second half, 89-86. Texas extended the lead in the remaining minutes and held on for the 99-92 double overtime victory.

Two nights later the Horns returned to action against Texas Tech. With the two previous games – an overtime and double-overtime affair – were the Horns headed to triple overtime against the Red Raiders? In the early going, overtime wasn't out of the question as both teams appeared to be evenly matched. But Penders got his team fired up after earning a technical foul midway through the first half, and the Longhorns played inspired basketball the remainder of the game. As a result, they came away with a convincing 82-68 victory. It was the 20th consecutive win at home.

Against the Houston Cougars in Hofheinz Pavilion, the Horns had a chance to establish themselves as the clear-cut frontrunners for the SWC crown. Houston had other ideas. The Cougars and Horns battled through both halves and still a winner was undecided. For the third time in four games, Texas was headed to overtime. In the overtime Houston established itself early and eventually pulled away for a 105-96 win. The Horns had run out of luck in overtime. UT was now in a race for the SWC title as it dropped to 12-5 and 4-2 in conference play.

After losing to Houston on the road, the Horns returned to the Erwin Center to host the Rice Owls. Almost 12,000 watched as Rencher and Tommy Penders Jr. led Texas in an 88-56 thrashing of the Owls. The younger Penders made four of five three-pointers for a career-high 12 points. With the win, Texas earned its place in a three-way tie for first place in the SWC with a 5-2 record.

The TCU Horned Frogs and Billy Tubbs were next for the Longhorns. In front of a near-capacity crowd in the Erwin Center, Texas sought out revenge for the early season loss at TCU, and one of only two losses in conference action. The trio of Rencher, Anderson and Freeman combined to score 73 points for Texas and the Longhorns won by a dozen, 111-99. The win, their 22nd consecutive at home, allowed Texas to maintain a share of first place in the SWC.

The Longhorns headed out on the road in their next contest against Texas A&M and a most hostile crowd of 6,370 at G. Rollie White Coliseum. The Longhorns were more than up to the challenge against their rival and its partisan crowd, as they escaped Aggieland with a 98-88 win.

In its next contest, UT hosted the struggling SMU Mustangs. The Horns ran away with an easy 91-65 victory, their fourth consecutive win, 23rd consecutive at home, and improved to 16-5 and 8-2 in the conference.

In the final non-conference game of the season, Penders knew his players were in for a tough fight as they faced John Chaney and the Temple Owls at the Alamodome in San Antonio. However, to everyone's surprise, the Longhorns had an easier-than-expected time with the Owls, defeating them 70-54 in front of a crowd of 16,716 and a national television audience.

The Horns got back into conference action in their next game on the road in Lubbock. If the Horns were to repeat as SWC regular-season champs, a victory over the Red Raiders, with whom they were tied for the SWC lead, would go a long way toward achieving that goal. The Red Raiders, in front of a rowdy home crowd, however, were the ones who took a giant step toward capturing the SWC crown as they disposed of the Longhorns with a 96-87 victory.

Back in Austin, the Texas players realized they could only focus on their own games and hope Tech would falter down the stretch if they were to somehow slip in through the back door for the SWC title. The first game they wanted to concentrate on was Baylor. The Bears, who had not been impressive all season, were not any different this time around against Texas. The Horns, with extra motivation after the tough loss in Lubbock, beat up the Bears, 109-75. Texas had won for the 24th consecutive time at home, the second-longest streak in the country behind Coppin State's 30, and one shy of the UT record.

In the regular-season home finale and final home contest for senior guards Terrence Rencher and Roderick Anderson, as well as center Rich McIver and forward Tremaine Wingfield, Texas faced the Houston Cougars. Rencher scored 23 points and did his part in assuring he and the three others departed victorious in their final home game, which they did by a final score of 96-82. The win was the Longhorns' 25th in a row at home and tied the school record. For the season, they were 13-0 in the Erwin Center. The overall record for the Horns improved to 19-6 and 10-3 in SWC play.

Texas closed out the regular season with a road game against the Rice Owls at The Summit in Houston. Although the road hadn't been too friendly to the Horns much of the season, Texas jumped to the early lead and never looked back. Texas cruised to a 108-74 victory. Texas finished the regular season with a 20-6 record, giving Penders his sixth 20-win season in seven years with the Longhorns. They were the No. 1 seed for the SWC Tournament.

Before the SWC Tournament, several players and Penders received accolades for their performances throughout the season. Penders was named SWC Coach of the Year. His team was destined for its sixth NCAA Tournament appearance in Penders' seven seasons at the school.

The SWC Tournament

In the opening round of the SWC Tournament, Texas didn't play. Because Baylor had banished itself from postseason play due to an alleged NCAA violation, only seven teams remained. That meant that the Longhorns, who were the No. 1 seed and were matched up against the No. 8-seeded team, were without an opponent. The bye meant a rest for the players.

In their first game of the tournament, the Horns defeated Rice in the semifinals, 78-75.

In the finals, it was only fitting that the two best teams from the regular season, which had tied as regular-season champs, battled it out for all the marbles. The game was tied at 92. In Texas' fourth overtime game of the season, the Horns held on for an exciting 107-104 victory and won their second consecutive tournament title, as well as an automatic berth to the NCAA Tournament.

The NCAA Tournament

In the first-round of the NCAA Tournament West Regional in Salt Lake City, the Horns battled the higher-seeded Oregon Ducks. In the final minute Texas led by as many as 23 points, but the Ducks cut into the margin for the final score of 90-73.

The win gave Penders a 5-1 record in the first round of NCAA Tournament games at Texas, and a 3-0 record against first-round opponents that were seeded higher. Next up for Texas was a battle against the Maryland Terrapins and All-American Joe Smith.

Against the 10th-ranked Terrapins, the Longhorn players and coaches knew they were in for a tough struggle. A combination of tough Maryland defense and poor Texas shooting down the stretch allowed the Terps to pull away for an 82-68 victory. The Longhorns finished with a 23-7 record and the fewest number of losses in a season since 1978, the year of the NIT National Championship. They also ended the season ranked 24th in the ESPN/*USA Today* poll, marking the first time in school history that the Horns were ranked in a final poll in two consecutive seasons.

The Off-Season
Penders Hires New Assistant

In an effort to improve on the tutoring that would be necessary for the young backcourt in the upcoming season, Penders hired one of his former point guards at Rhode Island – Carlton "Silk" Owens. Owens replaced Melvin Haralson, who left for an assistant coaching position at North Texas.

Chapter Eleven

Youth Has Its Benefits, 1995-1996

Going into the 1995-96 season, Penders knew he couldn't replace players like Rencher and Anderson, but he hoped to try to fill the voids to a certain extent. To do that, Penders had a wealth of talent coming in including the likes of McDonald's All-American Kris Clack of Austin's Anderson High School, DeJuan "Chico" Vazquez of Austin's Reagan High School, and 6-foot-10-inch Dennis Jordan, a junior college transfer. Despite their obvious talents, they were still a young, inexperienced group. With the right combination of younger talent mixed in with the remaining veterans such as Reggie Freeman and Sonny Alvarado, Penders believed the 1995-96 campaign could end much like six out of his first seven years in Austin had with a run by his team in the NCAA Tournament.

The Regular Season

The Longhorns opened the season at home against North Texas. The Horns made their debut with a convincing 88-67 victory over the Mean Green from Denton.

For their first road game of the season, the Longhorns headed north to Chicago and the home of the DePaul Blue Demons. The Horns left Illinois with an 88-84 victory. Texas improved to 2-1 on the season.

In its next game, Texas returned to Austin for a contest with the Roadrunners of UT-San Antonio. Reggie Freeman had a stellar offensive performance, this time scoring 25 in a 110-98 victory.

In Louisville, the Longhorns, for the second time in the young season, faced an opponent ranked in the top 25. The first contest against Utah was a disappointing last-second loss. Texas players hoped this one would be different. It wasn't. Louisville won the game going away, 101-78, and Texas dropped to 3-2.

After six days off for the Christmas break, UT visited the Lamar Cardinals in Beaumont. Due to considerable foul trouble for several Texas players including Freeman, the Cardinals remained close until late in the game. With Freeman out, freshman guard Titus Warmsley had a chance to shine. He did. Warmsley had a breakout performance scoring 18 of his 21 points in the second half as the Horns escaped with a 96-82 victory.

In the next game, the Longhorns remembered Chapel Hill a year earlier and a game they let get away against the then second-ranked Tar Heels. This year, in the Erwin Center, with that disappointing loss still fresh in their minds, the Horns wanted revenge. They also wanted to prove that despite the two losses earlier in the season to ranked teams, they were a quality team capable of competing with anybody.

This time, they secured a 74-72 victory. With the upset, Texas improved to 7-2.

In its final Southwest Conference opener, Texas hosted the Rice Owls in the Erwin Center for the last time as conference foes. After a poor shooting performance in Nebraska, the Longhorns hoped to get back on track offensively against the Owls. The only offense of the game, however, came from Rice's Tommy McGhee, who scored almost half of Rice's total output with a career-high 35 points. McGhee and the Owls led from start to finish and left Austin with an 80-69 victory. Texas had lost two consecutive games for the first time since December of 1993 and dropped to 7-4 on the season.

Against the TCU Horned Frogs, Penders started two freshmen for the first time since he had arrived at Texas. It was, however, a senior, Sonny Alvarado, who got the Longhorns back on the winning track. Alvarado scored a career-high 32 points on 13 of 20 shooting from the field, and Texas earned its first SWC victory of the season 103-88. The Horns improved their season mark to 8-4 and 1-1 in the SWC.

In the next game against the Aggies in College Station, UT, which had relied so heavily on its inside game against TCU, had to look elsewhere for offense due to the early foul troubles of Alvarado. Penders opted for the perimeter game, which had been absent in recent contests, with the hopes that any one of several Texas players would regain the long-distance, sharpshooting touch. The rediscovered Texas perimeter offense allowed the Horns to improve to 2-1 in conference play with an 86-70 win.

The Horns, in the weak SWC, had had few opportunities, if any, in recent years to beat a SWC opponent that was top-25 caliber. The Red Raiders were just that at No. 22 with an impressive 15-1 record and 5-0 mark in conference. The Longhorns made it a battle and had a chance to win the game late, but Texas Tech, in front of a sellout crowd of 8,892, eked out the one-point victory, 79-78.

Following the disappointing defeat in Lubbock, the Horns hoped to regroup against the Oklahoma Sooners in Austin. Penders watched his team – once again – fall on hard times shooting the basketball. The Horns lost in overtime, 67-65. Freeman, who suffered a bruised knee injury, had 20 points and was the only Horn to score in double figures.

In a battle for second place in the SWC, Texas hosted the Houston Cougars. Freeman, who was ailing with his bruised knee, saw limited action, but still managed to score 17 points – seven fewer than his average – as the Longhorns tripped up the Cougars, 80-63. The win gave Texas sole possession of second place at 5-2 and improved its overall record to 12-6.

At Autry Court in the final appearance by the Horns as foes in the SWC (Texas to the Big 12 and Rice to the Western Athletic Conference), Kris Clack became the latest in a line of surprise offensive performers for the Longhorns. The freshman had an impressive night to say the least. Clack scored a career-high 25 points, grabbed 10 rebounds, and blocked three shots as Texas easily handled the Owls, 79-64.

Continuing on the road in SWC action, the Longhorns ventured up to Fort Worth to take on TCU. The Horned Frogs never knew what hit them as Texas led at the break, 58-28. In the second half, the Horns continued their domination and won in a rout, 102-81.

The Longhorns returned to Austin to host their foes from College Station. The Aggies, who were barely above .500 with an 11-10 record coming in, fell behind early and never had a chance. Texas, which led by 15 at the half, coasted in the second half to the 69-50 final score and the team's fourth consecutive win.

After defeating the Aggies, the Longhorns headed up to Dallas for a matchup with the

SMU Mustangs and an attempt to extend their win streak to five. At Moody Coliseum, the Ponies tried to run with Texas early. But SMU, which was overmatched, was unable to maintain the frenetic pace. When the final buzzer sounded, the scoreboard showed the Mustangs had run out of gas as they fell to the Longhorns, 101-66. With its fifth win in a row, Texas improved to 16-6 overall and 10-2 in the conference.

The Horns traveled to Rhode Island and Penders' old stomping grounds for a game that had been scheduled earlier in the season but was cancelled due to a blizzard. Through the first half and deep into the second, Texas stayed within striking distance of the Rams, a solid team from the Atlantic 10 Conference. When it was finished, the Longhorns, which shot a solid 47 percent for the game, struck last and slipped out of the northeast with an 81-77 win. With the win, Texas improved to 18-7 on the season.

For the second time of the season, the Horns met the Houston Cougars in a battle for second place. A Hofheinz Pavilion crowd of 7,420 watched as both teams tried to improve their chances of making the NCAA Tournament as well as earn the No. 2 seed in the upcoming SWC Tournament. The Cougars, which trailed by seven points with five minutes remaining, went on a 17-0 run to close out the game and the Horns, 86-76. The win gave Houston sole possession of second place in the SWC and dropped Texas' record to 18-8 overall. The Longhorns finished their final SWC regular season with a 10-4 record.

The SWC Tournament

In the last-ever SWC Tournament, the Longhorns – the No. 3 seed – took on the No. 6-seeded Baylor Bears in the quarterfinals at Reunion Arena in Dallas. Unlike the last meeting of the two teams in Waco where the game wasn't decided until the final few minutes, this one was over by the half as Texas held a commanding 46-24 lead. In the second half Texas posted another 40 points to finish off the Bears, 86-65. With SMU's upset of Houston in another quarterfinal contest, Texas would face the Mustangs in the next round.

In the tournament semifinals with SMU, the Longhorns were unable to shake the Mustangs in the first half. After the intermission, Texas blew a six-point halftime lead completely open and saddled the Ponies with an 89-67 loss. At 20-8, the Longhorns faced the No. 7-ranked Red Raiders in the SWC Tournament Finals.

Heading into the game, both the Longhorn players and coaches believed the third time would be the charm and the Longhorns would put an end to the Red Raiders' 21-game winning streak. At the half, the streak appeared to be in serious jeopardy with Texas holding a 34-28 lead. In the second half, the Red Raiders made several adjustments and were able to reclaim the lead. But Tech, which had won convincingly all season, was never able to pull away. With 3.2 seconds remaining, Tech was still in front by two when UT's Reggie Freeman was fouled and sent to the line for a one-and-one. The tie seemed almost certain. To everyone's surprise, including his own, Freeman missed the first free throw and the Red Raiders escaped with a 75-73 victory.

And so it was, the book was officially closed on 82 years of Southwest Conference basketball. Texas Tech had earned the final regular-season and tournament titles and was headed to the NCAA Tournament as a high seed. The Longhorns also hoped to attend the Big Dance.

Following the game, Texas Tech received a No. 3 seed in the East Regional and the

Horns received an at-large bid as the No. 10 seed in the Midwest Region. Up first for the Horns, the No. 7-seeded Michigan Wolverines.

The NCAA Tournament

In Milwaukee, the Longhorns had their hands full against a tough Michigan team that had finished its regular season with a 20-11 record after battling through a tough Big 10 schedule. Despite the name and tradition of Michigan basketball, the Horns were not intimidated. In fact, Penders and his team welcomed the challenge. Michigan was the type of team Penders loved to coach against because he didn't need to provide any extra motivation for his players. Just the idea of upsetting a top, highly respected team was enough to get the juices flowing.

The Longhorns played loose and led by as many as 13 points in the opening half of play. In the second half, the game was much tighter. The Wolverines fought their way back and with less than a minute remaining, the Longhorns' lead was down to four, 78-74. Michigan then made a driving layup with less than five seconds to cut the lead to two and then, deja vu. Just as Chris Webber had done three years earlier in the NCAA Championship game against North Carolina, Michigan called for a timeout it didn't have. Technical foul. Brandy Perryman sank both free throws for Texas and the Longhorns left the Bradley Center with an 80-76 first-round upset.

The second round didn't get any easier for the Horns as they took on the No. 2-seeded Wake Forest Demon Deacons and 7-foot All-American center Tim Duncan. Duncan was ineffective against Texas for most of the game suffering from a case of the flu. With Duncan limited, the Horns took advantage. Texas jumped out to the early lead and remained in front through the break and deep into the second half. Then, with less than five minutes remaining, a lid seemingly enveloped the Texas basket. The basketball gods were apparently not wearing burnt orange as the Longhorns failed to score a single point in the final four minutes of the game. With the offensive collapse of Texas, Wake Forest capitalized. In the end, the Demon Deacons were advancing to the Sweet 16 with a 65-62 victory.

Texas had made it to the second round of the NCAA Tournament, bypassing most, if not all expectations anyone had and finished the season with a 21-10 record and a near-miss at the Sweet 16. The blend of youth and experience Penders was unsure of before the season had worked.

The Off-Season Stephen F. Austin Shows Interest in Assistant Trilli

Less than a month after the season ended, assistant Vic Trilli was listed as a finalist for the head coaching position of Stephen F. Austin, a Southland Conference school located in Nacogdoches, Texas. But finally, after a week of speculation, the Lumberjacks decided Trilli wasn't their man. Trilli, who interviewed twice with the school, said he was quite happy to remain with Penders and the Longhorns. "I've got a great job at Texas, and it's only going to get better, moving into the new conference."

III. The Final Years

Chapter Twelve

Welcome to the Big 12, 1996-1997

The 1996-1997 campaign was the season of "big" for the Longhorns with the move from the defunct Southwest Conference to the Big 12. Prior to the start of the season, the media had big expectations of the Horns as they were picked to finish second in the Big 12 behind only Kansas.

How big a season the Longhorns would have, nobody knew. The only certainty was the Horns faced some "big-time" opponents with the nation's second-toughest schedule. Among those to test Texas were defending NIT champion Nebraska, a Sweet 16 team in Arizona, as well as seven other teams that made NCAA Tournament appearances the previous season.

The Regular Season

In the season opener at the Erwin Center, the Horns came out fast and furious against the Nebraska Cornhuskers. A crowd of 12,821 watched anxiously as the Longhorns let a 16-point lead slip away in the second half, only to regain their composure in overtime to earn a hard-fought 83-81 victory. Texas improved its opening-game record to 7-2 under Penders.

In the second game of the season and against Penders' former club the Rhode Island Rams, the Longhorns lost another double-digit lead, but this time it turned into a double-digit deficit. But the Longhorns stormed back for an 86-79 victory.

Just two games into the season, Penders and the Longhorns received a minor blow when Titus Warmsley, a sophomore point guard who had received limited playing time and averaged just 2.8 points his freshman season, announced he had decided to transfer. Warmsley said he might possibly transfer to Montana State-Billings and play for family friend, Coach Craig Carse.

For the first road game of the season, the Horns opened in the Sunshine State against the Florida Gators. Texas, which had found non-conference road games to be tough sledding in the recent past, had a solid performance. The Longhorns won in convincing fashion, 82-64. For the first time since 1990 and only the second time since 1981, the Longhorns had started the season with three straight victories.

Back in Austin, the Horns played host to North Texas. After a sluggish first half, the Horns pulled away late for a 71-56 win. Texas improved to 4-0 on the season – its best start since 1982 when the Longhorns, under the guidance of Abe Lemons, started 14-0 and were ranked No. 5 in the country.

After a week in which the Horns lost at Arizona and defeated Fresno State at home, The *Associated Press* rankings found Texas at No. 14. Texas took its new ranking to Oregon as it faced the Oregon State Beavers. The Longhorns, which led by as many as 15 points in the second half, managed to hold off the Beavers in the end to escape with an 86-83 triumph.

Several nights later the Horns continued their West Coast swing with a matchup against another top-10 team – ninth-ranked Utah. The Utes, which trailed by six at halftime, 34-28, responded in the second half and cruised to an 80-68 victory over the Longhorns. The loss dropped UT to 6-2 on the season.

Following the two games out west, the Horns took 10 days off for Christmas break. After the respite, Texas headed to the opposite coast and Rhode Island to take on the Providence Friars. The 10 days off was apparent as the Horns struggled throughout the contest. The No. 18 Longhorns fell to 6-3 on the season with a disappointing 74-66 loss.

With two consecutive losses on the road to end 1996, the Horns returned to the Erwin Center hoping that the new year and a return to familiar surroundings might result in a different outcome. In Texas' Big 12 opener against Oklahoma State, the 18th-ranked Horns found the range – three-point range – early and often. UT won its conference opener easily, 92-58. With the strong overall team performance and a 7-3 record, the Horns were ready for the real test – a meeting with the top-ranked Jayhawks in Kansas.

In Lawrence, Penders tried an approach different from what anyone, including Kansas and Coach Roy Williams expected from Texas. Instead of the familiar fast-paced style of basketball that had earned Texas the nickname "Runnin' Horns," the Longhorns opened the game with a matchup zone and an offense more reminiscent of Princeton's methodical style. For one half it worked as Texas trailed by only six, 27-21, at the intermission. In the early going of the second half the Longhorns stayed close and even led 44-41, but then Kansas found an offensive groove and went on a scoring run. The Horns never recovered and the Jayhawks ran away with an 86-61 win. Texas dropped to 7-4 and 1-1 in Big 12 play. Freeman led the Horns offensively with 22 points.

Back in Austin, Texas finished up the final game of the three-game home stand, including Louisville and Oklahoma, against the feisty Missouri Tigers. In the second half, the 23rd-ranked Horns were in a situation strikingly similar to one a week earlier in which they lost to Louisville in overtime only after a 15-point second-half lead had evaporated. This time, after the 15-point lead had been reduced to two, the Horns managed to hold off the Tigers in regulation to win the game, 78-74.

On the road in Waco, the Horns took on the Bears. The players on the 23rd-ranked Texas team knew they were in for a battle. Unfortunately, the blowing of the whistle continuously interrupted that battle. For the night, officials called 54 fouls – 27 on each team. When the whistle blowing finished, the Horns were on the short end of a 76-72 score and had suffered their second conference loss in seven tries.

Following an impressive performance against OSU in Oklahoma, the Horns returned home to face the Baylor Bears in a grudge match. The game ended with a 70-67 win over the Bears. It wasn't a large margin of victory, but a win nonetheless. It improved the Horns' overall record to 14-7 and 8-3 in the Big 12.

In their next game, the sickly Longhorns headed north for a matchup with Nebraska. The Texas team, which included five players sick with the flu, was without question, limited against the Cornhuskers. Despite that and an 11-point deficit at the half, the Horns managed to cut the lead down to two in the second half. However, the depleted

In 1974, Penders (right) became head coach at Columbia. Since that time, he has seen a lot of change on and off the court, including hairstyles and clothing.

Penders, with wife Susie, is introduced as the 22nd men's basketball coach at the University of Texas in 1988.

At his introductory press conference, Penders flashes the Hook 'Em Horns sign for the first of many times in his 10 years.

Penders, who became the winningest basketball coach in school history, meets Cliff Gustafson, who was the winningest baseball coach in school history. Gustafson also left UT under a cloud of controversy as the winningest baseball coach in NCAA Division I history.

Karli (here in 1989), the littlest Penders, grew up on the sidelines at UT basketball games.

Penders with Dodds' wife Mary Ann flying on a state airplane.

Tommy Penders Jr. (left) starred at Austin Westlake High School - the same high school Luke Axtell and Chris Mihm attended - before playing under his father at Texas.

Dodds and Penders don cowboy attire at the 1989 Houston Rodeo.

Louis Pearce, Dodds, Penders and daughter Karli during happier times at the Houston Rodeo in 1989.

Penders flashes the Hook 'Em sign after a 1990 game with daughter Karli alongside, and assistant Jamie Ciampaglio in the background.

Penders, well-known in his own right, mixed company with the likes of golf legend Arnold Palmer and country music legend Willie Nelson.

Penders (second from right), Dodds (second from left) and alum Mike Myers (front left) all pose for a photo during dinner. Penders flew to Dallas on Myers' plane before he was hired.

The University of Texas men's athletics coaching staff gather for a picture in front of one of several fountains on the UT campus in the mid 1990s. (L to R): Dave Snyder, tennis; Penders; Eddie Reese, swimming; John Mackovic, football; Cliff Gustafson, baseball; Stan Huntsman, track; and Jimmy Clayton, golf. Only Reese and Snyder were still employed by the university for the '99-'00 season.

During his 10 years in Austin, Penders led the Longhorns to several net-cutting ceremonies in the SWC Tournament.

Penders looks on as caddie for legendary football coach Darrell Royal.

Penders' vocal coaching style was misinterpreted during his final season in Austin when he was accused of verbal abuse.

In the end, even divine intervention couldn't prevent the removal of Penders.

During his time at the University of Texas, Penders never shied away from challenging SWC officials. In 1991, he served a one-game suspension for his forthrightness.

At the resignation press conference, Penders and Dodds shake hands one final time.

Penders had only two losing seasons in 10 years at Texas. Some games during those seasons were even painful for him to watch at times.

Penders gives an interview to Bill Simonson at a 1998 tribute party, which Simonson and his station organized. Simonson received Luke Axtell's faxed academic progress report, but unlike Craig Way, never read it over the air.

Penders speaks to a crowd of more than 500 while wife Susie and daughter Karli look on.

Penders and wife Susie with former players Ron Baxter and Alex Broadway (right). Broadway witnessed Wendlandt in the dorms on numerous occasions during the final season.

Penders shakes hands with Eddie Oran at the tribute party, while administrative assistant Leslie Parks looks on.

After 10 years at Texas, Penders, in his first year at George Washington, led the Colonials to a 20-9 record and a berth in the NCAA Tournament.

Penders, his wife Susie, son Tommy, daughter-in-law Amy, and daughter Karli all dressed up for Tommy's wedding in August 1998.

Penders (second from right) is joined by his current GW administrators (from L to R): Dom Perno, Asst. AD/Development; Jack Kvancz, Athletic Director; and Bob Chernak, VP for Student and Academic Support Services.

Longhorns were never able to take the lead and Nebraska eventually pulled away for a 79-67 win.

The Longhorns returned home after the loss to Nebraska and were confronted with another top-10 team. The Iowa State Cyclones, who were 18-4 and ranked seventh, were in town and ready to put the Longhorns to their next test. This time, however, and for the first time in five tries all season against top-10 teams, Penders and the Longhorns came out on top. In the low-scoring affair, which was witnessed by more than 13,000 fans, the Horns showed they could play a half-court game with the best as they beat the Cyclones at their own game, 57-56. The Longhorns improved to 15-8 and 9-4 in the Big 12 with the victory.

A sellout crowd of 16,175 turned out for the final home game in the careers of Sheldon Quarles, Dennis Jordan, Al Coleman and Reggie Freeman. Those four, along with their teammates, wanted to put on a strong showing for the appreciative Erwin Center fans, who had shown up in great numbers all season and had shown up one last time to watch the Horns battle Texas A&M. It wasn't one of the team's best performances of the season but it was enough as the Horns prevailed with a 68-57 victory. The victory, Texas' eighth straight over the Aggies, improved the Longhorns' record to 16-9 and 10-5 in the Big 12, and secured a first-round bye and a No. 2 seed in the upcoming Big 12 tournament.

In the regular-season finale, the Horns traveled to the Rocky Mountains to take on another top-25 opponent in the 19th-ranked Colorado Buffaloes. The Longhorns appeared to be content with their No. 2 seeding in the upcoming conference tournament and were blown away by the Buffs in a lackluster performance, 83-60. Texas' Freeman awakened from an offensive slump to lead the Horns with 24 points. But Freeman's effort wasn't enough and UT closed out the regular season with a 16-10 overall record and a 10-6 Big 12 record.

At the conclusion of the regular season, Penders remained convinced that the Horns were a lock for the NCAA Tournament after managing 16 wins against an incredibly difficult schedule. Others weren't so easily persuaded. If Texas wanted to get off the proverbial tournament "bubble," a win in its first game of the Big 12 Tournament would go a long way toward accomplishing that.

The Big 12 Tournament

After a first-round bye in the first-ever Big 12 Tournament, the Longhorns played Missouri in the second round. The Tigers and their 14-16 record apparently lulled the Longhorns to sleep and with less than 10 minutes to play in the game, Missouri led by nine. Texas rallied and had several chances to pull within one late in the game, but the Horns never capitalized. As a result, the Tigers advanced to the semifinals with an 80-75 victory. Penders still contended that because his team had won 16 games against a difficult schedule, they should be rewarded with an at-large bid.

The NCAA Tournament Selection Committee apparently agreed with Penders and the Longhorns received a No.10 seed in the East Region and would face No. 7-seeded Wisconsin of the Big 10. Penders' point was further validated as the Longhorns had the fewest victories of any team in the NCAA Tournament, with the exception of the teams awarded automatic bids for conference championships. The Horns were only the sixth team in the 1990s to receive an at-large bid with 16 victories.

The NCAA Tournament

In the opening round of the Big Dance, Penders and his Longhorns were out to prove they were worthy of the at-large selection. Any of those Texas doubters, and there were plenty, had better take note. Up first was Wisconsin.

At the first-round NCAA East Regional game in Pittsburgh, the Badgers, which had finished the season with an 18-9 record, were believers just six minutes into the game as the Horns jumped out to an early 15-3 lead which Texas never relinquished. At the final buzzer, Texas was advancing to the second round with a 71-58 victory. The win marked the seventh time in eight NCAA first-round games that Penders, in his nine years at Texas, had guided the Longhorns to the field of 32. To everyone's surprise, Texas would be facing Coppin State, which had upset the No. 2-seeded South Carolina Gamecocks.

In the second-round NCAA Tournament matchup, Texas had to compete not only against Coppin State, but also against a partisan crowd of 17,509 in the Pittsburgh Civic Arena that had adopted the Eagles — a decided underdog — as their team. The crowd was disappointed midway through the second half as the Longhorns had put the crowd favorite at a decisive 51-39 deficit. However, Coppin State, spurned on by its adoptive fans, went on a 19-4 run and took the lead, 58-55. But Texas' senior leader Reggie Freeman scored 15 of the Longhorns' next 17 points and the Longhorns escaped at the end with an 82-81 victory. For the first time since 1990, the Longhorns were headed to the Sweet 16.

The doubters had been silenced.

Up next was the Louisville Cardinals, a team familiar to Penders and his Longhorns and one the Horns sought revenge on after a heartbreaking 85-78 overtime loss earlier in the season at the Erwin Center. In front of a crowd of more than 30,000 at the Syracuse Carrier Dome, the Horns had an eerily similar start against the Cardinals. In fact, at halftime, Texas led the Cardinals by the same margin they had in Austin earlier in the season, 37-31. But the second half proved to be very different. Louisville waltzed to an easy win, 78-63. Texas finished its season with an 18-12 record and an appearance in the Sweet 16 for the second time in Penders' nine-year career in Austin.

Chapter Thirteen

The Off-Season of Activity

Since Assistant Coach Jamie Ciampaglio resigned following the 1991-92 basketball season, the off-season months from the conclusion of one season to the start of the next had been relatively quiet on the Forty Acres. Besides the annual basketball banquet or talk of potential recruits, there wasn't much to discuss when it came to Texas basketball. That all changed following the 1996-97 season and before the start of the 1997-98 season.

Rutgers Shows Interest in Penders Again

The annual basketball banquet following the 1996-97 season was still a month away, and there was a flurry of activity surrounding the men's basketball program.

In fact, the season had been over just 24 hours when Penders was first informed that a school had interest in him possibly becoming its next head coach. It was a school with which Penders was quite familiar, and the same school he had passed over for Texas almost nine years to the day. It was none other than Rutgers University and long-time friend and Athletic Director Fred Gruninger.

Although Rutgers' recent interest in Penders had just surfaced publicly, the interest of Gruninger on behalf of the school was actually the culmination of numerous things that began during the 1995-96 season.

Penders said it was during that season Dodds told him he would get a new contract of at least five years and it would make him one of the top two or three highest paid coaches in the Big 12. However, like so many contracts in the past, the deal was slow in coming. Penders waited for the contract to be completed. During that time, Penders, who had worked on previous contracts with advice from long-time friend and agent Joe Glass, was contacted by Craig Fenech, an attorney from New Jersey. Fenech, who had been instrumental in getting former college coach John Calipari a professional coaching contract, contacted Penders about the potential of coaching in the professional ranks. At the time, Penders explained that he was happy at Texas and in the midst of negotiating a new contract. Fenech volunteered to review his present contract and act as a liaison. Penders was relieved to have someone else step in to handle the business side of his dealings with the university. "I didn't want to deal with it anymore because it was stressful."

In the fall of 1996, Fenech flew to Austin for his first meeting with Dodds. In that meeting the two discussed the general terms of Penders' future contract and how they were going to arrive at the final terms. Fenech expressed to Dodds that they hoped to have the contract done before the beginning of the 1996-1997 season. Dodds said they would work on it.

According to Penders, what was "par for the course" as far as contracts were concerned, the contract was not completed before the season. Instead of getting closer to a completed contract, negotiations had stalled. Penders said this was solely a result of Dodds and his refusal to return Fenech's phone calls to discuss the contract. Penders said on more than one occasion Fenech brought the situation to his attention and he in turn questioned Dodds about it in the hall. "DeLoss would say, 'I'm busy. I'm on the basketball committee and I'll get back to him.'"

By January of 1997 and more than halfway through the season, Dodds had still not discussed Penders' contract with Fenech. Fenech, who was becoming increasingly frustrated, told Penders that one option would be to seek employment elsewhere. He said numerous jobs would be opening up in the coming months if he was interested. "I'm not going anywhere. I want to stay here," Penders told Fenech. "Just hammer it out." By March and the NCAA Tournament, still no contract.

In a phone conversation Fenech had with Dodds early in the month, Dodds expressed that he was having problems getting the contract completed. He told Fenech that university president Robert Berdahl had no urgency in acting on the contract because he was leaving to become chancellor at California-Berkeley. As an addendum, Dodds told Fenech that Berdahl didn't like Penders. He told Fenech in order to overcome these two hurdles Penders should get involved in another job. This way, according to Dodds, he could have some leverage with his higher-ups.

After the discussion with Dodds, Fenech called Penders and told him what Dodds had said. Penders couldn't believe it. "That's nonsense Craig. Bob Berdahl and I had a great relationship." At the end of the conversation, Fenech told Penders in an effort to get the "leverage" Dodds said he needed, he would call Rutgers officials and see if they were interested. And maybe this might get the ball rolling on the new contract.

In the next few weeks, Penders and the Longhorns made it through the first and second rounds of the NCAA Tournament. Behind the scenes, Fenech had contacted Rutgers and just like nine years earlier, they were interested. However, before any Rutgers officials could speak with Penders about the opening, they had to get permission from Dodds.

Penders said when the team arrived in Syracuse for their game against Louisville in the Sweet 16, newspapers all along the East Coast were reporting Penders was a main target of Rutgers. Rumors were everywhere. To see what was happening, Penders called Dodds back in Austin.

"There's a lot of stuff in the newspapers up here," Penders told him.

"Oh yeah, I meant to tell you that the AD from Rutgers (Gruninger) called and asked for permission to talk to you."

"Did you give him permission?" Penders asked his boss.

"Yeah," Dodds answered.

"I really don't want to go there," Penders told Dodds. "I'd like to get this contract done."

"Maybe this will help get it done," Dodds said. The conversation ended.

Following the loss to Louisville, Penders and the team returned to Austin, where rumors were running rampant. In an attempt to see where contract negotiations stood, Penders tried to contact Dodds. Like Fenech had experienced several months earlier, Penders couldn't locate Dodds and Dodds wouldn't return his phone calls.

Finally, Penders contacted Dodds. He told Dodds that Rutgers had contacted him and expressed an interest in him flying up to see the campus.

"I think you ought to go up and talk to them and interview with them," Dodds told him.

"I don't really want to do that. It's not in good faith. If things (contract) are going to get done here," Penders countered.

"If you talk to them and they offer you a job, then maybe I'll have something," Dodds said.

Penders didn't understand.

"You mean to tell me that I need to get leverage after a Sweet 16 season and we have the best recruiting class coming in the history of the school, and I have to go talk to another school?"

"Yes," Dodds answered.

Penders, with frustration mounting, wanted to call President Berdahl, but because he had been told Berdahl didn't like him, in addition to his outgoing status, Penders opted to call University Chancellor Bill Cunningham. In the call, Penders explained to Cunningham that he had no intentions of going to Rutgers. But he was concerned how Cunningham and other administration officials viewed him as the basketball coach at Texas. Cunningham told Penders he was thought of highly and university officials definitely wanted him to stay.

"Tom, we want you to stay here. What's wrong? What's going on?" he asked Penders.

"DeLoss said he can't get this contract done unless I talk to Rutgers, so I've got to go up and talk to Rutgers."

After his discussion with Cunningham, Penders called long-time friend and university athletics council member Bob Moses. Same thing. Moses said all the people he knew, including the regents, wanted Penders to stay.

Although Penders had received affirmation from several Texas officials, Rutgers officials were putting on the heat for him to come to New Jersey. Fenech had spoken with the Rutgers vice president and had been told they would offer Penders a deal that was "too good to refuse."

With that in mind, Penders called Dodds the evening before he left for New Jersey.

"DeLoss, they are going to do the same thing to me that you did to me when I came here. It's going to be a lot of money. I'm not going to ask you to match the money. I just want you to promise that you'll come through with what you promised me last year and the fall. That you're going to give me a new contract that would put me in the top three in the Big 12."

"I can't promise you that at this point," Dodds replied.

Penders was confused. With the trip to New Jersey less than 12 hours away, and an athletic director who wouldn't assure him that he would receive a new contract, Penders had run out of options. He had to go and at least listen to what Rutgers had to offer, even if he really wasn't interested. A professional courtesy of sorts.

About two hours after the phone call with Dodds and late in the evening, there was a knock at Penders' front door. It was Dodds.

Deja vu all over again. With him, Dodds had a handwritten piece of paper. On it, much like Penders' original contract, Dodds had written out the terms of the new contract. For Penders, it wasn't enough.

"I've got to go up to Rutgers. I can't go on this (handwritten contract). Can't you get somebody else's signature?" Penders asked Dodds.

Dodds tried to convince Penders to accept the terms on the handwritten piece of paper, but it was to no avail. Penders retired to bed and Dodds visited with Penders' wife Susie. The next day Penders flew to New Jersey, where he met up with Fenech.

In the meeting with Rutgers officials, which lasted for six hours, school representatives made it abundantly clear that they wanted the third time to be the charm with Penders. After 1985 in which the school opted for another coach, and 1988 when the coach opted for another school, this time Rutgers officials wanted Penders over the other candidates which reportedly included Drexel's Bill Herrion, Old Dominion's Jeff Capel and Xavier's Skip Prosser.

To get Penders, Rutgers officials thought they had the answer – 700,000 of them in fact. Rutgers was offering Penders a seven-year, $700,000 per year contract minimum, with incentives to make more. This was definitely indicative of a school desperate in its search for a coach to rebuild a program that had gone 11-16 the previous year, its fifth straight losing season. Penders was impressed. He tested them for more and asked for 10 years. Rutgers officials never wavered.

With $7 million the final dollar amount discussed, Penders was still set on staying at Texas, although he never openly expressed it. Instead, Penders returned to Austin while Fenech remained behind to negotiate the contract.

Soon after his return to Austin, Penders heard from Dodds. Dodds told him that he had received approval from Berdahl and Cunningham for the new contract. The contract, which was still the handwritten piece of paper from Dodds, was for five years at a minimum of $550,000 a year, plus bonuses. At last. It took just a trip to New Jersey and an ungodly offer from another school to get the contract approved.

The next day, Penders held a press conference in Bellmont Hall announcing his intentions to stay. Throughout the first few minutes Penders discussed his coaching philosophies and talked about his visit to Rutgers. He said the New Jersey school offered a "great opportunity." Finally, he got to what everyone wanted to hear.

"I've always said that if I ever resign, or when I retire, I'll depart with the knowledge that I've left behind a much better situation for my successor. This was the case at every school that I've moved from.

"With this year's accomplishment, the returning players, a recruiting class that is ranked in the top-10 nationally, the timing would be perfect for such a scenario. The time might be right to make a move, and Rutgers would be the perfect move if I were to leave Texas.

Penders paused. The room was silent, the tension building. At last, he said what he planned to do. "I'm announcing today that I'm retiring effective April 1, year 2010, if I'm still able to walk to the podium," he said with a big smile.

University of Texas fans rejoiced. The man who had taken Texas basketball to a new level was staying.

After the public brouhaha, Penders expected the contract to be expediently processed. He should have known better. For four months, there was no word on the contract. Fenech was growing restless by the minute. "Why won't they get this thing done?" he repeatedly asked Penders, as if he knew the answer.

Penders said throughout this time, he was still being paid based on his old contract. It wasn't until August, four months after the press conference, when Fenech received a contract.

In the contract however, Penders noticed something was awry. In his previous contracts, there was always a clause that stated he could be terminated if he "knowingly violated a material provision." In other words, if he intentionally broke a rule. With the latest contract, the words "Knowingly violated ... " were struck through. The current wording essentially said if Penders broke any university rule, state rule, NCAA rule, or Big 12 rule, whether it was accidental or not, he could be terminated. Penders pointed this out to Fenech. "That's ridiculous," Fenech told Penders. "We want the same wording that you had in your last contract."

Fenech went to Dodds. When Fenech asked Dodds if he should talk to new UT interim president Peter Flawn, Dodds told him that Flawn wouldn't sign off on the contract. He told Fenech that he would be better served if he went up the chain of command, beginning with university attorney W.O. Shultz. When Fenech approached Shultz, who had insisted on uniformity in all coaches' contracts, the attorney told Fenech the contract Dodds had written out wasn't worth the paper it was written on. Shultz said Dodds had no authority to sign the contract. Essentially, Fenech concluded, Shultz was saying if he didn't want the contract, he didn't have to take it. But the wording was not going to change.

Fenech called Penders and told him he had reached a dead end. Penders was disappointed, but not surprised by Shultz's response. "It's kind of unethical to offer me a new contract and then change the wording so I'm day to day," Penders would recall later.

After pondering their next move, Fenech and Penders decided to call Ed Sharpe, a high-ranking member of the administration. Sharpe was more receptive to the idea of getting the new clause, but insisted he didn't have the authority to overrule Shultz. Running out of options, Fenech then called Bill Cunningham. Cunningham reiterated what Sharpe had said, and told Fenech he needed to try and work it out with Shultz.

Fenech had had enough.

"Tom, I can't take this any further. You're going to need help. Maybe there's a UT alum that has some clout."

Immediately, Penders thought of well-known Houston attorney and prominent alum Joe Jamail.

Penders called Jamail and explained what was happening. Jamail told Penders to send him copies of the previous contracts as well as the new one the university was offering.

After Jamail had received and perused all the documents, he called Penders back. He said he couldn't understand why they wouldn't give Penders the wording he had requested, especially since it had existed in all his previous contracts. Jamail then told

Penders he would get the wording he wanted. He said it would all be "straightened out."

Shortly thereafter, Penders received another call. It was Cunningham. Cunningham told Penders to expect the contract to be completed in the next 24 hours. Within 24 hours, Penders received the unsigned contract, which included the new wording that would, in the future, be referred to as the "Jamail Clause."

The night before the contract was to be signed by all parties, Penders decided to call Dodds and thank him for finally getting it done. "I call DeLoss to tell him we got it done and I'm real happy. It's over with and thanks. He starts swearing at me."

Penders said that among the terms Dodds called him was a "mother******." He said Dodds told him he had gone over his head and then hung up.

Penders called back.

"DeLoss, who were you talking about that I went over your head with? You told my attorney to talk with Chancellor Cunningham, Peter Flawn, Ed Sharpe and W.O. Shultz, which he did."

"You went and talked to Joe Jamail," Dodds answered angrily.

"Well what department does he work in here?" Penders asked quizzically.

"He's an alum," Dodds said.

"Yeah, he's also my lawyer and he's representing me now," Penders said, surprising Dodds.

"You think Jamail will get the other coaches this clause?" Dodds asked sarcastically.

"Probably, if we ask him," Penders shot back.

Dodds hung up on Penders a second time.

Penders said he was really bothered by Dodds' reaction. As a result, Penders called both Cunningham and Jamail and told them about Dodds' tirade and what he had said. Both assured him that the matter would be resolved.

The next day Dodds left an apology on Penders' answering machine at home. He then called Penders at his office and apologized again. It was the last time the two men spoke formally until Penders' final weeks at the school.

Trilli Leaves for North Texas

After three different schools in the previous two years had inquired about Texas Assistant Coach Vic Trilli for their vacant head coach position, only to go with another candidate, one school finally made Trilli an offer. He accepted.

The 44-year-old Trilli, who coached under Penders from 1990-1997, left the Longhorns to become head coach at the University of North Texas in Denton. Trilli was hired to replace Tim Jankovich who resigned after compiling a 10-16 record his final season.

Penders Adds to Coaching Staff

Following the departure of Trilli, Penders promoted Carlton "Silk" Owens to Trilli's role as the off-campus recruiter. Owens, 32, was the starting point guard on Penders' 1988 Sweet 16 team at Rhode Island and had just completed his second season as a UT assistant.

In addition to Owens, Penders hired another coach in Rob Wright, head coach from Dallas' Carter High School. Wright, whose nephew was then-Texas sophomore Anthony Goode, compiled a 92-18 record at Carter and his squad was the only 5A team in Texas to reach the regional finals three consecutive years.

Penders Dismisses Top Recruit From Team

Just two months before the start of the season, Tom Penders showed bad behavior wasn't tolerated from his players in the classroom or on the court – even if it meant a blow to the talent level of his team.

Penders dismissed 6-foot-9-inch freshman forward Lamar Wright, who was one of the five prized recruits for Penders and a main reason why the incoming freshman class was considered top-10 nationally. Penders said Wright was released because he repeatedly reported late, if he reported at all, to classes, team meetings and individual workouts.

According to Penders, after Wright attended several meetings with the head coach and assistant coaches, he was warned a third and final time. Penders told the freshman, who was ranked the 23rd best high school player in the country, if he had another misstep, he would be dismissed. The next day Wright was reportedly late for two classes and an individual workout session.

"Maybe at some places it's OK to do that. But he's sticking out like a sore thumb here by doing this. We've had him running at Memorial Stadium so much, I'm surprised he hasn't burned a hole in the track."

The dismissal of Wright from the team was important in the final few weeks of Penders' tenure at Texas because Penders had set a precedent for suspending, or in this case, dismissing a player from the team for not making the necessary commitment to academics, even while the player was still academically eligible.

Penders Falls Ill

Several weeks before practices began, Penders began his regimen of getting into "game-shape," which included working out hard and meticulously watching his diet. A ritual he said he went through each year in preparation for the long season ahead. But this year, something was different. He wasn't feeling right.

The first sign of potential problems occurred on a flight to Florida, where Penders was scheduled to speak at a convention for the Florida Coaches Association. He said on the flight he had a fever and generally wasn't feeling well. After a sleepless night, Penders called back to Austin and spoke to his doctor. On the advice of his doctor, Penders went to a Florida hospital for an examination. Following the full exam, which included a check of his kidneys, heart, liver and gallbladder, doctors determined that there was nothing seriously wrong with Penders and that it was a case of intestinal flu. As with any flu, bed rest and fluids were suggested. However, Penders had a speaking engagement later that day and asked the doctor for something to relieve his stomach pain. The doctor obliged and prescribed prescription-strength Ibuprofen. Later that day he gave the speech without incident.

The next day Penders flew north to Washington D.C. After speaking to a group of coaches at a clinic held at Dematha High School, Penders returned back to Austin feeling somewhat better. With two weeks before the start of practice, Penders and his wife decided to take a brief vacation to Mexico before the season got into full swing.

Penders said he wasn't feeling extremely bad in Mexico, but he didn't feel normal. "I just wasn't feeling myself. I felt a little listless and I seemed to be retaining water."

A week after returning from the trip, Penders and the Longhorns began practices. Almost two weeks into practice, Penders realized something still wasn't right. Despite being on the diet, he was still retaining water and hadn't lost any weight.

In late October, Penders, at the request of his wife, went in to see his doctor. With the results from his exam at the Florida hospital in hand, Penders' doctor told him it was evident that he had had an intestinal virus. After Penders told him he still wasn't feeling "right," the doctor ordered several tests.

The test results indicated that there was something wrong with the function of his kidneys. The doctor then prescribed a more extensive battery of tests. Penders had a choice – five tests, one a day for five days, or one full day of tests. He opted for the latter because this would allow him to have the tests run on a day the team wasn't scheduled to practice.

In early November, Penders went through a full day of tests. After all the tests were completed, it was determined that Penders had suffered an allergic reaction to the pain medication prescribed in Florida for his intestinal flu. His kidneys had not been able to tolerate the high dosage of Ibuprofen. As a result, his kidneys had begun a process of shutting down. With the overtaxed kidneys, fluid was building up in his body and putting pressure on his heart and weakening it. Penders was prescribed diuretics to alleviate some of the fluid buildup.

A weakened heart, which is serious in any case, was more so for Penders because of a pre-existing heart condition. Penders said while undergoing an extensive physical examination required to purchase a life insurance policy in 1991, he was diagnosed with cardiomyopathy, or a weakening of the heart muscle that impairs its ability to pump blood and can lead to cardiac arrest. At that time, it was determined that Penders' heart had the ability to pump at a maximum of 70 percent capacity of the normal heart.

Since the original diagnosis in 1991, Penders had received regular checkups and his heart had maintained its pumping capacity at 70 percent. However, the latest test results indicated that his heart had weakened considerably since his last checkup in July. With Penders' regular cardiologist out of town, the doctor told Penders based on the test results, he should not leave the hospital because his heart was too weak.

Penders convinced the doctor he was fine and told him he would call his friend Denton Cooley, a former UT basketball letterman from 1939-1941, and the Surgeon-in-Chief and President of the Texas Heart Institute in Houston.

Soon after, Penders called Cooley. After listening to Penders describe the chain of events and the results of his tests, Cooley recommended Penders come to Houston the next day.

The next day, Penders and his wife went to Houston. Cooley had arranged for the two to meet with the Chief of Cardiology, James T. Willerson. In that meeting, Cooley and Willerson explained to the Penders the results of his tests performed back in Austin. They were shocking. Since his last checkup, in which his heart was pumping at its normal capacity of 70 percent, it had dropped to around 45 percent.

Cooley and Willerson persuaded Penders to check into the Texas Heart Institute and have additional tests run. Penders agreed because he knew he was in the hands of two of the world's most respected heart specialists. When the test results came back, they showed a marked improvement. The pumping capacity of Penders' heart had already increased to 55 percent, indicating that it was on its way back to recovery and that the weakening was a direct result of his ailing kidneys. Despite that turnaround, the doctors recommended Penders have a defibrillator, or a device designed to restore a normal heartbeat, implanted as a preventative measure.

On November 6, just five days before the season-opening game, Penders had the defibrillator implanted.

"This procedure should allow Coach Penders to coach without risk of sudden cardiac arrest and to lead a normal life," Willerson told the media after Penders' surgery.

Penders remained hospitalized for several days. During his stay, Penders said he never received a phone call from Dodds. At one point Penders' wife called Dodds to tell him that everything was fine and to inform him that he could speak with Willerson if he had any questions about the procedure or the future health of his head basketball coach. Dodds never called.

After four days, with his kidneys functioning close to normal, and his heart steadily improving, Penders was released. Upon his release, Penders was instructed by his doctors not to travel out of state and not to fly. With those orders, Penders would have to miss the team's first two games in New Jersey at the Coaches vs. Cancer Classic.

His absence from the sidelines in those two games would mark just the third and fourth times that Penders had missed a game in his 27 years of coaching. The first occurred in 1972 when his mother died and he was head coach at Tufts University in Boston, and the second, in 1991, when he served a one-game suspension handed down by the Southwest Conference for criticizing game officials.

Chapter Fourteen

The Final Season, 1997-1998

After the most active of off-seasons, the Longhorn players and coaching staff were ready to put the off-court issues behind them and focus on the on-court issues such as the first game in the Coaches vs. Cancer Classic in New Jersey. Even without their head coach, for at least the first two games, the players, both new and veteran, were excited about the prospects of the coming season.

The Regular Season

In the season opener at the Meadowlands, the 22nd-ranked Longhorns battled the methodical Princeton Tigers in the first round of the Coaches vs. Cancer Classic. With Assistant Coach Eddie Oran at the helm, the Horns were never able to get things going offensively. Princeton, with its back-door cuts and walk-it-up-the-court style of basketball, outlasted the fast-paced, run-and-gun style of the Longhorns for a 62-56 victory.

In the consolation game of the Classic, No. 22 Texas faced No. 19 Georgia, who had lost to North Carolina State in the opener. The Horns were led by junior Kris Clack, who tied a career high with 25 points, and freshman Luke Axtell, who scored 19 points that included three of four from three-point range. Despite the 44 points from Clack and Axtell, UT wasn't able to stop the Bulldogs in the end. Eddie Oran's record as a head coach dropped to 0-2 with an 89-87 loss.

Following the two losses in New Jersey, the Longhorns returned back to Texas. But before the Erwin Center fans got their first glimpse of the 1997-98 version of Texas basketball, the Horns had a game in Denton against North Texas. In that game, two familiar faces were in the coaching boxes. Penders, who had returned from his heart surgery, was on the Texas bench, and Vic Trilli, who had left Texas just the season before, was on the North Texas bench. Against North Texas, Penders saw a team that looked very much like his own. The only difference was talent. In the end, Texas' talent was just too much for Trilli's Eagles. UT had earned its first victory of the season with a 116-94 win.

While Penders had successfully returned to the sideline with a win over North Texas just two weeks after having a heart defibrillator implanted, his health was still of concern to others, even though they never openly expressed it with him. In fact, his health status was one of three main topics discussed by the University of Texas men's athletic council in a two-hour long executive session meeting. In addition to Penders' health, Dodds told the *American-Statesman* that the future of football coach John Mackovic and the school's radio contract were also discussed.

Back on the court in the home opener, the Longhorns hosted the Liberty Flames. Against the school known more for its founder – the Reverend Jerry Falwell – than its basketball program, the Longhorns easily doused the Flames with the offensive leadership of freshman Luke Axtell. The Horns evened their record at 2-2 with a 98-70 victory.

Just a little more than two weeks after suffering a two-point loss – 89-87 – to Georgia in the consolation game of the Coaches vs. Cancer Classic, the Horns looked for redemption on the road in Athens. The Texas players expected this game to be different because not only did they have a few more games under their belt, they also had their head coach back. If everything were that simple.

The Longhorns never got on track offensively against the No. 22 Bulldogs. In front of a crowd of 6,806 fans, Georgia forced Texas into 22 turnovers and capitalized repeatedly. Even with the head coach back and the experience of a few more games, the Horns never mounted a serious challenge and came out on the short end of the 94-76 score. Sophomore forward Gabe Muoneke tied a career high with 20 points to lead Texas. With the loss, UT dropped to 2-3 on the season.

Back in the Erwin Center, Penders did something that hadn't been done at UT since the 1979-1980 season when he started three freshmen. Luke Axtell, Chris Mihm and Bernard Smith all got the starting nod from the head coach as the Longhorns played host to American University. The trio of youngsters paid dividends as they combined for 34 points in the Horns 78-62 victory.

In the next game, the Horns rolled out the welcome mat for the defending national champion Arizona Wildcats. In the hard-fought contest, which saw the Horns trim a 13-point deficit at the four-minute mark to four with less than a minute to play, the difference came at the charity stripe. Arizona made its free throws down the stretch, including three in the final 30 seconds, to win the game, 88-81. The loss, which was considered a positive experience by most, dropped Texas to 3-4 on the young season.

After the big game with Arizona, the Longhorns were tested three days later when the undefeated (5-0) Florida Gators visited Austin. Although the Horns weren't much better offensively shooting just 37 percent, they converted enough to come away with a big 85-82 triumph. With the win, Texas evened its season record at 4-4.

The Horns finished up their four-game home stand with a game against the LSU Tigers. In the first matchup with LSU since the 1994-1995 season, the Longhorns hoped to get over the .500 mark for the first time all year. After a less than 50 percent free-throw shooting performance in the first half, the Longhorns found the mark in the second half hitting 12 consecutive free throws to break away from the Tigers for a 69-63 victory. The win improved Texas' record to 5-4.

In their next contest, a nationally televised game on CBS against Illinois, the Longhorns tried to improve to 6-4 and give Penders his 200th win as coach at Texas. Neither was meant to be. If Texas had won, Penders wouldn't have been around to see it as both he and long-time Assistant Coach Eddie Oran were ejected from the game after each received two technical fouls for arguing foul calls. For the game, Texas was charged with 32 fouls including 16 in the third quarter – the same quarter Penders was ejected. Illinois, with its coaching staff courtside, ran away from the Horns with a 105-80 victory.

After the loss to Illinois, the Longhorns returned to the Erwin Center where they took on former Southwest Conference rival Houston in the final game of the early non-conference schedule. The contest was nothing reminiscent of the former battles in the now defunct SWC. The Longhorns, which led by 10 at halftime, turned up the heat defensively in the second half and pulled away with the 89-71 win, Penders' 200th at Texas.

Against Baylor in the Big 12 opener for both teams, the Longhorns and Bears battled in a rough-and-tumble affair. The rough came in the form of two technical fouls, two intentional fouls, one flagrant foul, and one ejection. The tumble came in the form of Texas' Kris Clack and Luke Axtell collapsing on the floor with injuries. Clack's injury appeared to be the more serious of the two as he left the Erwin Center floor in considerable pain with an injury to his knee. The initial report was an injury to the anterior cruciate ligament. Axtell suffered a moderate sprain of his right ankle just prior to Clack's injury and was listed as doubtful for the team's next game at Missouri. In their absence, Texas' Ira Clark scored his first double-double with 19 points and 12 rebounds, while Muoneke scored 18 points of his own. It wasn't enough, though, as the Horns lost, 87-81. Texas dropped to 6-6 and 0-1 in Big 12 action.

In Missouri, the Horns never had a chance. With Axtell and Clack out, the Horns took the court without their two main offensive leaders. It showed. By halftime the Tigers were ahead, 51-26. The second half wasn't any different and Missouri rolled to the 91-69 victory. Chris Mihm scored 14 points and Muoneke added 11 to lead the less-than-potent Texas offense.

Before Texas' next game against Kansas, the Longhorns got a much-needed break. Instead of a season-ending knee injury, which most thought Clack had suffered against Baylor, the junior would only miss two to four weeks with a sprained ligament.

The good news of Clack's pending return was quickly brought in check when No. 4 Kansas came calling. With an Erwin Center crowd of 13,296 and a national television audience watching, the Jayhawks came at the Horns from all angles and all distances. When the offensive display was complete, Kansas had carved up the Longhorns for a 102-72 victory. With the loss Texas fell to 6-8 and 0-3 in the Big 12.

In its next contest, UT traveled to Oklahoma for another Big 12 matchup. Against the Sooners, Texas played an inspired first half and led 41-36 at the break but the Sooners rallied for a 91-75 victory. Muoneke led Texas with 17 points and Vazquez added 16. Although it was a loss, the Texas players and coaches were pleased with the overall performance and thought the game was something positive to build on.

In a game against Nebraska, an audience of 12,882 filled the Erwin Center and cheered as the Horns had by far their best shooting performance of the year. For the game, Texas shot 55 percent against the Big 12's second-ranked defense and waltzed to a 105-91 victory. Mihm scored a career-high 29 points, Axtell added 25, and Clack continued to rebound from his injured knee with 22 points in the winning effort. With the win, Texas improved to 2-4 in the conference and 8-9 overall.

In its final non-conference game of the season, Texas traveled to California to take on Jerry Tarkanian and the Fresno State Bulldogs. Without the services of freshman Luke Axtell who remained in Austin with an upset stomach, the Longhorns offense wasn't the same. Despite a perimeter game that made only six of 26 from behind the three-point arc, the Horns still had a chance to win the game late. But Fresno State clamped down on defense in the final minutes to emerge with a 90-82 win.

Returning back to conference action against Iowa State in Ames, Penders expected to get a spark for his offense with the return of Axtell to the lineup. But Axtell, who had missed the previous game due to a stomach virus, came up lame during warmups with back spasms. With Axtell's absence and a less productive performance from Mihm (10 points), the Longhorns dropped to 8-11 overall and 2-5 in conference play with an 85-82 loss.

After another disappointing conference loss, Texas returned to the Erwin Center to host Oklahoma State, a team Penders and the Longhorns had handled rather easily in recent years. Even with a sub-par year, the Longhorn players had hopes of continuing their dominance over the Cowboys, who had a 14-3 record coming in. Axtell returned to the lineup for the first time in three games and provided a much-needed lift for the Horns. As a team the Longhorns shot 59 percent or 13 of 22 from three-point land, which was more than enough to defeat the Cowboys, 88-73. The win improved Texas' record to 9-11 overall and 3-5 in Big 12 play.

In the Longhorns' final game at G. Rollie White Coliseum in College Station, Texas hoped to overcome its road woes that consisted of only one win in eight tries all season. Playing the 6-12 Aggies appeared to be a likely cure. The Aggies had other ideas and with 5:30 remaining in the game led the Horns by five points. But UT rallied. With less than a minute remaining, Texas' Chris Mihm followed up on a Kris Clack miss and gave the Longhorns an 81-80 lead. On its ensuing possession, Texas A&M missed a shot in the final seconds and Texas escaped G. Rollie White for the last time with an 81-80 win.

Almost a week later, the Horns returned to action in Austin against Oklahoma in what was expected to be a physical battle. Texas wasn't able to play physically very long when its two big men, Mihm and Muoneke, got into early foul trouble. As a result, Oklahoma's Corey Brewer was let loose on the inside and the Sooners left Austin with an 81-74 victory. The loss dropped Texas to 10-12 overall and 4-6 in the Big 12.

Mihm to Transfer?

Following the loss to Oklahoma, what turned out to be more disconcerting than the loss itself, was the rumor that future star center Chris Mihm was considering transferring from the program. When Mihm was questioned by the *American-Statesman* about the matter, he said he didn't know where or when the rumor started. If Mihm didn't know any particulars about the origin of the rumors, all he had to do was pick up the previous day's paper to see who was perpetuating them. It was in the commentary of *American-Statesman* sports columnist Kirk Bohls, who second-guessed Penders throughout the article.

Bohls said Penders wisely took Mihm out with 13:13 left in the game when the freshman picked up his fourth foul. But then Bohls questioned why Penders waited until less than two minutes remained in the game to put Mihm back in. Penders said after the game "... if he had to do it over again, he would have put him back in at the five- or six-minute mark." But Penders also said the reason he kept Mihm out was he had confidence in senior Ira Clark, who had "picked us up before in those situations." He also said if he had sent Mihm in earlier, Oklahoma coach Kelvin Sampson would have gone right at him and had his players bait Mihm into committing a foul.

Bohls concluded his column by classifying the incident as a "highly sensitive, explosive situation." He said Penders should "... swallow his pride, admit he made a mistake and work harder at developing the type of half-court offense he promised the Mihms during recruiting." He added that Mihm's parents were not particularly "thrilled by Penders' use of him and even met with Penders privately after the game."

With Bohls' last statement, one had to wonder: how did Bohls know Penders met with the Mihms if it was a private meeting? And how did Bohls know it was such an explosive situation?

Two days after the Oklahoma game, Mihm finally put the rumors to rest. He said he wasn't upset with Penders' move in the Oklahoma game, just "confused a little bit." "But Coach Penders explained it to me and explained it well," the freshman said.

Mihm said the rumor of his transfer, which had apparently been swirling for several weeks, was never substantiated. "I blew it off. I thought it must just be one of those rumor-type deals, but it was getting strong. I kept hearing more and more about it. But I didn't know where it was coming from. It was strange."

The whole incident with Mihm should have been a red flag to anyone following the program. A head basketball coach at a Division I school being asked by the parents to explain why he chose not to play their son? On top of that, rumors circulating that the player was unhappy and he had a desire to transfer elsewhere. Something smelled funny.

In Manhattan, Kansas, the Horns tried to put the mini-controversy behind them as they took on the Kansas State Wildcats. Against a K-State squad that had defeated Missouri and Nebraska by a combined 78 points, the Longhorns held tough. After trailing by 11 points with less than three minutes, the Horns rallied and were within striking distance. Unfortunately, Texas struck out and the Wildcats won in a close one, 83-79. It wouldn't get any easier in the next game as the Horns headed to Lubbock.

In a season where Texas had a difficult time winning games, especially those on the road, the odds of winning a game against Texas Tech in Lubbock Municipal Coliseum – an arena where Texas hadn't won since 1992 – were slim and none. Admittedly, the Horns' previous five losses in Lubbock were by a combined total of 17 points, but it still appeared as if UT was cursed on the South Plains. This time it was different as the Horns pulled off a stunning 82-80 road win. Clack equaled his career high with 26 points and pulled down 10 rebounds while Mihm scored 18 points and grabbed 17 rebounds, tying LaSalle Thompson's UT freshman record in the winning effort.

Back at home the Horns hosted the Aggies in front of 13,421 fans in the Erwin Center. Mihm continued to post impressive offensive numbers. The freshman center scored a game-high 25 points on 12-of-14 shooting from the field and the Longhorns defeated the Aggies going away, 87-74.

In another attempt to reach .500 for the first time all season, the Longhorns traveled north up I-35 to Waco. In the early going UT looked well on its way to a .500 record and a mini three-game winning streak when it led Baylor by as many as 13 points. In the second half the Bears managed to fight back and with less than five minutes remaining, Baylor had the lead. The Longhorns never answered and Baylor handed Texas an 80-75 defeat.

In their next contest the Longhorns traveled further up I-35 to Stillwater, Okla., for their final conference road game. Oklahoma State came out a completely different team than the one defeated back in Austin in late January. The Cowboys set the tone early and at the intermission held a 40-25 lead. The lead grew larger in the second half and OSU walked off the floor with a payback, 80-58. With the loss, Texas was assured its first losing season since 1992-1993, and only its second losing season in 11 years.

In the regular season home finale and final home game for seniors Brandy Perryman and Ira Clark, Penders hoped to finish the season in front of the Erwin Center crowd on a positive note. He had no idea it would be his last home game as well.

Against Colorado, Texas set the pace early jumping out to a 12-point lead midway through the first half. It didn't last. The Longhorns struggled the remainder of the game and the Buffaloes overcame the deficit and eventually led by a dozen. At the final buzzer, the Buffs had won the contest by an 81-64 margin. Texas finished the season with its third straight loss and a regular-season record of 12-16 and 6-10 in the Big 12. With that finish, the Longhorns were seeded No. 10 in the Big 12 Tournament and would face No. 7 Texas Tech.

In Kansas City at the Big 12 Tournament, it was "do or die" time for Texas. Win and keep playing, or lose and the season was finished. With no chance of reaching the .500 mark and a bid to the NIT Tournament, the Horns' only chance at postseason play was sweeping through the Big 12 Tourney and getting the automatic bid to the NCAA. It would be an uphill battle, but anything was possible.

However, before Texas' first game against Tech, any realistic hopes of running the table in the conference tournament took a hit when the Longhorns' leading scorer, Kris Clack, went down with a separated shoulder in practice. It was just the latest in a laundry list of injuries suffered by the team all season which included a deep thigh bruise suffered by Vazquez in the last game of the season against Colorado. Clack was listed as doubtful against Tech.

Before the Horns left Austin for Kansas City, they had one more distraction thrown their way when it was reported in the *American-Statesman* that sophomore guard Anthony Goode was pondering a transfer due to his lack of playing time. Goode had appeared in 14 games all season and averaged 2.2 points per game and had 26 assists and 23 turnovers. "It's been a very disappointing year for me. I was discouraged at first but I've sort of gotten over it."

The Big 12 Tournament

Despite the distractions since the regular season finale loss against Colorado, the Horns came out ready to play against the Red Raiders. For the first 20 minutes Texas dominated Tech, and at the half held its biggest halftime lead of the year at 47-30. In the second half, the Red Raiders came storming back. In the end, it was Carr who had a chance to tie the game with a three. He missed and Texas held on for the 86-83 win to advance to the second round of the Big 12 Tournament. Next up for Texas was a date with the No. 2-seeded Oklahoma State Cowboys.

Against OSU, the Texas players and staff knew they had their hands full against a team they had managed to defeat earlier in the season only after converting 59 percent of their shots from three-point range. It would take a similar effort if Texas had any chance of toppling the No. 25-ranked Cowboys.

In the first half, the Longhorns hung around. The second half was much the same as Texas managed to keep OSU within striking distance. However, with just over six minutes remaining in the game, the Horns' chances of overtaking the Cowboys dropped considerably when Clack went down with an ankle injury, his second injury in a week and third of the season.

The Horns kept it close long enough for their leader to get taped up and return to the floor with just over a minute to play. Upon his return, Clack scored on a driving layup that pulled Texas within two with less than a minute remaining in the contest. Then, after OSU missed its free throws, Clack dished off a pass to Brandy Perryman, who hit a three that gave Texas a shocking 65-64 upset win. With the improbable victory, the Longhorns were advancing to the semifinals to take on the Sooner State's other team, Oklahoma.

The Horns could almost see the light at the end of the tunnel. Two more games, albeit tough ones, and they were back in the NCAAs. Against Oklahoma in the semifinals, it was a struggle from the start. The Longhorns had evidently run out of gas and their star's multiple injuries had finally caught up with him. Texas converted 19 of 55 from the floor for a season-low 34.5 percent, and 13 of 28 from the free-throw line for 46.4 percent. Those numbers meant a Texas loss, 68-55.

So it was done. The University of Texas men's basketball season was finished. Although the season-ending record was 14-17, the team finished strong down the stretch. Something to build on for next year with the loss of only two seniors, Brandy Perryman and Ira Clark.

Chapter Fifteen

The Final Days

Following the loss to Oklahoma in the Big 12 Tournament semifinals, the mood in the locker room was somber. A season full of expectations by many, including the players, was over. Despite the end of a season, which is disappointing for all but one team, Penders, as coaches are apt to do, was upbeat. He told the team how proud he was of their effort and the way they played in the tournament despite injuries, which included Clack's separated shoulder and sprained ankle and Axtell's back. He then, as was customary following the conclusion of each season, told the players that after they returned to Austin he would meet with each one of them the following week to discuss their plans for the upcoming spring and summer. The timing of this speech was unusual for Penders. In years past this type of talk normally occurred after a loss in the NCAA tournament, not the conference tournament. This was unfamiliar territory for Penders and his staff – just the second time in his 10 years at Texas that his team was not going to the NCAA.

Sunday, March 8
The Meeting

Less than 24 hours after the conclusion of the season, the first of what turned out to be many off-season meetings was held. However, this meeting wasn't one Penders had referred to the night before in his post-game locker room speech. In fact, Penders wasn't even in attendance at this meeting and had no knowledge of its taking place until much later. Instead, this was a secret meeting between four players and Athletic Director DeLoss Dodds, held at Dodds' home. Those attending included three freshmen – Luke Axtell, Chris Mihm, and Bernard Smith – and one sophomore, Gabe Muoneke.

The meeting, each player was told, would be a review of the season and how everything went, or how each respective player thought it went. According to Bernard Smith, the meeting wasn't out of the ordinary since Dodds had periodically checked with many of the players throughout the season to see how their entire college experience was going. He figured this was somewhat of a continuation of sorts.

Axtell and Smith arrived in one car; Mihm and Muoneke in another. After the athletic director greeted each player, the four sat down and began discussing the season. Just minutes into the conversation, the casual tone and reflection on a disappointing season abruptly changed. Two players, Axtell and Muoneke, took the offensive and began voicing their displeasure with the head coach. Both made it very clear to Dodds, who was busily taking notes – if Penders returned the following season, they would not.

Muoneke's reason for wanting to change schools – he wasn't getting the ball enough, or as he described it, not enough "touches." He told Dodds he was very disappointed in the 1997-98 campaign, his second, because he had not improved as a player the way he had hoped and expected.

Numbers for the two seasons, however, indicated the exact opposite. During his freshman year, Muoneke averaged 15.2 minutes and 5.9 points per game. In his sophomore year, both numbers increased dramatically – 10 more minutes of playing time per game (25.9 minutes), and almost twice the point production (10.4 points per game).

Despite the numbers, Muoneke explained to Dodds that with all the hard work he had put in the summer before the 1997-98 season, he should have touched the ball more often. "He felt this was going to be his year," Smith said. "And when that didn't come about and he wasn't getting the ball and plays weren't run to him, he was disappointed."

According to Smith, who was Muoneke's suitemate during the season, this wasn't something Muoneke concocted for the meeting, but was something he had discussed throughout the season and openly voiced with Smith, his closest friend on the team.

Axtell, on the other hand, who averaged 13.3 points per game on the season – the fourth highest scoring average all-time for a freshman at UT – was not concerned with his on-court production. Instead, he was bothered by Penders' coaching style.

He told Dodds he did not like the way Penders treated some of the players on the team, what would later be termed "verbal abuse" in news reports. Axtell said it wasn't necessarily how Penders interacted personally with him, but with some of the older players. "Luke took dislike in Penders getting on the older players," Smith said. "He really didn't like the way coach approached some of the players and some of the things he said."

According to one such "older" player, Kris Clack, a junior at the time, Penders and his style were nothing out of the ordinary. "With any coach in the country, they get in your face and try to motivate you and get you going. That's all he ever did," the former McDonald's High School All-American said.

"Anytime that he would say something, you couldn't take it personally. You're out there to try and win the game and he's out there to try and win the game. If he thinks you're not ready to play or not motivated, he's going to do anything he can to get you motivated, to get you angry to go out there and want to play. That's all he wants to do."

Smith, a former prep star himself from Houston, said he agreed with Clack. "Most of the stuff Coach Penders would say was motivational stuff. He knew what it took to get you motivated."

When asked if he cussed, Smith said sometimes, but they weren't harsh words directed at specific players. "It was just coaching," he said. "He wasn't harsh at all. Any other coach would have laughed at him (Penders) because they say a lot harsher things to their players."

Clack added that all the claims of mistreatment of the older players, or "verbal abuse," were incorrect, especially in what turned out to be Penders' final year. He said the heart ailment that kept Penders from coaching the team's first two games of the 1997-98 season also prevented him from being as vocal during the year.

"The verbal abuse was a bunch of BS if you ask me," Clack said, "because he couldn't be really aggressive with us. He didn't have any energy because he was just getting off of this (heart) surgery. He couldn't even come out yelling and screaming like he usually does."

Although the heart played a significant role in Penders not being as animated as usual in practice, Clack said Penders also realized he was dealing with a team full of youth and inexperience, including three freshmen starters, the first time that had happened on a Longhorn squad since 1984.

"He hardly did any kind of disciplinarian-type things. On occasion he might raise his voice, but it wasn't like what I'm used to because we had a young team and it was a rebuilding kind of year."

Once again, Smith concurred with Clack. "I didn't notice a difference (in his coaching style), but some of the older players noticed a difference. They were telling us he wasn't getting on us as much. I would talk to him and he would just say, 'We're a young team.' He couldn't really get on Chris, Luke and myself as hard as he did the other guys in the past because they were a lot older. He really didn't get on us all year."

In response to the allegations of Penders mistreating players, Dodds told the four players, "I'll talk to him and see what's going on." Smith said later that Dodds did not appear to be too concerned about the charges. "He wasn't shocked. I think he knew that it was just part of coaching."

Before the meeting concluded, one of the players broached the subject of Penders and late-night phone calls to players. The player said he had never personally received any calls, but had heard about it from others. Dodds said he would also look into that.

When asked about late-night calls, Clack said he received calls in the evening, and he had even been at the house of another player when Penders called one night. In all cases, though, he said conversations were always casual talk about the game.

"He did that (last year) when Reggie (Freeman) was here because I would be in Reggie's room and he would call and they would just talk about the game. It was nothing irate. He even called me sometimes to see how I was doing after a game. We talked about the game, what happened in the game, and maybe why we lost the game. It was always basketball-related."

After all voices had been heard, Dodds asked Smith, "Bernard, do you have anything to say?"

"I really don't have much to say," the quiet freshman said. "I'm just listening to everybody else."

The meeting ended after just an hour of discussions, and the four players returned to campus.

Smith said following the meeting, and even during the meeting, he was incredulous of what was occurring. Although, admittedly, he never thought at the time it would lead to the coach leaving the program.

"'Why the hell am I here?' was going through my head during the meeting," Smith said. "I didn't think what they were saying could bring someone down. I didn't think this was going to hurt Coach Penders. After the meeting I was kind of in disbelief. You can only take so much when you hear about a certain person and some stuff is not true. You hear stuff just out of the blue that you never heard of before. It's more shocking."

Monday, March 9
Tying Up Loose Ends

Penders' wife, Susie, knew this was the first time since the 1992-93 season her husband wouldn't be coaching in the postseason. With that in mind, she asked him to take a vacation, which would be a first with their 15-year-old daughter. Penders agreed and Susie immediately began making plans for the trip. Meanwhile, Penders had business to take care of at the office and left for Darrell K. Royal-Texas Memorial Stadium, home of Bellmont Hall and all the athletic offices.

Upon arrival at Bellmont Hall, Penders recognized that his secretary was upset. She said the acting director of basketball operations, Jimmy Gonzalez had been "in her hair and making her feel uncomfortable." She asked Penders to intervene and talk with Gonzalez about the matter. Penders told her he would take care of it. Soon after their brief discussion, he sat down and wrote a note to Butch Worley, senior associate athletic director.

In the memo Penders told Worley he would address the situation that week with Gonzalez, but next week he would need Worley to look over the matter while Penders vacationed in St. Martin with his family. "Give him (Gonzalez) some other things to do for a week," the note said.

After writing the note to Worley, Penders decided it was time to reduce the stacks of paper that had collected on his desk. Later, he said every year during the last few weeks of the season, when everything gets hectic as the season winds down and postseason play heats up, there is never any time to answer correspondence or anything else. "I'm trying to catch up and I look through the academic reports (at this time)."

In the collection of papers, several academic reports were uncovered. Among those, the most prominent was that of Luke Axtell. It wasn't a full report, but a one-page letter from Othell Ballage, the head of academic support, to Senior Assistant Athletic Director Curt Fludd, which warned Fludd that Luke was behind in his studies, hadn't been attending study hall, and hadn't been meeting with his tutors.

Penders put the report aside and told his secretary to schedule an appointment with Axtell for the next day, if possible. While Penders went through more correspondence the next few hours, his secretary called to inform him that Axtell had been contacted and the two would meet tomorrow afternoon at 3 p.m. Penders then went through several more pieces of mail and left for the day.

Tuesday, March 10
Penders Meets With Axtell

Penders arrived at the office before his scheduled meeting with Axtell and tried to go through more correspondence. Around 3 p.m., the 6-foot-9-inch freshman finished up his classes for the day and headed over to Bellmont Hall for his meeting with Penders. Axtell arrived just before 3 p.m. After the two greeted each other, Penders closed the office door, and Axtell sat in a chair across the desk from Penders. Axtell sat with both his arms and feet crossed, chin to his chest, and eyes firmly fixed on the floor in front of him.

"Luke, I'm here. Look at me," Penders began the discussion. "I want eye contact. I want to make sure you are understanding this."

Unaware that Axtell had already made his intentions of transferring clear to Dodds in a meeting just two days before, Penders began reading the academic report to Axtell. For the duration of the meeting, Axtell appeared uninterested in what the coach had to say, much less being in his office.

"I'm doing alright," Axtell responded at one point. "I don't want to be hassled."

"Well, if you keep this up, you're going to be in big-time trouble," Penders said. "At the very least you're going to have to go to summer school. And I know you don't want to go to summer school because you told me before you didn't want to have to deal with summer school."

"I'll catch up," Axtell answered.

"You've got to do something right away," Penders said. "You've got this week to get caught up."

Penders continued with several questions regarding the academic report. "Why aren't you going to study hall?"

"I don't like study hall," Axtell said, in an acknowledgement of sorts.

"You're not meeting your tutors. You have to go to study hall and you have to meet with your tutors," Penders sternly told him.

"I've been meeting with them," Axtell said.

Penders was stunned. Not convinced of what he just heard, Penders asked, "Are you saying this is a bunch of garbage? This thing I'm reading, that I just read to you?"

"Yeah, that's not true," the freshman said.

"If you're lying to me I'm going to have to suspend you," Penders said in a disciplinarian tone.

"Big deal. The season's over," Axtell fired back.

Although surprised and disappointed in Axtell's last remarks, Penders was quick to remind him of a similar situation that occurred just a season earlier.

"Yeah, the season's over. Big deal," he said. "I suspended and threw off Lamar Wright in September before we ever played a game if you remember. This means get your butt to class."

"If you suspend me, what does that mean?" Axtell asked, somewhat awakened by the coach's remarks.

"That means you don't have any team activities, weight training, and you're suspended from all team duties," Penders informed him.

"I don't want to lift weights anyway," Axtell said defiantly.

Penders had heard enough. He reasserted one last time to Axtell that he needed to improve on the "student" in student-athlete by going to study hall and seeing his tutors. Axtell left.

Before Penders went home for the day, he wrote a memo to Dodds explaining how he would like to meet with him as soon as possible regarding a possible replacement for Jimmy Gonzalez. Penders said Gonzalez was trying his best to perform the duties of director of basketball operations, but it just wasn't a fit. "He didn't know what the job entailed ... I knew he was going to be there through August and then we were bringing in somebody else," Penders said later.

Among the duties for the position were helping groom the athletes, getting them summer jobs, talking to the parents, and getting involved in the recruiting process. Penders said it was important this new person be in place before the spring recruiting season, which was just around the corner. In the note to Dodds, Penders tried to convey the importance of filling the position in a timely manner. After he finished the note, he left for the day.

Later that evening from home, Penders called assistant coach Eddie Oran and told him to run a check to see how Luke was doing academically. Penders said he would wait to hear back from him. In the meantime, he was going to take a few days off and hit the links.

Wednesday, March 11

Penders played golf and did not conduct any official university business.

Thursday, March 12

After he returned home from playing his second round of golf in two days, Penders received a phone call that evening from his secretary. She told him that Dodds wanted to meet with him the next day. Penders was pleasantly surprised by Dodds' prompt response and was looking forward to discussing the new director of basketball operations position. He also told himself that while he was at the office, he'd "kill two birds with one stone" and visit a few more players about the past season, and discuss their plans for the upcoming off-season.

Friday, March 13
Penders Meets With Players and Dodds

Upon arriving at the office, Penders had his itinerary set. He was to first meet with Gabe Muoneke at 12:30 p.m., followed by Chris Mihm at 1:30 p.m., Dodds at 2 p.m., and finally, backup center Marlon Drakes at 4 p.m.

At 12:30 p.m., Muoneke sat down with both Penders and Oran to discuss his future. Penders began the meeting by telling the forward that he expected him to clean up his act for next year, his junior season. He told him he didn't want to worry about any more of Muoneke's "shenanigans." Penders was referring to Muoneke's quick temper and outspokenness in several games during the previous two seasons, particularly his sophomore season, in which he earned numerous technical fouls. "You should be more mature by now, and I'm not going to put up with it any longer."

Penders also told the forward that he wanted him to stay in the country this season and try to improve as a player. "I want you to play basketball this summer and not go to Africa like you did last year," he said. (Muoneke had spent two months in Nigeria visiting relatives the summer before his sophomore season.)

What Muoneke said next caught both Penders and Oran completely by surprise. "I'm thinking of transferring," he told his two coaches.

Penders, not believing what he had just heard, responded. "You're kidding me! What's the reason?"

"I want to play outside. I want to play the wing position," Muoneke said.

"Yeah Gabe, and I want to be quarterback for the Dallas Cowboys, too," Penders said facetiously.

Oran said he thought the whole thing was a joke. "Gabe has been known to joke and I thought he was joking."

Muoneke wasn't.

"I think I should be further along (in development)," he said.

After the last remarks, Penders searched for and quickly found several sheets of paper that refuted Muoneke's claims.

"As a freshmen you averaged five points a game and three rebounds," Penders said. "And this year you averaged 11 points a game and six rebounds. You also played more minutes. The only problem I have with your development is you losing your temper and that kind of thing. But, if you really want to transfer, we'll talk about it after the semester break and after you talk to your dad. Have you talked to him yet?"

"No, I haven't talked to him," he said.

"OK, I'll call him tonight and we'll talk," Penders told the youngster.

The meeting ended. Muoneke left the office with both coaches in shock.

Oran said he couldn't believe after all Penders had done for Muoneke the previous two seasons, as far as defending him and his tirades, that Muoneke wanted to transfer. "I just couldn't believe he was going to leave, because I thought Tom was very protective and supportive of him."

After Muoneke left, Oran returned to his office, and Penders regrouped in preparation for his meeting with Mihm.

In the 1:30 p.m. session, Mihm and Penders discussed how they were both very pleased with the 7-footer's performance his first year as a freshman. Penders showed Mihm his impressive numbers for the season, which included an average of 24.8 minutes, 12.4 points, and eight rebounds per game. He also showed how Mihm's numbers compared favorably with the statistics of former Kansas' standout center and current NBA player Greg Ostertag.

"You had a damn good year," Penders told Mihm. "You made the all-freshmen team. Your numbers for a freshman were way beyond what I expected and you've done a great job in school. What are you going to do this summer? Do you want to go to Pete Newell's Big Man Camp?"

Mihm said he planned on attending the camp, which was music to Penders' ears. After several minutes of idle discussion, the two shook hands and Mihm put his arm around Penders. "Thanks. I really enjoyed this year," he told the coach.

Penders was encouraged. Just minutes earlier he had listened to Muoneke talk of transferring, and now Mihm, who was arguably the future of Texas basketball, was a complete 180-degree turn.

At 2 p.m. Penders headed down to Dodds' office, expecting to discuss the director of basketball operations position. Soon after the two men sat down and finished the trivial talk, Dodds dropped the bomb. "Four players came to my office yesterday and said they want to transfer," Dodds said. "They had some complaints – and one of them was verbal abuse."

Penders was dumbfounded. He had no idea how to respond. In fact, as Oran had thought just an hour before with Muoneke's remarks, Penders thought it was a joke.

"Are you kidding me? My practices are open. Parents are there," he explained to Dodds, trying to refute the claim.

Penders then asked Dodds which players might be transferring.

"Chris Mihm, Bernard Smith, Gabe Muoneke and Luke Axtell," Dodds said in order.

"Gabe Muoneke did say something about it. I just had a meeting with him earlier," Penders said. "If he wants to transfer I don't have a problem with that, although I don't think he should. It would be in my opinion less than catastrophic since we have this kid Courtney Joseph all set to come in. So it's not a big deal. Luke Axtell?

"My only concern with Luke is grades right now. He's having big-time trouble. That may be the best thing," Penders said, suggesting that it might best if Axtell left the program. "If he's not going to go to class, I'm not going to chase his ass around. He's defying the academic support people. Right now, I'm probably going to have to suspend him."

"You can't do that. He's doing well," Dodds said quickly.

"Who told you?" Penders asked.

"He did," Dodds answered.

"That's not the reports I'm getting from Curt Fludd and Othell Ballage. I just got a report and I had a meeting with him on Tuesday. Let's get Eddie to come down here."

Dodds called Oran, who had returned to his office, and asked him to come down. When he arrived, Penders immediately started asking questions.

"Eddie, have you found out what Luke Axtell is doing?" Penders asked.

"No, Curt Fludd is not around. I can't get a hold of him," Oran said.

"I want you to find out for sure what he is doing – whether he is going to study hall, whether he is meeting his tutors ... in general, what he is doing academically," Penders said, instructing Oran to pursue the matter.

"I'll try him on Monday. This is Friday, and spring break has already started," Oran said assuredly to Penders.

"Have you heard anything about him wanting to transfer?" Penders asked his long-time assistant. "No," Oran responded.

"I had a meeting with him on Tuesday, DeLoss, and he didn't say one word about transferring," Penders told the athletic director. "I chewed him out basically for academics and told him to get on the stick. And if he doesn't get his act together maybe he won't even be playing here next year."

Penders then asked Oran about verbal abuse. Oran laughed.

"DeLoss, that's the most ridiculous thing," Oran said.

Dodds then took a piece of paper he had been perusing for the duration of the meeting, crumpled it up, and said to the two men, "That takes care of that."

"Did you ever call Chico Vazquez at 3 a.m. and chew him out?" Dodds then asked Penders.

"What, are you nuts? Call Chico," Penders fired back.

Dodds then crumpled up another piece of paper and discarded it into the trash. "Well, that takes care of that too," he said.

Penders then moved on to the matter of Mihm and his alleged desire to transfer.

"I just talked to him. Eddie, what's his beeper number?"

Oran called Mihm's beeper and within minutes, Mihm was back at Bellmont Hall, this time in Dodds' office. Soon after he entered and before Dodds could pose a question, Penders told his star center, "Chris, I got a couple of questions."

"Yes," Mihm answered.

"Have I ever verbally abused you in your opinion or any of your teammates?" Penders asked.

"No sir," Mihm said.

"Do you have any thoughts about transferring?" Penders continued with his line of questioning.

"Well, only if everybody else does. But I really like it here and I like the coaches," he told the three men. Although Mihm's last response was reason for celebrating, Penders maintained his composure and continued to oversee the conversation, probing for more information.

He asked Mihm about another player. "Do you know anything about Bernard?"

"No, I think Bernard's happy. I don't think there's any problem," Mihm said about his freshman teammate.

"All right. You can go," Penders told him.

Before Mihm exited, Penders yielded the floor to Dodds. "DeLoss, do you have any questions?"

"No. Go ahead, Chris," Dodds said.

After Mihm's departure, Penders told Dodds he would call Bernard as soon as he returned to his office. Before the meeting concluded, Dodds made it very clear that his main concern was Mihm.

"The whole key here is Mihm. We've got to keep Mihm," he told the two coaches.

"Mihm has no interest in transferring unless everybody else goes," Penders told Dodds confidently. "And if Muoneke goes, I don't think it's a big deal. And Luke, I don't want Luke to transfer and he has no reason to transfer."

Soon after he arrived back in his office, Penders called Gabe Muoneke's father. When Penders asked about his son's desire to transfer, the elder Muoneke said he had no knowledge of anything of that nature. He told Penders he thought his son was happy and he knew that he loved the school. He assured Penders he would talk to him. Hanging up the phone, Penders knew now that the only player he was aware of who was seriously considering a transfer had a father who was supportive of his cause.

He then called Bernard Smith's mother. Not surprisingly, he received a similar response. She emphatically denied hearing anything of her son's intention to transfer – in fact she said just the opposite. She told Penders that Bernard had said he loved the school and the coaching staff, specifically Penders.

Two phone calls, two denials of transferring. Penders was breathing somewhat easier, although he was confident before he ever made the calls that the players in question would be back next year, his 11th season as head coach.

The Visitor

Around 5 p.m. that afternoon, Robert "Bob" Utley III, a University donor and Penders' friend of eight years, showed up at Penders' office unannounced. Although Utley hadn't previously told Penders he would be stopping by, it wasn't completely out of the ordinary for him to do so. The last time such a visit occurred was the day of the football team's debacle with UCLA, five months earlier to the day.

Utley, according to Penders, was someone who stopped supporting the athletic program following the departure of Abe Lemons. However, when Penders arrived in 1988, Utley reappeared, as did his support of the basketball program, particularly Penders.

Throughout his tenure at Texas, Penders said Utley was someone he could regularly ask for advice on how to get things done for the program. Their relationship was such that the two went together with their families on a trip to Aspen one year. This visit, however, was unexpected, and the conversation got off to an inauspicious beginning.

"Tom, this would be a great time for you to get the heck out of here. You don't need all this hassle," Utley said.

Confused by the remarks and unsure if Utley had any previous knowledge of the players' meeting with Dodds and their thoughts of transferring, Penders asked, "What hassle?"

"With your health and everything that's going on," Utley answered.

"What do you mean, 'Going on?'" Penders asked, once again confused by Utley's remarks.

"You know what's going on," he said.

"It's no big deal. I'm not worried about anything," said Penders. "We've got a great team coming back next year. Next year we'll probably be picked to win the conference."

"Yeah, but we've been working on this deal with Host Communications, and you'll get the same money you get here at Texas," Utley said.

Penders couldn't believe what Utley had just said. He tried to remain calm. Although he may have wanted to, Penders wasn't in any position to tell Utley to leave his office, because it might result in Utley getting upset. For all he knew at that point, Utley had just come from Dodds' office. Instead, Penders decided to take note and inquire more about what Utley knew.

"All this sounds pretty interesting, Bob, and it's something I would consider," Penders said inquisitively. "I've always wanted to be in television. I don't know if I want to do it yet. And, I haven't talked to Jim Host, who's a good friend of mine. I would like talk to him."

"Tom Hicks (a University of Texas regent) is going to buy Host Communications," said Utley. "Tom Hicks and I are close friends and we've talked about it."

"I need to talk to somebody," Penders quickly answered. "Tom Hicks or Jim Host and get something in writing. I'm not going to make that kind of decision."

"What's your timetable?" Utley asked.

"I don't have a timetable. I'm going to St. Martin tomorrow with my wife and daughter. When I come back, it's business as usual."

The conversation ended, and Utley left Penders' office. Penders had no time to ponder the conversation he just had with Utley. Instead, he had to tie up a few more loose ends before heading out for the day and a week of vacation. After he wrapped up several more items, Penders decided he'd had enough and called it a day.

The week's events had been bizarre to say the least, and the vacation to St. Martin was very much needed. This trip would not only allow him to spend some precious time with his family, but also take him away from the strange happenings of the past week. At least he hoped it would.

Axtell Calls

Before Penders escaped to the Caribbean, there was one last bizarre phone call. It came late that night, around 11 p.m., just before Penders had retired to bed. It was Luke Axtell. Axtell cut to the chase soon after Penders answered the phone.

"Coach, I'm really sorry I never brought this up to you in the meeting the other day and I shouldn't have waited, but I'm really thinking of transferring."

This had become an all-to-familiar subject for Penders and his conversations of late.

"What for? What's the deal?" the coach asked.

"I don't know. I'm just not comfortable," Axtell said. "You've been hassling me about grades."

Penders stopped him mid-sentence. "Luke, I hassle every player about grades since I've been here, unless you're doing straight-A work." Penders then suggested to Axtell that maybe it was a little premature for him to make such a big decision and it would probably be in everyone's best interest if Axtell gave it more consideration the next week.

"Why don't you just think about it over the vacation?" Penders both asked and recommended at the same time. "In the meantime, I'm still checking on your situation, and if you're not doing what you said you were doing in school, then I'm going to suspend you from the team."

"If that's what you got to do, then that's what you got to do," Axtell answered.

Penders believed this response was somewhat of an admission from Axtell that he had indeed not been doing what he had told him in their meeting just three days before.

"Are you telling me that you were lying to me?" Penders asked bluntly.

"No, no, I'm not telling you that," Axtell carefully responded.

Penders told Axtell once again to think about it and they would talk about it when he returned from his trip. The conversation ended, and Penders retired for the night.

Saturday, March 14

Penders, his wife and daughter flew to St. Martin.

Sunday, March 15
Several University Supporters Promoting Host

On the family's first full day in St. Martin, Bob Utley made another surprise appearance in Penders' life – this time by phone. The medium may have been different, but the subject was much the same. For an hour, Utley reiterated to Penders how it was time for him to move on.

At one point, Utley said in a foretelling manner, "DeLoss is never going to give you what you need to get it done here, Tom."

"Well that's not a good attitude to take," Penders, who was trying to remain optimistic, responded. "You've got to keep working on those things. Just because he says no or we can't get this or can't get that, there are ways to get it done. My job is to get the most I can get for our program to help us win. That's my job. That's part of it. I don't look at that as a big deal. I would rather not have that obstruction. I'd rather have cooperation, but I can deal with it. I'll fight for it. I'll get it done."

"Tom, it's not going to happen. It's not going to happen," Utley said, maintaining his position. "All this is done, Tom. The contract is done. It's all a done deal."

"What? What are you talking about?" Penders asked Utley. "What about DeLoss Dodds?"

"Oh, he's all for it," Utley responded. "He's been talking to Jim (Host) since January."

Penders was puzzled by Utley's last remarks, particularly the month. If what Utley said was true, the university had been trying for two months to get Penders a job at Host, all without his knowledge. He listened intently for the remainder of the conversation, most of which was done by Utley, while he took down notes. Utley continued on about the need for a change. Finally, Penders told him he would think about it, and they ended the conversation.

In addition to the call from Utley that day, two other powerful members of the University of Texas community called Penders about the Host deal, including Mike Myers and long-time friend and athletics council member Bob Moses.

Moses encouraged Penders to strongly consider the Host deal.

"I heard about that thing," Moses told Penders. "Maybe with all this stuff going on that would be a good thing to do."

Myers, a well-known Longhorn supporter who initially flew Penders and his wife to D/FW Airport on his own personal jet for the first meeting with the selection committee, also made an unexpected call to Penders. He also promoted the position at Host.

Through all the calls, Penders listened and tried to glean more details from each caller. He was surprised that of all the calls received regarding the move to Host, none of them were from Jim Host himself.

What he thought and hoped he was getting away from when he left Austin had followed him to St. Martin. Unbeknownst to him, it would only get stranger in the days to come.

Monday, March 16

Penders received several calls during the day from Oran on recruiting. However, there were no other calls promoting Host. For the most part, the day was relatively quiet. Unfortunately for Penders and his family, it turned out to be the only day like that the whole week.

Tuesday, March 17

Oran called several times during the day to discuss a variety of things including updates on recruiting as well as what happened at the meeting between Dodds and the players. Although the conversations were short, the Dodds meeting was the main topic. Both Oran and Penders discussed how incredulous they were that the athletic director would do such a thing. Axtell's academic status wasn't discussed at any length.

"When this thing (information about the secret meeting) hit me in the face on Friday, I wanted to know what the hell was going on, and Eddie was uncovering it," Penders would say later, referring to his meeting with Dodds.

The one time Axtell's situation was the topic of discussion; Penders was inquiring whether or not Oran had learned anything new about it. He told Penders he had not been able to contact Fludd.

Penders Suspends Axtell

Later that day Oran called Penders again. This time, he told him, he had actually seen the progress report.

"He isn't doing so well and he could fail everything right now," Oran told Penders.

"How about the attendance?" Penders asked.

"He's been to only a few study halls in two weeks, and he hasn't met with his tutors," Oran said.

Essentially, with those words to Penders, Oran had refuted everything Axtell had told Penders in their meeting a week before and confirmed that the written academic status report from Othell Ballage to Curt Fludd, which would later become the subject of controversy, was, in fact, accurate as Penders had suspected.

"Suspend him," Penders said.

"Do the same thing we did with Lamar Wright," he continued. "Go tell Dave Saba (sports information director)."

Soon after Penders ordered the suspension, the phone began ringing incessantly. One of the first callers was Saba, asking Penders how he wanted to handle the situation.

Penders repeated to Saba what he had already told Oran. "Do it the same way we handled the Lamar Wright incident. (Identify it's) for academic reasons, because I don't want anyone thinking it's something else."

Penders said his experience in the past had been any time a press release isn't specific in its reason for an action such as a suspension, the media, public and anyone else concerned with the matter automatically suspect the worst.

Dodds Calls About Suspension

After he spoke with Saba about the press release, the phone rang again. It was Dodds. It was the first time the two had talked since Penders had arrived in St. Martin, even though Penders had tried, unsuccessfully, on numerous occasions to contact Dodds and further discuss the meeting he had held with the players.

Now, seeing that Axtell's suspension was of interest to him, Dodds called Penders. "I don't think you should suspend Luke. He's a wealthy kid from Westlake. Tom, let's don't do this," Dodds said. "Before we put this out on the wire and before this is official."

Penders interrupted his boss. "This is official."

"Remember, this is a well-to-do kid from Westlake," Dodds informed him again.

Penders refused to reply.

When Dodds recognized Penders was not responsive to his pleas not to suspend Axtell, Dodds asked to speak with Penders' wife, Susie. Penders handed over the phone to his wife. It was obvious that Dodds hoped Penders' wife wouldn't be so hard-line on the decision and might convince her husband to change his mind.

Dodds continued along the same lines with her and pleaded with her to convince her husband not to go through with the suspension. She matter-of-factly told him "it wasn't her decision." Dodds soon realized that Penders' other half was not going to help his cause either. Out of desperation, Dodds asked one last time for her to talk with her husband. He said he would call back in 15 minutes to see if anything had changed.

When Susie hung up the phone, she told her husband what Dodds had said. Penders stood firm with his decision to suspend the freshman from Westlake. He told her he was going to get cleaned up and shower before they went to dinner. He said if Dodds called back while he was in the shower, "Tell him, 'Forget about it.'" In Penders' eyes, the suspension was a done deal.

Dodds, as promised, called back a few minutes later. Penders was done with his shower and opted to speak with him. Once again, Dodds pleaded his case and asked Penders to reconsider his decision.

"You do what you think you have to do," Dodds said, "but I don't think you ought to do this because he is a well-to-do kid from Westlake."

"You know, I threw off a not-too-well-to-do kid from Dallas in Lamar Wright in September and nobody gave a crap. I can't have a double standard," Penders told Dodds.

In a last-ditch effort, Dodds asked Penders again not to suspend Axtell. He said if Penders suspended Axtell, there would be considerable ramifications.

Dodds' pleading was to no avail. The suspension was non-negotiable.

After the final conversation between Dodds and Penders, Saba was informed to write up the press release. Three paragraphs long, it stated that Axtell was suspended from the team indefinitely because of academic reasons and cited his refusal to go to study hall or meet with tutors. Later that afternoon, the story was put on the wire.

Wednesday, March 18
Axtell Responds

When the morning papers hit newsstands the next day, it was apparent a small battle was brewing behind the scenes of the University of Texas basketball program, and Luke Axtell fired the first shot.

The sports front page headline of the *Austin American-Statesman* read, "Axtell, Mihm, 2 Others Unhappy With Penders." Although the quotes were seen in the March 18 edition of the paper, they were made the night before by the freshman, who after hearing he had been suspended from the team, went out of his way to contact the *American-Statesman* from West Texas, where he was vacationing on spring break.

Axtell told the reporter that he and three teammates – Mihm, Muoneke and Smith – had met with Dodds on March 9, the day after Texas was eliminated from the Big 12 Tournament, to tell him that they could no longer play for Penders and wanted to transfer. He said the players were unhappy over a variety of issues, including Penders' treatment of them, verbal abuse, and his failure to develop them into better players.

"I think there's a lot of dishonesty in the program, and it starts at the top," the paper quoted Axtell. "Things are said to people that have no truth, and I was fed all that stuff. Most everybody wants to get out. You can't play for somebody you don't respect, and you can't respect somebody who lies to you all the time.

"I love the university, and I love Austin," Axtell said. "But it wouldn't matter if Dean Smith came here as an assistant coach. (Penders) is still running the show." Axtell told the paper that he had asked for and received his release from the university by Dodds.

Axtell continued, "Other people (teammates) have failed classes and nothing happened to them. He's (Penders) trying to get me back for saying some things. He found out I was trying to transfer, and he's running my name in the dirt. My mind's made up. When I told him I wanted to transfer, he said that's not a smart move, but that we would talk about it after spring break."

In addition to Axtell's statements, his parents responded and were quoted in the same article. "The best word to describe us is dismayed," Axtell's father, Calvin, said. "No one contacted Luke and us that this was about to happen."

Two of the three other potential transferring players, or representatives on their behalf, were also quoted in the article. Muoneke was contacted in Houston and said he was uncertain about his future and acknowledged that he was considering leaving.

"I'm thinking about my future," Muoneke said. "I've played two years of college basketball, and I'm two years behind. I'm disappointed in how I've developed. I'd love to put the blame on myself, but I wouldn't be being honest. I played with all those guys who were big-name recruits in high school tournaments. There was a reason I was recruited over those guys. Now it's a joke to even compare me to them, and that upsets me."

Mihm was out of town, but his father, Gary, was quoted in the article. He said his son might change schools if some of the other players decide to leave. "Chris has said he will consider transferring if the other guys leave," the elder Mihm said. "If the guts of the team were gone, he would consider transferring."

Mihm also told the paper that they had spoken with Dodds about the situation. "We have inquired about what the procedure would be," Mihm said, "but we haven't implemented it."

Penders In The Dark

As the Texas basketball program became the hot topic among sports fans throughout the city on Wednesday, Penders was oblivious to the whole situation back in St. Martin. He and his family had planned to resume their original plan of daily fun in the sun. After yesterday's mini-interruption with the Axtell suspension, it was time to put Austin and the university behind them and get back to the business at hand – rest and relaxation. Then the phone rang, and rang and rang...

Among the many calls Penders received during the day, one of the first was from Bob Moses. This time, however, Moses wasn't calling about the job with Host. Rather, he called to tell Penders about an article in the paper that he thought Penders might find "interesting." Moses told him he would fax it to him shortly. Penders told him thanks and said he would be looking for it.

After the conversation with Moses, the phone rang again. It was a reporter. Penders told the reporter he stood by his suspension of Axtell and he was sorry that Axtell had a desire to transfer. "I suspended Luke for academic reasons and academic reasons only," Penders said, not realizing the scope of the situation because he had yet to see Axtell's actual comments.

When told that Axtell accused him of verbal abuse, dishonesty and failing to develop players, Penders responded, "I won't even dignify those comments with an answer. It's like asking someone, 'When was the last time you beat your wife?'"

Penders reiterated to the reporter the reason for the suspension. He said Axtell "refused to go to study hall or meet with tutors, and his performance was indicative of that. Our players know they have to take care of the academic side of things before they take care of basketball."

In a break from the phone calls, Penders received the fax from Moses. After reading the whole article, Penders was furious. Not because of any player comments, but because of a reference to one day – Sunday, March 8.

According to the article, Axtell was quoted as saying the players had met at Dodds' house on that day, not Thursday afternoon in Dodds' office, as Dodds had previously told Penders in their meeting on Friday. Penders was livid and decided it was imperative that he call Dodds and discuss the issue with him personally. Before the call to Dodds, he first wanted to get some advice from others about how to handle a situation that was growing worse by the minute.

He called Moses first.

Penders told Moses he read the article and he was very upset. He told Moses the main reason for his displeasure was because, according to the article, the date Dodds met with the players was different from the date Dodds had told Penders in their meeting. He then asked Moses, "What is going on?"

Moses wasn't sure. "I don't know, but you better have a one-on-one with him."

Penders agreed and said he planned on calling Dodds later that day. They finished the conversation and Penders decided to get some more advice and called another friend, Darrell Royal.

When Penders told Royal about the situation, Royal was genuinely concerned. He told Penders he ought to get on the next plane back to town and barge into Dodds' office and confront him about the whole situation.

Penders Confronts Dodds by Phone

After he listened to both Moses and Royal tell him how they would have handled the situation, Penders picked up the phone and called Dodds.

Dodds answered the phone and Penders began with the first of many questions.

"How could you do this?" he asked Dodds. "How could you meet with my players on Sunday, and not tell me until Friday?"

Dodds, somewhat surprised by the phone call, stumbled and justified the reason for his delayed response regarding the meeting, telling Penders he was busy that week and hadn't had the time to tell him.

"That's inexcusable and it's unethical," Penders angrily responded.

Before Dodds responded to the charges, Penders' wife, Susie, grabbed the phone and put in her two cents. She, like her husband, asked Dodds how he could do such a thing without telling Tom. She continued telling him how wrong it was for him to hold a covert meeting.

Apparently tired of taking the heat, Dodds interrupted her. "That's it. I'm not covering for anybody. I didn't call the meeting. Bill Wendlandt organized that meeting," Dodds told Susie.

"Bill Wendlandt?" she asked, puzzled by Dodds' remark.

Penders heard his wife say the name Bill Wendlandt and immediately took back the phone.

"Who is Bill Wendlandt and what's he have to do with my program or UT?" he asked Dodds.

Before Dodds answered, Penders continued on his diatribe. "That still doesn't explain the five-day gap of not telling me about the meeting," he said. "It's obvious to me what you were doing. You were waiting until vacation started and then when I was gone you were probably going to have it leaked that there was a meeting."

Dodds was silent.

After Dodds tried to explain why everything happened the way it did, which obviously was not to Penders' satisfaction, the two finished the conversation.

(NOTE: Wendlandt later confirmed with *The Associated Press* that he did, in fact, organize the meeting. However, he said he only did so at the request of the Axtells and the Mihms.)

The Wendlandt File

Bill Wendlandt played at the university in two different stints during the early 1980s. According to the *1998-99 Texas Basketball Media Guide*, those years are conflicting. Despite that, it is known that Wendlandt left the team after his first stint while playing under Abe Lemons, and returned to the team to play under new head coach Bob Weltlich.

In Weltlich's first year, 1982-83, in which Texas had a 6-22 record, Wendlandt averaged 15.3 points and was named the team's most valuable player.

In hindsight, Penders said it was during that phone conversation with Dodds when Wendlandt's name was first mentioned that he realized "the lines were drawn in the sand."

"It was beyond (the point of no return)," he said, remembering back to the call. "It was obvious to me what he was doing and what he had done. Publicly, I had to say what I felt would keep the gas off the fire."

With the phone call to Dodds done and still very angry, Penders was now confronted with the challenge of responding to questions from the media regarding Axtell's accusations. As the phone rang each time, Penders maintained his composure and the professionalism he had learned from 27 years in the business. Although the situation with Dodds was definitely different from anything he had ever experienced in the past, he answered the same questions over and over, never telling the reporter on the other end what he was really thinking about his athletic director. Instead, he told reporters, when asked, he had no problems with Dodds or him meeting with players.

"DeLoss can meet with the players any time. I'm very comfortable with that because I don't hide anything," Penders was quoted in the March 19 edition of the *American-Statesman*. "As long as DeLoss tells me what's going on, if he thinks I should be there and calls me, that would be my only concern."

After being confronted by Penders, Dodds decided it was an appropriate time to comment on the situation. In a statement released by the school, he said: "We are concerned, and this is a family issue, as all team matters are in athletics. We care about our student-athletes and we care about our coaches. The most critical aspect of resolving team matters is communication between the two. This process is under way."

During the barrage of calls that day, mid-afternoon St. Martin time, which is two hours ahead of Austin time, Penders received a call with a familiar, friendly voice on the other end. It was Oran. He was calling to tell Penders about the firestorm developing as a result of the academic suspension of Axtell, and Axtell's subsequent remarks quoted in the paper. Oran asked Penders what he wanted him to do.

Penders told Oran since he couldn't be there to answer all the questions, that Oran should make himself available to media, and if requested, go on the air and do the local sports talk show circuit. "Go on the radio," Penders told Oran. "You handle that for me. That's what I'd do if I was there."

Oran assured Penders he would take care of it.

The Fax

With all the information regarding Axtell's academic status report still at his disposal, including grades for specific courses, and the green light from Penders to answer questions from the media, Oran wrote down the grades for each of Axtell's courses on the report. Instead of going on the air and being interviewed as Penders had suggested, the soft-spoken Oran opted to give the media the information it needed via fax, so in the end, they wouldn't need to interview him. He gave the report to basketball secretary Leslie Parks with the instructions to fax it to several local media outlets.

Within an hour, Parks faxed out the progress report to two radio stations, KVET-AM, the flagship station of University of Texas sports, and KJFK-FM, a radio station with an all-talk format and a sports show on in the early evening time period.

The Broadcast

Late in the afternoon, with media calls tapering off, Penders and his family prepared to head out to a much-anticipated dinner cruise. Just minutes before leaving, Penders received one last call regarding the same topic he had answered questions about all day – Luke Axtell's suspension and his comments, or so he thought.

On the other end of the phone was Craig Way, color commentator for men's athletics on KVET-AM. Obviously not wearing his color commentator hat at the time, Way, who also co-hosts a radio talk show on the same station, was calling to ask Penders if he would come on the radio show and comment on Axtell's grade situation. He told Penders he had "all the information," which was in the form of a fax he had received at the station.

Thinking "all the information" Way was referring to was the same information he had discussed with other members of the media that day regarding Axtell's suspension, Penders declined Way's invitation and told him he was pressed for time. He told Way he and his family were on their way out the door for dinner, and told him to call Oran if he had any questions about the situation.

"Call Eddie and he will talk to you," Penders told Way. "I talked to him and told him to be available for radio and media. He'll handle it."

Penders and Way ended their conversation. Soon thereafter, Penders and his family left the hotel for dinner.

It was at this point that there was a major lack of communication between Penders and Way. Way assumed Penders knew about the fax and knew what "all the information" meant when he mentioned it to Penders.

Conversely, Penders assumed when Way was speaking of "all the information," he was talking about information regarding Axtell's academic status, not anything specific about grades in individual classes.

"He didn't say, 'I have a fax in front of me that has his grades,'" Penders would say later. "I didn't know what he had. And he certainly didn't say, 'I'm going to read (this) on the air.' I thought maybe he found out from Saba because I had had a long conversation with Dave about telling the media what's going on, to just tell them that I had reason to suspend him."

Regardless of the miscommunication at the time, Way felt compelled to go on the air with the information. Shortly after his conversation with Penders, Way read parts of the report on the air.

Driving down the road, Christine Plonsky, senior associate athletic director, heard the report being read by Way. From her car phone, she immediately called Saba and told him she had just heard a report on Luke Axtell's academic status being read over the air. She asked Saba if he would go to the radio station and get a copy of the report. He agreed and immediately left.

If the report, which Way had just read, was released by UT officials, it would be considered a violation of the Buckley Amendment, an amendment enacted in 1974 by Congress that was designed to protect students' privacy and prevent schools from haphazardly releasing student files. Any school that violates the Buckley Amendment could lose federal funds.

Soon after he arrived at the station, Saba encountered Way and asked him for a copy of the academic report. "Craig, what happened?" he asked Way.

"Here, that's what I was given," Way answered, showing Saba the faxed report. "It was faxed to me." The conversation was short, and Saba returned back to campus with the report in hand.

In a separate incident, the True Orange Fax Service, a newsletter on Texas athletics, quoted Penders as saying, "I had no option. He is failing three out of four courses (this semester) and when (academic advisor) Curt Fludd called his mother, she said, 'We're not going to deal with academic issues – that's Penders' problem.' When she said that, that was the last straw."

Mollie Axtell responded and said that was not exactly the case.

"Luke asked us at the beginning of the semester if we'd take a hands-off approach and not be hovering parents," Axtell said. "When Curt called I said we promised Luke we'd leave it between him and his coach."

Axtell went on to add that her son was failing not three classes, but one.

Alex Broadway, a basketball administrative assistant, gave a sworn statement a week later on March 26 that confirmed the Axtells had essentially turned over the academic situation of their son to Penders and his staff.

"As part of my duties I am responsible for monitoring the attendance and performance of the University of Texas basketball student athletes," the notarized statement said.

"As a part of the process I would routinely meet with Curt Fludd. During our meetings we would discuss the academic progress (class attendance and grades) of the players. Sometime during the early part of February 1998, we discussed the fact that there were some bad academic reports concerning Luke Axtell.

"Mr. Fludd and I would routinely contact the parents of any player who was performing poorly in class or having problems with attendance.

"It was during this meeting that Mr. Fludd called Luke's mother, Molly (sic) Axtell.

"It was routine for Mr. Fludd to use the speaker phone so that I could listen or answer questions if necessary. During the conversation with Mrs. Axtell, Mr. Fludd was using the speakerphone.

"Mr. Fludd told Mrs. Axtell that Luke had received some bad progress reports and was on the verge of flunking some classes, which would result in Luke having to take summer classes in order to maintain his eligibility. Mrs. Axtell's response was that they had numerous talks with Luke and that Luke and his parents had decided that they would treat Luke more like an adult and allow him to be more responsible. Mrs. Axtell felt that Luke was the coaches' responsibility and that the coaches should deal with it.

"Mr. Fludd thanked Mrs. Axtell and that was the end of the conversation."

Broadway said after the conversation, Fludd was stunned by Axtell's response, and it was at that point they informed Penders about Axtell's grade situation.

That evening, Dodds received a call from the Axtells. They were troubled by the broadcast of Luke's grades. Dodds assured the family that the issue had been referred to the university's legal counsel and was currently under investigation.

Dodds also made a phone call of his own. Dodds called Oran and asked if he could meet the next morning. Oran agreed. After deciding on a time convenient for both, they agreed to meet at the Capitol Marriott the next morning around 8 a.m. Oran would say later that he expected the meeting with Dodds to be about Dodds and his meeting with the players 10 days earlier.

In St. Martin, Penders and his family returned from their dinner cruise and retired for the evening, completely unaware of what was happening back in Austin. About 2 a.m., Penders was clued in to the stirrings back home when he received a phone call from Bill Simonson, a sports talk show host on KJFK, the only other radio station that received the fax.

Simonson said he had received a fax prior to his show that day before, and it was regarding Luke Axtell's grades. He asked Penders what he knew.

"I'm wondering if you knew anything about it?" Simonson asked.

"I have no idea what you are talking about," Penders answered, trying to awaken from his sleep. "What are you talking about? Fax?"

"It's something about academics," Simonson answered. "I just threw it away (after I received it)."

Penders, still not completely sure what Simonson was talking about since he had never actually seen the fax, told him he didn't know anything about it. Simonson told Penders he would let him get back to sleep, and the conversation ended.

Thursday, March 19
Oran Meets with Dodds, Others

Oran, as discussed the night before with Dodds, drove to the Capitol Marriott for his scheduled meeting with the athletic director. To his surprise, when he arrived just before 8 a.m., Dodds wasn't there – but Butch Worley, senior associate athletic director, was. When Dodds arrived minutes later, he had company. Accompanying him was Patricia Ohlendorf, UT vice provost and general counsel to the president (Ohlendorf has since been promoted to vice president of administration). Oran, who had expected to meet only with Dodds, was stunned.

For approximately the next half-hour to an hour, Oran listened as the three discussed the events that would take place later in the day. Oran was informed that he would be meeting again with Ohlendorf, as well as university attorney W.O. Shultz, to discuss the fax. There would be a variety of questions, which he would have to answer to the best of his ability. After the discussion was over, all four dispersed and made their way back to campus.

The Investigation Begins

Back on campus Ohlendorf began the investigation into the fax and subsequent broadcast, interviewing several people. "We are trying to determine the circumstances concerning the disclosure to the public of the academic records of Luke Axtell," Ohlendorf was quoted in the March 20 edition of the *American-Statesman.* "We did a number of interviews and feel like we are making progress. We're looking at a number of things. What actually happened. How the information was made available. Whether or not UT policy was violated."

As a preliminary part of her investigation, Ohlendorf also called Penders in St. Martin. Ohlendorf informed him she was conducting an investigation into the faxing of Luke Axtell's grades and asked Penders what he knew about it.

"I was told about the article this morning," Penders told her. "That's the first I knew about it. I didn't know anything about it prior to that," he said, obviously forgetting about the wake-up call from Simonson in the early hours of the morning.

Ohlendorf told Penders that once he arrived back in town they needed to meet regarding the situation. He said that would be fine.

UT Lawyers Question Oran

On the way to his first meeting with Ohlendorf and Shultz, Oran saw Parks exit Dodds' office. She had just been questioned by Ohlendorf and Shultz and looked like she was "in shock," according to Oran. Knowing full well that she had been the one to actually push the button that faxed out the academic report, Oran quietly told Parks, "I'll take care of it."

In his meeting with Ohlendorf and Shultz, Oran was instructed early on that he needed to tell the truth. They informed him that his career was "on the line."

Oran said, as a rule, the questions asked in the hour-long session were trying to get him to implicate Penders.

"Why are you protecting Tom?" and "Would Tom do that for you?" were a couple of the questions asked.

Oran said it wasn't too long after the meeting started and in response to one of the questions, when he said, "I did it. I did it," admitting that it was he who sent the fax, not Parks.

Regardless of his statement, Ohlendorf and Shultz continued to plod on. After they asked several more questions, the two soon realized, simply by the amount of time Oran was taking to answer their questions, he had had enough. They knew he was obviously under a lot of stress and was very tired.

Oran would say later that he had had hardly any sleep that week, and particularly the few nights before the interviews. Because of that, he sometimes took two or three minutes to answer a question. "There was a lot of silence," Oran said.

Finally, Ohlendorf and Shultz relented and suggested that Oran get some rest. They told him to plan on meeting again on Saturday. Oran agreed. He said he would see them then and left.

After the meeting, Oran made his way over to the office of Rob Wright, another assistant coach. Oran told Wright he needed to use his phone because he feared that his phone might be tapped, and he wasn't supposed to be in contact with Penders.

From Wright's office, with both Wright and the other assistant coach Carlton Owens present, Oran called Penders.

"Tom, I'm sorry. I released the fax. I didn't know you couldn't do this," Oran told Penders.

Oran then told Penders how he had met with Ohlendorf and Shultz and the questions asked were very one-sided, trying to get him to point the finger at Penders. He told Penders he was going to meet with them again on Saturday for more questions.

"Eddie, I've never heard of this. I don't know that what you did was wrong," Penders said, trying to assure his assistant, even though at the time he was unsure of any violation, including the Buckley Amendment. "But if you made a mistake, you made a mistake and don't worry about it. Chancellor (William) Cunningham has always said if you make a mistake and you admit it, and it wasn't intentional, then nothing will happen to you." After approximately 15 minutes, the conversation ended.

According to Wright, soon after Oran's conversation with Penders ended, Oran was told by a secretary in the office that he and Leslie Parks needed to meet with Dodds in Dodds' office. The two left several minutes later.

After lunch, Oran once again returned to Wright's office. This time he told Wright he was going to use the phone in the film room, an office adjacent to Wright's.

From there, Oran called Penders a second time. This time, however, Oran was much more emotional. According to Wright, Oran began to cry during the conversation. Wright said Oran repeatedly apologized to Penders expressing his regret for what had happened with the fax and taking complete responsibility for it being sent. He said Oran told Penders at one point that "he didn't mean to get him (Penders) in trouble." After several minutes of discussion on the phone with Penders, Wright said Oran closed the door.

The conversation lasted several more minutes. It finally came to an end when Penders, recognizing his assistant was tired, told him, just as university attorneys had done just an hour or so before, to go home and get some rest. Oran agreed and left for the day. Minutes later, Penders received another call. It was Wright.

"What the hell is going on?" he asked Penders. "What's this Eddie is talking about? What'd he do?"

"You heard him," Penders said, referring to the conversation that had just taken place.

"Is he going to be in trouble? Is he going to get fired?" Wright asked inquisitively.

"No, he didn't do it on purpose. He didn't do it with malice," Penders pointed out. "As far as I know, it's not a violation."

Wright, seemingly appeased by Penders' words, told him he would talk to him later and the conversation ended.

The Axtells Respond

With so much action going on behind the scenes on Thursday, the Axtells decided to go public and released a statement regarding their son's academic status, the suspension, and the broadcast of his grades by the radio station.

Our son, Luke Axtell, is behind in his schoolwork. He has missed approximately 20 days of school for basketball and will make every effort, now that basketball season is over, to catch up. However, Luke is only midway through the current semester and has received no final grades. In the fall semester, Luke fulfilled all academic requirements for eligibility required by the NCAA, the Big 12 Conference and the University of Texas. Luke talked to Tom Penders on Friday, March 13, and told Penders that he planned on transferring. The conversation ended with an agreement that the two would talk again after the university's spring break.

While on our spring vacation, a friend in Austin telephoned to inform us that Luke had been suspended from the basketball team by Tom Penders for academic reasons. We heard about the suspension after it had already appeared on the 6 o'clock news. We were amazed by this unprecedented action by Penders. To the best of our knowledge, Luke is the only player to be suspended by the UT athletic department for academic performance when the athlete is not in violation of NCAA standards.

What appalls our family is that Tom Penders chose a public venue to suspend our son. Luke was given no warning of suspension, even though Penders had ample opportunity to do so. Additionally, someone in the athletic department has chosen to make confidential information public regarding Luke's grades and interim progress reports, some of which are false.

We have been told this is a violation of federal law. We have discussed their improprieties with DeLoss Dodds, athletic director at the University of Texas. We have been assured by Dodds that this issue has been referred to the university's internal legal counsel and is under investigation.

Dodds has granted Luke a blanket release to talk to other schools.

Although the tide looked like it was turning against the popular, most successful basketball coach in school history, the news wasn't all bad. Bernard Smith announced he had no plans of transferring from the school and said he had a good relationship with Penders.

That evening, with the controversy regarding the fax now stirring up all kinds of interest and unwanted phone calls, Oran went into hiding. Under the name of Eddie Smith, he took up refuge at Barton Creek Country Club, a place he called home for several days.

Friday, March 20
Penders Acknowledges Oran's Role

Penders was quoted in the *American-Statesman* regarding his knowledge of Oran and the fax.

"Eddie told me this afternoon," Penders said from the Caribbean island of St. Martin, where he is vacationing. "I heard from the university lawyer (Patricia Ohlendorf) they wanted to investigate. Eddie just said he didn't know he couldn't do it. He thought that with all the things that were being written and being said on radio, he didn't think there was anything wrong with it.

"Eddie apologized. I had no idea he did it. I didn't tell anybody to do anything. I'm not an expert on the laws. He said there weren't transcripts. He said he was sorry he did it, that he made a mistake. He didn't go into detail on it. He was very hurt, very down about it. He's a good person. If he made a mistake, it was unintentional."

When asked later about his knowledge of the Buckley Amendment, Oran said, "I don't know if I actually heard the words Buckley Amendment, but I knew there were certain restrictions on what you could release and what you couldn't release. I thought releasing transcripts was wrong."

On Friday evening, Oran received a message on his answering machine. It was Ohlendorf. She asked him to contact her so they could confirm a time for their meeting the next day. Oran decided it could wait.

Saturday, March 21
Reality Sets In

The next morning Oran called Ohlendorf. She instructed him to meet with her and W.O. Shultz at the president's office, located in the main building, or "The Tower."

After eating breakfast, Oran and his son headed into town for the meeting. Just minutes into their trip, Oran turned on the radio to KVET and a sports call-in show called The Press Box. He couldn't have prepared himself or his son for what they heard next, but it was indicative of how serious the situation was and how strongly those following it felt about it.

"They ought to fire Eddie Oran," the caller said.

"That's you, Daddy," Oran's son said immediately after the caller's comment.

"That's me," Oran answered back.

UT Lawyers Question Oran a Second Time

Oran and his son arrived at the president's office, with Shultz and Ohlendorf waiting to begin the second round of questions. Before the first question was asked, and in an effort to get the younger Oran out of the room, one of the questioners asked the youngster to go get them some colas and look at the aquarium.

Oran said they used a number of requests and tactics to get his son out of the room so he wouldn't hear all the questions concerning his dad, but through it all, the youngster stayed by his father's side. "He just stood there and patted me on the back. They kept saying, 'Your daddy is a good person and nothing is going to happen to your daddy.'"

Although it was a different day and different meeting place, the questions remained much the same: "Why are you protecting Tom?" "Would Tom do this for you?"

Also, at one point when his son was out of the room, Oran was told, "You realize you can lose your job."

"Yes," he answered.

Oran, as he had done in their meeting on Thursday, admitted that he was responsible for sending the fax.

"I did it," he told them repeatedly.

The comments appeared to fall on deaf ears as the two continued to question why he was protecting Penders. Then the two went on to another subject: whether or not Oran was aware that Penders was going to tell the media on Thursday that he had faxed the progress report on his own. They asked him about Friday's *American-Statesman* and Penders' quotes. Oran told them he wasn't sure.

After an hour of questions, Ohlendorf and Shultz told Oran they were done with their questions and he and his son were excused. The two left.

That afternoon, Penders and his family returned to Austin.

Sunday, March 22
Wendlandt Speaks Out

As readers across the city of Austin opened their papers and respective sports sections, they had a chance to see the opinion of someone who was surprisingly familiar with the brewing controversy at the University of Texas and its basketball program. In the "Letters to the Sports Editor" of the *Austin American-Statesman*, Bill Wendlandt spoke out on behalf of Axtell.

"University of Texas basketball player Luke Axtell is an honest, talented kid who had the courage to stand up and tell the truth. He deserves to be judged by the facts as opposed to unsubstantiated information, which is being passed around by uninformed people.

"What 19-year-old kid in the country with a scholarship and playing time at stake would go public after witnessing the bashing Axtell has taken?

"Here are the facts: 1) Axtell has never failed a course or been ineligible in high school or college; 2) His current grades reflect that he missed approximately 20 days of school for basketball; 3) Axtell is committed to improving his grades and met with his academic adviser before spring break to develop his plan to do so; 4) Axtell and his teammates never gave DeLoss Dodds or anyone else an 'ultimatum.' They merely stated their concerns and future intentions.

"These are good kids who have a talent level we have rarely seen here. Let's support them as Longhorns and enjoy their future success at the University of Texas."

BILL WENDLANDT
Austin

Penders Meets With University Attorneys

Ohlendorf and Shultz went over to the office of Roy Minton, who, along with Joe Longley, represented Penders.

Ohlendorf asked the questions. Before she started, she made it very clear why they were there. "We know there's no verbal abuse," she said. "That is not why we are here. This is about the Buckley Amendment issue."

Ohlendorf then began.

"Did you tell Eddie Oran to fax the grades?" she asked.

"No," Penders answered.

"When did you know about it?"

"When you told me about it. Eddie told me about the article," responded the coach, reminding Ohlendorf of her call to him that Thursday morning.

"Do you know about the Buckley Amendment?" questioned the attorney.

"Not until now. Roy and Joe have been reading it to me," he answered.

Penders said after each question and his response, which was sometimes as long as three or four minutes, Ohlendorf put a check mark in her notebook. Then, she moved on to the next question. All in all, there were approximately a dozen questions, none of which made Penders the least bit uncomfortable.

As the meeting continued, Penders shuttled back and forth between the room where he was being questioned and a room downstairs that had a television. On the set was an NCAA Tournament game, which featured his former team, the Rhode Island Rams, with whom his son Tommy was an assistant, and the Stanford Cardinals. Because he had a vested interest, Penders wanted to see as much of the game as possible. It was obvious that Penders was not terribly concerned with the investigation and whether he was guilty of anything. He knew he had done nothing wrong.

After about an hour, the question-and-answer session, which had not been recorded by any of the parties, was complete. Feeling he was finished with his part, Penders went back downstairs to watch the game while his attorneys continued the discussion with Ohlendorf and Shultz.

With just the attorneys present, the legal experts and their lingo took center stage. Ohlendorf told Minton and Longley that, as the university attorney, she had three issues on the agenda she wanted to discuss. First was the suspension of Luke Axtell and the circumstances surrounding it. Second was the release of confidential information. And the third and final issue was how they believed the media was encouraged to use the disclosed confidential information.

With the university investigation having entered its third day and its focus solely on the release of confidential information, Ohlendorf made it clear to Longley and Minton that this was the topic of most concern to the university. She said she was prepared to make a finding that Penders knew about Oran and his distributing the grades. She explained that although Oran had not officially claimed Penders had any knowledge about the fax, she said Oran had casually mentioned it in an earlier meeting at the Marriott. She said in that conversation, he made it very clear that Tom knew what was going on. However, she said, later that day, at the meeting with Shultz and Ohlendorf on campus, Oran changed his tune. He said Penders had no knowledge of the fax.

With that information, Minton was confident Ohlendorf and Shultz and the university had no proof. Recalling the meeting, he would say later, "Even though she was close to certain in her own mind (about the evidence), it certainly didn't appear to me that they had proof."

And that's essentially what he told Ohlendorf and Shultz. "If you all have it, pull back the curtain and show me your evidence."

Minton asked the university attorneys in what way could their evidence hurt their case if they told him. "If you've got something that is conclusive, where does it hurt you to tell me?"

There was no good answer to that question, and everyone in the room knew it.

Minton said in the legal profession it is almost always true that the opposing counsel has some proof, but it's never as good as they want you to believe. Minton then broached another subject and one that would force them to reveal their evidence – a lawsuit.

"If we file a lawsuit, all this is going to come out, and it is going to be something that a court is going to decide," Minton said.

Ohlendorf and Shultz knew that wasn't a route the university wanted to take. At that point, they countered. They said there was a position as a color commentator with Host Communications ready for the taking if Penders wanted it. Minton said in his 40 years in the business, nothing really catches him by surprise, but this was something that definitely got his attention. They continued, explaining the terms of the contract including a salary of $550,000, plus incentives, or the same amount Penders was currently making as head coach.

Both Longley and Minton agreed it was a good stopping point. With an offer of a job they were both unaware of, they needed to discuss it with their client. All agreed enough issues had been discussed to keep them busy for the next few days, if not weeks.

The meeting concluded. Ohlendorf and Shultz left.

From what Minton had just heard in the meeting, as well as conversations he had had previously with Penders, it was apparent that Dodds wanted him out, with or without cause. He would say later that in just his first few days of involvement with the case, he recognized there was nothing in Penders relationship with the university, contractual or otherwise, that would give him the right to remain as head coach, especially if the athletic director wanted to move him into another position as he had done recently with former coaches such as John Mackovic and David McWilliams.

"It was clear to me that DeLoss had decided that Tom Penders shouldn't be coach anymore and I became convinced that DeLoss Dodds was going to unilaterally transfer him," Minton would say later. "I did not think that it would be in his best interest to let that happen."

As the basketball game neared its end, Minton and Longley entered the room and interrupted Penders viewing of the final few minutes.

"What's this Host deal?" Minton quickly asked Penders.

"Oh, Bob Utley and all these people have been telling me about this," he answered.

"Patti Ohlendorf said if you resign you'll make $550,000 a year minimum, with incentives from Host to make more," Minton told him.

"What else are they saying?" Penders asked.

"They think you had something to do with the fax, but they can't prove it," Minton said.

"They also said you're guilty of fueling the media," Longley added.

"Fueling the media?" repeated Penders, this time as a question.

"Is that illegal if I did it? And what exactly do they mean by that?" he asked.

"They said you called the media and told them all about Luke," one of the attorneys said.

"Un-uh," Penders fired back. "I didn't call one media person. They called me," Penders said assuredly to his attorneys.

"Am I supposed to say no comment? Nobody told me I couldn't say anything and all I was doing was defending myself and my reputation, which I think I have a right to do."

"Tom, what they're saying is (not true) and we all know that," his attorney said. "But if they want to terminate you, they can."

"No, they can't," Penders said, shocked at what he had just heard from his attorney. "I got my contract. They can't just do that," he said.

"Technically, you're right, Tom. They can terminate you, and we'll sue them. But, they already said if you sue them it's going to take up to three years, and you have to get permission through the Legislature to sue the University of Texas."

Minton was referring to sovereign immunity, a legal doctrine that, under some circumstances, protects the federal, state, and tribal governments within the United States from lawsuits which would cause those governments to pay out money, real estate, or goods from the governmental treasury. The University of Texas is considered to be a part of the state government because it is a state-funded institution. The basic idea behind sovereign immunity is that property held by the government is in trust for all the citizens of that particular government. The public treasury and public property are, therefore, to be used for the benefit of all the citizens equally – not just a few individuals (such as the people who file lawsuits). If, through lawsuit, a plaintiff can collect money from the government for some wrong the government has done him, the public treasury will be reduced for the benefit of that one person. There will then be less money to provide services to all the other citizens of the government. All the citizens will suffer because of the drain on the public treasury caused by a single citizen.

Penders, upset at the discussion, responded. "I don't care, let's sue them. This is ridiculous. This whole thing is untrue. That was no investigation."

"We know that," said his attorney. "They didn't ask you to sign anything. They weren't taping it. They didn't want anything for the records. But the reality of it is, it's going to take three years."

"Fine, let's sue them," Penders said, reiterating what he had said just moments earlier. It was almost as if it was a challenge or a dare to him.

"We've got to come up with a figure," Minton said.

"Well, figure out what I could make in the next 15 years. That's the normal span in a coach's career. Until I'm 66," Penders said. "Plus what inflation will be; I suspect around $20 million."

Even with the prospects of suing for what he felt he was rightfully owed by the university, Penders recognized, as did his attorneys, that his relationship with the University of Texas, specifically Dodds, appeared to be at a point often referred to in divorce court as "irreconcilable differences." This was a divorce of enormous proportions, and Dodds was filing for it. What bothered Penders most was not that Dodds insisted on parting ways, but the way in which it was being done.

"If he wants me out, there is a right way of doing it and a wrong way of doing it. The right way is to just reassign me, and they don't have to really even have a reason. If they're going to do that, then go ahead and do it," he told his attorneys.

They both agreed.

What lay ahead for Penders was doing the right thing for his career. He had to make a decision. Did he really want to file a lawsuit against a school that he genuinely cared for after committing 10 years of service and in the process create a tremendous amount of turmoil for both his family and the university? Or would he rather settle the dispute and move off quietly to Host as a color commentator, making a salary commensurate with his current pay rate? It was a difficult decision, but it was a choice nonetheless.

The attorneys and Penders agreed to meet the next day and discuss the situation again to further examine their options.

Minton Calls Host

Although not exactly sure of the day in recalling the sequence of events in 1998, Minton said it was around this time – soon after he initially heard about Host and potential employment for Penders – that he first called James Host to discuss the matter.

"You know about this job that he's (being offered)?" Minton asked Host

According to Minton, Host responded, "What job?" or words to that effect.

Minton said Host was very gracious about the whole matter. Even though a specific job hadn't been set up for Penders as far as he was aware, Host said, they liked Penders and would work something out with him. However, he added that Penders should complete everything with Texas before negotiating a contract with Host.

"Host said 'Get your stuff finished down there, Tom, and then come over here and see me. Don't leave that job based on the idea that this is going to be a part of the university. I'm independent of the university,' " Minton recalled. "(Host continued), 'I think we have a place for you. I think we have something good for you. But I don't want you to make your mind up on what you're going to do there based on what you think you can do with us.' "

"These words were exactly the opposite of what Patti and W.O. and others affiliated with the university were saying," Minton said. They had guaranteed that Penders already had a job lined up with Host, while Host insisted on Penders getting separation from the school. It was a case of the left hand not knowing what the right hand was doing.

Oran Publicly Admits Sending Axtell's Report

Later that evening, Oran, in an ironic twist, distributed another facsimile to several media outlets, this time taking full responsibility for the release of Luke Axtell's academic progress report.

In the report, Oran said he was never ordered to release Axtell's grades and never discussed it with any party, including Penders, prior to releasing the grades to KVET and KJFK. He said he had decided to fax the information he received from the academic support staff only after he read a quote in the *American-Statesman*, which he described as "inaccurate," apparently referring to the quotes Axtell had made regarding his flunking only one course, physical science.

"I took it upon myself to let the local media know the truth ... I was never ordered to do this action and never discussed it with anyone until after being interviewed by the (UT) attorneys," Oran said in the fax.

"I did not realize that I could be in violation of any law," the statement read. "I apologize if I have embarrassed Luke Axtell, our program, or the University of Texas. It was totally unintentional."

Monday March 23
Penders and Attorneys Plan Course of Action

Penders met again with Longley and Minton. For the bulk of the meeting, Penders discussed his options in taking a position with Host. Penders had resigned himself to the fact that his time at Texas was coming to an end. Although he didn't like it, he accepted it. He had no choice but accept it. The offer on the table from Host lessened the blow to a certain extent.

"If they give me a million dollars, plus this Host deal," it would be acceptable, he told Longley and Minton. With this settlement, he would explain later, Penders would have the security of knowing that he would have made more than if he had stayed at the university. Penders said if he decided later that he liked television and radio, he might stay in it.

Minton suggested, in agreement with his client, that taking the Host job would be in his best interest. He said instead of getting into a long and messy lawsuit, which could take years to conclude and severely damage his reputation, Penders should, as the song from the popular 70s rock group, the Steve Miller Band is titled, "Take the Money and Run."

"It was in Tom's best interest to get the best deal that he could and take that money and go somewhere else and make as much, or more money, and be a half million plus."

Following the meeting, Penders' lawyers began working on terms of a settlement.

Penders Speaks Out

That afternoon, Penders decided he had heard enough and wanted to try to answer any questions regarding the continuing saga. However, this was no ordinary news conference. Instead of being held on campus with the University of Texas backdrop, it was held in the driveway of Penders' front yard. He had been told he couldn't convene the press on campus while the investigation was still pending.

With more than two dozen reporters present, Penders defended his name and character, which had both taken a bruising, if not outright beating, since he had left on his trip to St. Martin just nine days earlier. With his wife and daughter, and assistant coaches Eddie Oran, Carlton Owens and Rob Wright present, Penders, for the first time, publicly acknowledged that a change might be in order.

"If the University of Texas doesn't want me to be the head coach, in my contract they can always reassign me," Penders said. "I would gladly work for them in some other capacity when that time comes, but I still feel I'm one of the best coaches in the country. I'll let my record speak for itself."

He said that Muoneke was still considering transferring, and Mihm was waiting to see how the situation played out before he made a decision on leaving. When asked about Mihm's possible transfer, Penders said, "I think it would be a tremendous mistake for him to leave the University of Texas and sit out a year, after what he's developed into this year."

Penders also spoke highly of Axtell. He said Axtell would be welcome at the team meeting, which was scheduled for later that evening.

"I had no problem whatsoever with Luke. He's a good kid who played hurt. He tried to play through his back problems. We were a better basketball team with Luke. I never had a heated conversation with Luke – about basketball, at least."

He continued, "You've got to remember these are 18- and 19-year-old kids. Maybe I was too soft on him. But I was totally shocked by this."

Penders also told reporters he had retained the services of Roy Minton and said that they had met the day before with university attorneys. "I can't comment on that. That's confidential," Penders said. "All of us huddled yesterday (Sunday) and talked. That's all I can say."

Veterans Clack and Vazquez Defend Penders

Across town at the Givens Recreation Center, juniors Kris Clack and DeJuan "Chico" Vazquez held a press conference of their own, with both speaking positively of Penders and his program.

Clack would say later the reason they decided to have a press conference, which he said they did on their own volition, was to show their support for Penders.

"We wanted to help our coach out because I didn't think what was going on was fair," Clack said. "We wanted to come out and express how we felt about it. There had been nothing positive said and I guess they (the public) felt everybody on the team felt that way. We wanted to come out and say, 'We don't feel this way.'"

Tuesday, March 24
Penders Receives Contract Offer With Host

Just two days after meeting with Ohlendorf and Shultz for the first time, Penders' attorneys received and presented him with a contract from Host. After he perused the document for several minutes, he soon realized it was not the $550,000 annual salary that had been discussed earlier.

"Everything is great here, but it's only $350,000," Penders said. "And I haven't talked to Jim Host yet. Can I talk to Mr. Host?"

Minton said the university expected him to make a decision within 48 hours, but he personally was in no rush for Penders to make a decision.

"I'm not making a decision until I talk to Jim Host," Penders responded.

"That's fine," the attorney answered.

The meeting ended a few minutes later, leaving Penders unsatisfied with the terms of the contract.

Following the meeting, Minton called and spoke with Ohlendorf and Shultz. He said they were equally surprised that the amount was less than the $550,000 they had originally committed to.

"The Host job did not turn out to be the kind of money that Patti and W.O. were under the impression that it was," Minton would say later.

Penders, unsatisfied with the amount, decided to be proactive and call Jim Host. In their brief conversation, Host told Penders he would be unavailable the next few days, but he knew Penders wanted to discuss potential employment. Host told him he would be in San Antonio for the Final Four and they could talk at that time. Penders said that would be fine, and set up an appointment to meet with Host that Friday, March 27. Until then, the job with Host was on hold.

As the situation continued to get more serious, the removal of Penders, in the public eye, seemed almost inevitable. Behind the scenes it was even more apparent as Joe Jamail, the renowned Houston-based attorney and one of Penders' biggest supporters throughout his tenure at Texas, made his intentions clear that he was "not going to get involved" with the situation.

Wednesday, March 25
Investigation to be Completed Soon

Ohlendorf told *The Associated Press* that administration officials had not reached a conclusion to their probe, but it would likely be completed Friday.

"When we look at policy violations and law violations, we have to look at all the surrounding information, and we haven't reached any conclusions," Ohlendorf said.

Penders Remains Willing to be Reassigned

When contacted by *The Associated Press* regarding the ongoing developments, Penders reiterated his willingness to accept another position within the university.

"As I've said many times, I have a contract that has four years remaining," Penders said. "There is a reassignment clause in there, and they could reassign me for any reason. If they want to do that, that's their prerogative.

"I love the University of Texas, and if they decided to reassign me because they wanted to make a change, I would probably work for them and raise money or whatever they want me to do," he said.

Penders "Out at Texas," According to Report

For the first time since the controversy began, it was publicly reported that Penders days as head coach were numbered.

On Wednesday night, a source close to the university told *The Associated Press* that

Tom Penders would not coach the Texas Longhorns the following season. The source said Penders was considering an outside opportunity that would take him away from coaching, or he would be reassigned, possibly as early as Friday.

Penders said this was news to him.

"I have not had one phone call from Mr. Dodds, who is my boss. I haven't heard anything about my job status changing."

Dodds said he wouldn't comment on the matter until the completion of an investigation.

UT Official Refutes Rumor of Penders Firing

The *American-Statesman* quoted an unidentified university official on Penders' employment status with the school. "It's not true. He has not been fired. Tom Penders, as of now, is the coach at the University of Texas," the official said.

Minton was also quoted by the paper and said he was unaware of any change in his client's employment. "I'm not aware of anything like that. I hear everything, but the people I'm talking to are not dealing with those rumors. They're putting something together to give to the (UT) president."

In a related matter, Ohlendorf had a phone conversation with Donald L. Evans, chairman of the Board of Regents for the University of Texas System. Evans told Ohlendorf that the University of Texas had nothing to offer Penders in regards to the Host offer.

Muoneke Announces Intent to Transfer

Also in the *American-Statesman*, Gabe Muoneke said it was time for him to move on to another program because of the difficulty he had with Penders' system.

"It's kind of like transferring out of a biology class you're having trouble in and starting over in another one. I just didn't do well in Tom Penders 101."

He told the paper that he hadn't received a formal release from Dodds, as Axtell had earlier in the month, but he suggested to Dodds that he did want it.

"I haven't put it in a position where he has to give it to me."

Muoneke also said no one had tried to convince him to stay at the school.

"Except my girlfriend," he said. "Nobody wants me to stay, is the way I feel. I know if I asked them (teammates) if I should leave, they'd probably say no, but I shouldn't have to go ask them."

Muoneke also told the paper that there was no personal conflict with the coach. "It's not that. It's about my future. I don't have anything personal against the guy," he said.

Thursday, March 26
Penders' Defenders, Including Wife, Speak Out

Penders' wife, Susie, told *The Associated Press* that her husband isn't considering a television job and that she would be shocked if the University of Texas asked him to step down as basketball coach.

"That is always something that many people in the media industry have told him he would be great at when he was ready to retire from coaching," she said. "He has many network contacts ... But he loves coaching. That's who he is." She said she would be stunned if the university ousted her husband, the winningest coach in Texas history.

"I would think unless there was a valid reason, the university wouldn't have any interest in removing him from a job he has done so well," she said. "I would be shocked if someone asked him to voluntarily step down from a job he loves to do."

Yolanda Chevannes, mother of Vohn Hunter, a Texas signee and one of the top high school players in New York City, told *The Associated Press* that her son probably would reconsider if Penders wasn't the coach.

"Coach Penders came to our home in the Bronx, and Vohn just fell in love with him," Ms. Chevannes said. "We got a sense of family from him and his coaching staff. If Coach Penders isn't there, I don't think my son would want to go there."

Investigation Continues

Dodds told the *American-Statesman* that the investigation was moving along at a quick pace. "No decision's been made. But we're further along," he told the paper. "I think it's in the hands of the attorneys. It was a basketball matter. Now it's a Buckley Amendment matter."

Dodds said a violation of the Buckley Amendment was serious for the university because it could jeopardize federal money. However, Ohlendorf told the paper that the university was not in danger of losing funding.

"To my knowledge, a (federal) complaint has not been filed. It does not happen very often if the university takes corrective action, and usually they do," Ohlendorf said.

In addition, Ohlendorf made one of the more bizarre moves since the saga began when she offered an apology to the family of Luke Axtell on behalf of the university, even though the investigation was still ongoing.

"The university owes Luke and his family an apology for releasing Luke's grades, no matter how it happened," Ohlendorf said. "We've lingered too long without doing that, and we regret it very much." This was just the first of several apologies the university would offer to the Axtell family in the coming days.

Dodds Comments on Secret Meeting with the Players

Dodds, who had been relatively silent about the entire basketball program and the developing situation, also spoke with *The Associated Press* in an effort to clarify some previous statements made by Penders.

Dodds said there was a reason he did not tell Penders about the private meeting held at his house on March 8. "Several players asked to meet with me individually after we met as a group and asked me not to tell coach until we met," he said. "I kept my word to the players."

"I told them that once we had met individually, I would tell coach everything they said. I told them individually to go see coach and tell Tom the same things they were telling me. I contacted Tom as soon as I finished meeting with the players individually," Dodds said.

Penders Receives Phone Call on Possible Violations

That day in San Antonio, Penders received a phone call from a member of his staff that indicated the parents of one Texas basketball player may have been flown to a basketball game earlier in the season. If this was true, it would be an NCAA violation, because a player or his family cannot receive a benefit of value, such as plane tickets, from a school or its booster.

Those in question were Gary and Nina Mihm, parents of star Longhorns freshman center Chris Mihm. According to Alex Broadway, an administrative assistant on the Texas basketball staff, a booster flew the Mihms to the Texas Feb. 24 game at Oklahoma State on a private jet. Broadway said he learned about this from someone who was also on the plane. The person told Broadway the whole trip was set up by a booster, but the identity of the booster was never given. When Broadway told this information to Penders, he smelled trouble and knew he had to react, and promptly.

"I just assumed that it was set up by Frank Douglass because I knew he had use of the plane. I didn't know it was him, but I knew I had to report it. The rules at Texas say that if you hear of a possible violation, you're to report it to the compliance director for investigation. So right away I got ahold of Barbara down in San Antonio and arranged to meet with her."

Players Meet With Wendlandt

With everything moving fast and furiously behind the scenes, Broadway said that same day another secret meeting was held. This one involved Bill Wendlandt and several players.

According to Broadway, Bill Wendlandt was seen in Jester Dormitory, home to many student-athletes. Broadway said Wendlandt was visiting with players Ira Clark and DeJuan "Chico" Vazquez near the athletic elevators – elevators designated for use by athletes only – that were located behind the athlete's dining hall.

Broadway said after he saw the interaction between Wendlandt and the players, he asked both Clark and Vazquez what they had discussed. "I asked them what was going on and they said in so many words what was going on, about what was going to take place. He (Wendlandt) told them what was going to take place, as far as what was going to happen with the program and coaching. There was going to be a coaching change. He also told them not to be so hard on Luke and Chris because they are going through a lot right now."

Friday, March 27
Penders Meets with University Compliance Director

In a hotel room in the San Antonio Hyatt, which was headquarters for the Final Four festivities, Penders met with compliance director Barbara Walker. No one else was present. Walker listened as Penders described what Broadway had told him. He told her that he suspected it might be Frank Douglass, but he wasn't sure. Walker listened intently as Penders described the events with great detail as he recalled Broadway's description to him. After 45 minutes, the two finished the conversation, which had been taped, and Penders left.

Release of Investigation Results Hits Snag

Back in Austin, Ohlendorf said the investigation was still ongoing and would likely continue through the weekend.

"We won't be issuing any statement today," she said. "I don't think anything in terms of resolution will be done until Monday. The best-case scenario would be Monday afternoon."

The *American-Statesman* speculated that the delay could have been as a result of both Penders and Dodds being out of town in San Antonio as part of the Final Four. It also quoted school officials, saying they planned on working on the case through the weekend.

Penders: "Somebody's Behind This"

Although the *American-Statesman* was unable, of late, to get an interview from Penders regarding the ongoing situation at his school, television station KDFW of Dallas did not encounter the same problem. In the interview, Penders revealed some interesting things.

From the Final Four in San Antonio, Penders blamed the controversy regarding his program on a man with unknown motives.

"Somebody's behind this. There's somebody talking to these kids, somebody orchestrating this," Penders said. "I know who this person is, and I hope, in the end, this person will be exposed."

When asked if he thought someone was after his job, Penders said, "I don't think, I know. There is a person, and I'm not even going to say he's affiliated with the university, who is spending time in the dormitories, and he's hanging around the kids, and this is something that will come out eventually. I don't want to say names."

According to one player, who requested anonymity, Bill Wendlandt was one individual regularly seen in the dorms during Penders' final season at Texas. In addition to personally visiting with players in the dorm, the player said, Wendlandt and several other individuals routinely called players and told them about future events that would be happening with the basketball program, including the ouster of Penders. He said the individuals also said some not-so-flattering things about Penders. "They were just saying negative stuff like he had a drinking problem," the player said.

The player said because he was never approached during the season, there was never any reason for him to suspect anything was happening behind the scenes. It was not until the close of the season that he took notice of the situation, when he personally began to receive calls. He said with what he actually experienced and what he heard from other players, the phone calls and dorm visitations picked up considerably at season's end.

"This all happened at the end. During the season I never heard any of this stuff," he said. "I had never heard of any of these people. I think when they finally talked to me, I think they had been talking to different people for a while. Some people (players) knew for a while. I didn't really know until the end of the season, that's when I found out."

Minton Discusses Host with Media

When asked by a *Dallas Morning News* reporter if Penders would be fired, Minton categorically denied that any such item was being discussed behind closed doors and even went so far as to say that if such a thing occurred, it would be grounds for a lawsuit by his client. "If they make a decision we don't agree with, we'll see them in some courthouse some day," Minton was quoted in the paper.

Minton's words confirmed that no deal had been struck regarding Penders' impending removal, including the negotiation of a contract with Host. In the same interview, Minton for the first time publicly confirmed that Penders had been encouraged to leave his position as coach and take the television deal with Host before the Axtell situation took place.

"The university has been talking to Host Communications for six weeks," Minton told the paper.

Axtell Attorney Demands Another Apology

Obviously Ohlendorf's apology on behalf of the university the day before was not enough for Axtell and attorney Sherry Rasmus. Rasmus was quoted in the *Dallas Morning News* saying that Axtell was not academically ineligible according to rules of both the NCAA and the university.

"We want an official and formal apology for the release of his records and the resulting smear of Luke's name – an action that has caused Luke tremendous embarrassment," Rasmus told the paper. "When this is all said and done, we want to see (an apology) in an official posture, under the seal of the university."

Rasmus added that the release of Axtell's academic report had subjected the freshman to public criticism from a variety of people. "Luke has taken a lot of abuse through the talk show media. It has been hurtful and mean-spirited."

Saturday, March 28
Negotiations Heat Up

With the action heating up down the road in San Antonio at the Alamodome and the Final Four, it was getting even hotter in Austin as attorneys for both sides continued to pound away at resolving the head basketball coaching situation.

In a meeting of Ohlendorf and Minton, Ohlendorf gave Penders' attorney the first written settlement offer. In it, the university and Penders "... agreed that effective May 1, 1998, the Head Basketball Coach Agreement between the University and Penders shall terminate and neither University nor Penders shall have responsibility to perform their respective duties and obligations under such agreement."

In the issue that had been a main sticking point with Penders in negotiations – salary – the university agreed to pay Penders $400,000 in $100,000 annual installments. In addition, the agreement prevented both sides from filing lawsuits against each other.

Item number two of the settlement specifically released the university from any wrongdoing and stated:

"Penders releases the University, The University of Texas System, the Board of Regents of the University of Texas System, and the officers and employees of each in their official and individual capacity from all obligations under the Head Basketball

Coach Agreement and from all claims and causes of action Penders may have, whether presently known or unknown, that arise directly or indirectly from the acts or omissions of University, The University of Texas System, the Board of Regents of The University of Texas System, or the officers or employees of each with regard to any statement or action that may have been made or taken or alleged to have been made or taken by Penders in his capacity as head coach of University's intercollegiate basketball team for men."

Item number three of the settlement released Penders from any wrongdoing and stated:

"University releases Penders from all obligations under the Head Basketball Coach Agreement and from all claims and causes of action, whether presently known or unknown, that arise directly or indirectly from any statement or action that may have been made or taken or alleged to have been made or taken by Penders in his capacity as head coach of University's intercollegiate basketball team for men."

UT Delays Release of Investigation Findings Again

Although an offer had been made, Ohlendorf never let on with the media. In fact, it looked publicly as if both the negotiations and investigation were at a crawl, if not a complete standstill. She told reporters the results of the investigation, which she had said just the day before might be released on Monday afternoon at the earliest, were being pushed back another day.

"It's now probably Tuesday at the earliest," Ohlendorf told the *American-Statesman*. She said she had discovered at least four more people to interview and expected those additional sessions to delay the release of the findings.

Ohlendorf said the additional information she hoped to obtain "is similar to the other information, related to the academic information being released."

Minton was also quoted in the same article, saying: "I'm really just waiting on her (Ohlendorf)."

Sunday, March 29
Dodds Tells Media Penders Turned in Program

After Dodds learned from Barbara Walker that Penders had reported a possible NCAA violation, Dodds, according to Penders, made a pre-emptive strike. Dodds went public with the information and told the media about Penders' confidential meeting with Walker. This move was surprising because most – if not all – matters relating to possible NCAA violations are kept private. In fact, on most occasions, these matters are never made public unless serious violations are uncovered and possible sanctions might be handed down.

According to a representative from the university's compliance office, Dodds volunteering information to the media was not the standard. He said it is not common practice to discuss with the media a secondary-type violation, or a violation that provides a limited recruiting or competitive advantage and that is isolated or inadvertent in nature. "I don't think it's a written policy but certainly it's kind of an unspoken policy that we don't do it (speak to media) simply because the kid suffers more than anybody. The kid is involved and the kid has to answer questions. The kid has to have their life intruded on by so many people. We try to protect their privacy."

The compliance representative said only in the case of a possible major violation, of which the Mihms' plane ride was not considered, would a university official likely leak something to the media.

"When you get to a major violation, there's usually enough people involved, that somebody opens their mouth. Somebody finds the legitimate need to kind of cover themselves by telling someone outside the situation," the UT representative said.

Despite the unwritten policy, Dodds told the *American-Statesman* that Penders met with Walker and told her that the parents of freshman center Chris Mihm flew to the Oklahoma State game on Feb. 24 in a private airplane owned by a "UT alumnus," Rick Hawkins of Austin.

Hawkins, who was a season ticket-holder and a Texas Foundation member, told the *American-Statesman* that he was not a graduate of UT and had "never" attended UT in any capacity. He admitted that he flew the Mihms to the Stillwater game on his Citation V jet.

"I'm a graduate of Ohio University and proud of it," said Hawkins, chairman of a biotechnology company in Austin and a long-time family friend of the Mihms. "I was taking my son, his AAU teammate, and his coach to the Texas game, and I told the Mihms if they wanted to catch a ride, they could do it. "I wonder why he (Penders) turned it in now and not then," Hawkins said. "The timing is a little interesting."

Mihm's mother, Nina, denied the charges and also questioned Penders' motives. "I find it hard to believe he has Chris' best interests in mind," she said. "I'm just as shocked he's trying to find any dirt he can to muddy the waters. He is clouding the waters and trying to make everybody else look like they have something to hide."

Mihm also said no one in their family had spoken with Penders since Chris had attended the team meeting Penders called on Monday, March 23.

"Of course, he hasn't called," she said adamantly. "Nor has he spoken to Chris, who he claims is so close to him he's like a son. I can't believe he makes accusations like that without trying to find out the facts."

Dodds said that he had turned over the matter to Britton Banowsky, associate commissioner for administration and compliance of the Big 12.

"I don't have any real concern about it," Dodds said, once again commenting on the private matter. "But we're going to go ahead and check it out. From what I know, it's not a problem, and Britton was not too concerned about it. If the university had arranged (the trip), it's a violation, but they (the Hawkins and the Mihms) were friends previous to Chris' coming to Texas."

Penders would say later that Dodds' telling the media that he turned in the school worked exactly as Dodds had intended. He said the pre-emptive strike by Dodds allowed all those allegedly accused of any wrongdoing to voice their side of the story and get it out in the media before a real investigation into the matter took place. Penders said essentially Dodds made him play the part of villain for turning in his own school, and it worked, as evidenced by the reaction of Nina Mihm.

"Dodds used that with the Mihms to say that I wasn't interested in their son. But if I didn't do that, and this came up – and it would have – I'd have been fired for that.

They would have forgotten the faxing of Luke's grades. They would have used that (instead to get rid of me)."

Monday, March 30
Penders Defends Reporting Possible Violation

After being questioned in the media by both Mihm and Hawkins regarding the plane trip and possible violation of NCAA rules, Penders defended his actions.

"It's our procedure at Texas that if possible violations are brought to our attention, we have to go to our compliance director immediately and tell her about that suspicion," Penders told *The Associated Press*.

"I have had numerous phone calls relating to this issue. Everything else is confidential. The same people calling me may be calling other people. This was brought to my attention on Thursday, and I met with Barbara on Friday.

"I have no comment about the Mihms other than they are wonderful people. I have a job to do. I have to follow university rules or I could be terminated."

Ohlendorf said the university would review the issue "under our regular procedures," and added that it would not be part of the investigation into the circumstances surrounding the release of Axtell's academic progress report.

Release of Investigation Findings Stall Yet Again

Ohlendorf said the findings of the investigation into the fax may not be released until Wednesday – nearly a week after officials had first hoped to conclude the probe – because she had to interview three more people.

"The list could probably go higher. I'm not giving out the list of people we're interviewing. My inclination is it will go beyond (today)," she said. "We keep putting this off a day at a time as we keep getting information. We have a responsibility to be very thorough and fair, and that's what we are doing."

Penders reiterated in an interview with the *American-Statesman* that he was not familiar with the Buckley Amendment.

Dodds, from the Final Four in San Antonio, told the *American-Statesman* Monday night, "... everybody knows about the Buckley Amendment in college athletics. We live with it every day."

Dodds also said that he and other UT officials had looked into Penders' report of the possible rule violation. "We don't see anything there."

Despite those obviously slanted comments by his athletic director, Penders said he didn't think that the university had treated him unfairly during the investigation.

"I have never at any time felt like the school was handling my situation poorly," he told *The Associated Press*. "I'm taking the high road. I don't have anything but positive things to say about the university. I believe people are just trying to do their jobs. If other people want to speculate, that's their right."

Dodds also confirmed reports that Penders was involved in discussions with USA Collegiate, formerly known as Host Communications, about a possible television commentator's job.

"I have not heard he has a job with them. I don't think that's a done deal," Dodds said. "I know they've had some conversations, but I don't know any more about it."

Penders deferred any questions about the job at Host to his attorney. "That (television speculation), you'd have to talk to Roy about," he said. "He knows more about those things than me. I haven't talked to anyone at Host."

Penders, Attorneys Send Counteroffer to University

While Penders publicly deferred questions about Host to his attorney, privately his attorney sent a counterproposal of the settlement to Ohlendorf and the university.

The cover letter read:

"Enclosed is a copy of our revisions to the University's proposal which we submit in the spirit of compromise as a counter-proposal. The amount requested to be paid by the University is less than the present value of the future payments to be made under our client's current agreement with the University.

"I gather that we have a short time to get this settled so that both my client and your client come out feeling good about this, so please get me an answer as soon as you can, Patty."

It was signed by Minton.

In the settlement, the contents revealed that Penders was not satisfied with the university's offer of $400,000 over four years. Instead, he wanted $1.5 million to be paid in one lump sum.

In addition, the modified agreement changed the wording so that Penders would be released from any lawsuits as a result of actions by his assistant coaches or staff.

Item number three now read:

"University releases Penders from all obligations under the Head Basketball Coach Agreement and from all claims and causes of action [University may have], whether presently known or unknown, that arise directly or indirectly from [the acts or omissions of Penders; his assistant coaches and/or staff with regard to] any statement or action that may have been made or taken or alleged to have been made or taken by Penders in his capacity as head coach of University's intercollegiate basketball team for men."

Penders, also concerned about the future of his assistants, had a fourth item included that read:

"University acknowledges and will continue to honor the contracts of the assistant basketball coaches in accordance with their individual terms."

University Makes Another Offer

That same day, Ohlendorf responded to Minton's memo and modified version of the agreement with a letter of her own. The main focus was salary.

"I write in response to your letter of March 30 and your counter-proposal to the settlement and release offer The University proposed last week. I understand that you felt obliged to make the counter-proposal you submitted due to the desires of your client. Nevertheless, I must advise you, consistent with my previous statements, that the amount requested is well beyond what The University can agree to in good faith and when considering the circumstances described in our discussions.

The University will agree to pay Tom Penders $500,000 on May 1, 1998. As we have discussed previously, we will agree to make his resignation effective May 1, 1998, so that he has access to the special investment account funds totaling $157,237. If he is not employed by The University on April 30, 1998, he has no right to the special investment account funds. Tom Penders may continue to use the courtesy cars and other benefits accruing to his Head Coach position through May 1, 1998."

Ohlendorf's letter also revealed that an agreement had been worked out where the university would not comment on Penders and his resignation. "The University will not issue public statements regarding Tom Penders when he announces his resignation this week other than that he decided to resign his position, presumably to pursue other opportunities."

Last on the list of topics, Ohlendorf said the university could not, as requested in the modified agreement, release the assistants from any liabilities.

"The University is not in a position to enter into an agreement with Tom Penders to release the assistant coaches from liability for any claims or causes of action that The University may have. We have an employment relationship with the assistant coaches that is separate from Tom Penders. As I told you yesterday, Rob Wright and Carlton Owens have appointments through August 31, 1998. They also may be considered for continued appointment by the new Head Coach after he is hired. Eddie Oran's appointment status is the same although based upon information that we have at this time some disciplinary action will be appropriate."

She concluded: "Roy, I look forward to hearing from you. The University is making this offer in an effort to provide good choices for the future of all parties concerned. My clients are not in a position to offer additional funds. Their good faith is being extended to its limits."

Tuesday March 31
Minton Counters Back

Despite Ohlendorf's letter and explanation that the university had been extended to its limits, Minton, on behalf of Penders, requested more. Minton said Penders would be satisfied with $643,000, because with that figure, in addition to the $157,000 from the special investment account, as well as a supplemental payment of $100,000 for services performed in radio/TV, the total package would be $900,000. When coupled with the $350,000 salary over four years from Host, Penders would essentially make the same amount now being dissolved in his contract with the university.

UT Postpones Annual Basketball Banquet

With all the controversy surrounding the basketball program, the University of Texas athletic department indefinitely postponed the annual men's basketball banquet scheduled for that Friday at the Erwin Center.

More than 600 of the $20 tickets had been sold for the event, but the university opted to move it back to a later date.

Saba offered no explanation for the delay to the *American-Statesman*. "We have to wait and see what transpires and if the players are interested. After all, it's their event."

Investigation Nears End

Ohlendorf told the *American-Statesman* that the investigation into the release of the academic status of Axtell's grades was expected to be complete in the next couple of days. She said 20 people had already been interviewed.

"We have formulated some preliminary conclusions in our own minds, but we're looking through everything to see what supports those and what doesn't and seeing what else we have to track down."

The paper also quoted University Compliance Director Barbara Walker, who said that the university's position on the student privacy law is included in a nearly 3-inch-thick "Policy and Procedures Manual," which was updated this year for the men's department. "All of us are accountable for everything in it," Walker told the paper. "We're probably like a lot of other big organizations. You have policy manuals that you are held accountable for. What we try to educate our staff on is new rules that come through, particularly from my office."

Walker said that all UT intercollegiate athletic teams have meetings at the start of the academic year to cover a wide range of subjects, including the Buckley Amendment.

Coaches are not required to attend the meetings, but Walker estimated more than half do. No records are kept on those who do attend.

Host Working with Penders

Scott Willingham, vice president and general manager of the Longhorn Sports Network, told the *American-Statesman* that Host Communications had entered into talks with Penders about possible employment. He said nothing had been finalized.

"Tom has had conversations with Host Communications," Willingham told the paper. "Host likes Tom, thinks a lot of him, and thinks he's talented as far as being a broadcaster. He'll probably do some contract work with us. I think we're going to help him out as a friend. If he wants to be involved, we'll probably put him in the right place with the right people."

Clack Speaks Out

As "fallout" of the nearly month-long controversy, Kris Clack told the *San Antonio Express-News* the dividing lines were drawn and the Longhorns would be a team divided next season regardless of whether Penders is the coach.

Wednesday, April 1
UT Officials Expect Investigation to End Soon

Dodds told the *American-Statesman* that the University of Texas and its two-week-long investigation into the release of Luke Axtell's academic progress report would be concluded soon. "I think there is a chance it could be (today)," he told the paper.

Dodds also told the paper that he had completed his own inquiry into Penders' revelation that the parents of Chris Mihm had received a free plane ride to the Oklahoma State game from a Longhorn booster. "I don't think it's an issue," Dodds said. He said the report on the inquiry was mailed to the Big 12 office and he feels that it cleared the school of any wrongdoing.

Britton Banowsky, the Big 12's associate commissioner for administration and compliance, said he had spoken with UT officials about the matter and received a fax report that he had not yet reviewed.

"Based on conversations we have had and information developed by the university, it would appear there is a substantial pre-existing relationship between the involved individuals that would override any NCAA rules issue. We will work with them (NCAA) on it. I expect to have some resolution by the end of the week."

University Provides New Draft of Settlement

In the latest draft of the release and settlement agreement, the university chose to follow a godly approach – to giveth and to taketh away. It gave Penders what he wanted as far as settlement money was concerned, agreeing to pay a lump sum of $643,000 to him on May 1, 1998. However, it removed item number four from the agreement, which Penders had included so that the contracts of his assistant coaches would be honored.

In addition to the draft agreement and in anticipation that Penders' departure from the university would be announced the next day, April 2, the first draft press release describing Penders' resignation was written.

With "Draft #1 (for discussion purposes only)" and "4/1/98" handwritten at the top, the release began: "In a joint statement released Thursday, Tom Penders and the University of Texas announced that he will no longer be the head basketball coach effective May 1, 1998. His resignation comes as part of a mutual settlement package that resolves the issues that have arisen between the parties in recent weeks. Mr. Penders will receive a lump sum payment and a release from his duties and obligations under his coaching contract with the University.

The University will immediately commence the selection process for a new head basketball coach and the parties wish each other well in their future endeavors."

Throughout the release, numerous editing remarks were made by Ohlendorf, most notably the removal of the entire sentence identifying that Penders would receive a lump sum payment and a release from his duties and obligations.

In addition, at the bottom of the page, Ohlendorf wrote: "[Put a quote from Dodds re: Penders contributions over the years?]" and "[Put a quote from Penders re: UT?]" From its appearance, Ohlendorf wanted both parties to say something nice about the other so the split looked more amicable than it actually was.

Thursday, April 2

The phones were ringing and faxes were flying to begin the morning.

Early on, Penders told Longley he wanted to have a press conference announcing his departure. He asked Longley to tell Ohlendorf of his request. Longley did. Ohlendorf said the university was hesitant to do so, but she would look into the matter.

Penders said when he heard the university didn't want to allow him to hold a press conference, as the case was for Mackovic less than a year earlier, all bets were off. "If there's no press conference, there's no deal," he told his attorney.

He also told his attorney to tell university officials that he would come up with his own words for the press conference. "No one is going to tell me what to say." Despite the request, the university offered assistance. Penders refused.

Late in the morning, just after 11 a.m., Longley received a fax from the university. In it, there were two versions of the settlement agreement. Both included the lump sum payment of $643,000. However, one version included the paragraph honoring the assistant coaches and their contracts, while the other had the paragraph crossed out. Longley perused over both documents and then faxed them on to Penders.

In his cover letter to Penders, he told him that both versions "look fine as to form," but it was Penders' decision as to which one he wanted to sign. That was an obvious choice. With all the haggling he had gone through to get it included in the agreement, there was no reason to believe he would change his mind at the last second.

The letter from Longley also discussed Penders and his health insurance. Most importantly, at the end, Longley told Penders that Ohlendorf had agreed to allow Penders to hold a press conference at Bellmont Hall sometime that afternoon. "I informed her that you would prefer to hold it at 4:00 p.m. with the press being notified sometime prior to that time. She has not gotten back to me with regard to whether or not that is OK."

He concluded, telling Penders he would see him for lunch.

Penders, UT Reach Agreement on Release and Settlement

At 1:36 p.m., the agreement was officially complete, with the signatures of both Penders and interim President Peter T. Flawn. The final agreement included payment to Penders in the form of a lump sum of $643,000 on May 1, 1998. It also included that the contracts of assistant basketball coaches would be honored "in accordance with their individual terms, subject to any disciplinary action that University determines shall be taken for actions of such assistant coaches."

All that remained was the official announcement. A press conference was scheduled for 4:00 p.m. that afternoon.

Penders, Dodds and Ohlendorf Hold Press Conference

At 4:00 p.m., DeLoss Dodds and Tom Penders sat along side each other in what could be best described as an "awkward" situation to say the least. The two had not spoken in person for weeks. And it was Dodds, as far as Penders was concerned, who was solely responsible for all the previous events that led to this moment. Also sitting behind the orange-draped table was Patricia Ohlendorf, who was to announce the results of the investigation.

Penders read from the statement he prepared:

It is with mixed emotions that I resign from my position as head basketball coach at the University of Texas. I have been very fortunate. My position as head basketball coach has allowed me to meet many wonderful people. I've dedicated the last 10 years of my life to bringing the university a basketball program that everyone could be proud of.

I would be remiss if I didn't thank all the past and present players, coaches and fans who made it all possible. I will forever be grateful to the University of Texas for giving me the opportunity to represent their fine institution.

I think it is the proper time to step aside. The future is bright for Texas basketball and for me and my family as well. It is the time of my life to pursue other options and consider other challenges and other opportunities. I think that change is good for everyone at certain times in their lives.

I wish my players and everyone at the university the very best. No matter where I go from here, my wife and partner Susie, my precious daughter, Karli – who many of you witnessed blossom into a young lady – my wonderful son, Tommy, a graduate of UT and now a coach at the University of Rhode Island, and I will always cherish the great memories.

Immediately after Penders' speech, with the lights glaring and hundreds of people, including several players looking on, Dodds read from his prepared statement.

Tom Penders is a friend to the University of Texas and will be acknowledged as the man responsible for bringing Texas basketball to a new competitive level. Our ability to compete for conference championships and postseason play are directly attributable to Tom, his coaching, his staff, his players, and the kids he recruited to the University of Texas.

Tom has worked hard for the University of Texas for 10 years. And he's put UT basketball into the national limelight. He achieved that goal with a great personality, style, and provided an entertaining kind of basketball.

I want to personally thank Tom Penders, Susie, for what they've contributed to the University of Texas and our athletic program. And I want to thank them for 10 wonderful years as friends of the Dodds family. And I look forward Tom and Susie, to many, many more years of friendship.

Following Dodds' remarks, Penders and Dodds shook hands, and Dodds patted Penders on the back of the neck. After his remarks, all those in attendance anticipated Ohlendorf would read the results of the investigation, which had gone on for three weeks. Instead, Ohlendorf read a prepared statement of her own.

The University of Texas has completed its review of the public disclosure of academic information regarding a student-athlete. We have been in discussions with the student-athlete, with his family, and with his attorney. The university is going to take the following steps:

We will talk with assistant men's basketball coach Eddie Oran when he returns from a recruiting trip. We will discuss with him appropriate disciplinary action for his authorization of the release of academic information.

The university and the departments of intercollegiate athletics will take steps to enhance the knowledge of and implementation of the federal Family Educational Right to Privacy Act (Buckley Amendment).

Written notices regarding our responsibilities under the act will be distributed and the act will be highlighted in training sessions and staff meetings.

The departments of intercollegiate athletics will develop written guidelines related to suspensions of student-athletes by coaches.

The university appreciates the cooperation of all who participated in this review. Thank you.

When asked about the results of the investigation, Ohlendorf responded, "This is our statement."

So it was done. Tom Penders was out as head coach at the University of Texas. And the investigation by Ohlendorf, which was pushed back day after day, was pushed back yet again – indefinitely. As of this writing, the findings have never been released.

Chapter Sixteen

What Has Happened Since

Before Penders' resignation press conference ended, Dodds had a considerable slip of the tongue. To most present, including members of the media, it went unnoticed and unreported. But for those who were paying closer attention, it was obvious Dodds had something or someone else on his mind.

Immediately following Ohlendorf's remarks, Dodds discussed how he had visited with the players before the press conference and how they were all very emotional about Penders' pending departure. He asked that the members of the media respect that and take it into consideration when approaching the players about interviews. He also said that he had told the players there would be several involved in the search committee to find Penders' replacement, which they hoped to locate in a timely manner.

At that point, Dodds turned the floor over to Assistant Athletic Director for External Services Bill Little. "Now, I guess Bill Littlelandt, what you want to do is do Q and As?"

Littlelandt? Dodds had just combined the names of Little and Wendlandt. Both Bills and both involved with Texas athletics. One involved in an official capacity, the other not so official, but involved nonetheless.

The Day After

A day after the university officially ended its relationship with Penders, UT officials went to work on another strained relationship, that of Luke Axtell and his family.

The University of Texas, in a damage-control move and possibly with the hopes that Axtell might change his mind and return for his sophomore season, reinstated the freshman and apologized to him and his family. The university issued a statement:

The University of Texas and the department of intercollegiate athletics for men apologizes to Mr. Luke Axtell, a freshman student-athlete at the university. Academic information concerning Mr. Axtell was wrongfully released. This academic information should not have been released.

Further, the information inaccurately reflected Mr. Axtell's grades and current academic status. Mr. Axtell was not academically ineligible under university rules and his scholarship was never in jeopardy. Mr. Axtell's suspension from the team is lifted, and he is reinstated, effective immediately.

The University of Texas and the department of intercollegiate athletics for men sincerely regret any embarrassment this entire situation has caused Mr. Axtell and his family.

The Axtells' lawyer, Sherry Rasmus, said the family had been told of the university's statement.

"We appreciate the university's stance with respect to the apology and the wrongful release of Luke's transcript," she said. "We're interested in a little bit more information with respect to the investigation (conducted by UT), and that we don't have yet."

Search for Replacement

Two days after Penders' resignation, a committee was formed to find the new head coach. Among those on the committee were former players Jay Arnette, Courtney Jeans and Slater Martin; Tom Hicks of the Board of Regents; UT Associate Athletic Director Butch Worley; and current players Kris Clack and DeJuan "Chico" Vazquez, who served in an advisory capacity.

The committee had a wish list of coaches to review. Among those were Washington's Bob Bender, Clemson's Rick Barnes, Oklahoma's Kelvin Sampson, Wake Forest's Dave Odom, Florida's Billy Donovan, South Carolina's Eddie Fogler, North Carolina assistant Phil Ford, and last, but certainly not least, Utah's Rick Majerus.

Majerus was the main target of the search committee – and why not? Majerus had a week earlier led his Utah team to the national championship contest in which they lost to Kentucky. Could this be a situation like the one 10 years earlier in which Billy Tubbs propositioned Texas and Dodds about the opening following his team's loss in the NCAA Championship game? Only time would tell.

Axtell Heads to Plains of Kansas

While the university continued to seek out a new head basketball coach, Luke Axtell wasn't going to wait around for the search results. Axtell decided to transfer to the University of Kansas.

Axtell released a statement that said, "After visiting the KU campus, it was clear that the transfer was the best choice for me. I am grateful for the opportunities I was given at the University of Texas."

Rasmus said Axtell was concerned about a backlash from Texas fans regarding the firestorm controversy that occurred after Penders suspended him. "Luke had some real concerns about being blamed for everything based on what was said in the media and on radio shows," Rasmus said. "But he also knew that memories are sometimes short when you are scoring a lot of points per game."

"However, he is really positive about the Kansas opportunity. He was very impressed with Kansas coach Roy Williams and his staff and the university after visiting the campus."

Rasmus said Axtell and his family wouldn't seek legal action against the university in response to his grades being released because school officials had been cooperative since the incident.

She also said Dodds had already requested that the Big 12 waive a rule that required Axtell to lose a year of eligibility as a result of his transfer. If the waiver was granted, Axtell would have to sit out a year but he would receive a fifth year of eligibility.

Search on Hold

The search for Penders' replacement had stalled, but university officials maintained that Majerus was the man they wanted. Clemson's Rick Barnes was also being mentioned with greater frequency around Bellmont Hall, but no firm decision on a final candidate had been made.

The main sticking point with Majerus was money. He made $1 million per season at Utah, and the University of Texas would not pay the new basketball coach more than what first-year head football coach Mack Brown was making – $750,000. Barnes had received $668,000 from Clemson the year before.

Majerus, who is a close friend of Penders, also gave Texas officials a list of criteria that must be met before he considered another job including weight rooms, training facilities, and an academic advisory board.

There was also an increased concern around the athletic department that both Majerus and Barnes might lose interest because of the protracted discussions they had had with university officials. That obviously played a role with Washington's Bob Bender and Oklahoma's Kelvin Sampson, who both withdrew their names from consideration.

UT Names Barnes New Head Coach

On April 13, 1998 – 11 days after Texas' winningest coach resigned – the University of Texas announced Rick Barnes as the 23rd men's basketball coach. Barnes, a 43-year-old native of Hickory, N.C., who had compiled a career record of 202-134 as head coach at George Mason, Providence and Clemson, signed a five-year, $700,000 a year contract.

Barnes Meets with Axtell

After Barnes was named head coach, one of his first orders of business was to talk with Axtell. Axtell met with the new head man and never wavered on his decision to transfer. Rasmus said Axtell's meeting was simply a courtesy. "Coach Barnes, through the university, asked to meet with Luke and Luke agreed to do that. But there isn't anything more to do or say. He has decided on Kansas."

"I respect Luke's decision," Barnes said. If there was any hope that Axtell would return to Texas, there was none now. The meeting with Barnes made it official.

Goode Leaves Texas

Less than a month after taking the reins at Texas and the departure of Axtell, Rick Barnes suffered another loss when Anthony Goode, a product of Carter High School in Dallas and once-projected point guard of the future at Texas, announced his intent to transfer to the University of Texas-Arlington.

Goode, who had been rumored to be transferring after limited playing time at Texas, said he made his decision to transfer only after not being asked by Barnes or members of his staff to stay at Texas. "My mind wasn't made up until last week. They never took it upon themselves to ask me to stay, so I took it upon myself to leave."

University Promotes Ohlendorf

While some players and coaches were leaving the University of Texas, some in administration were moving up. A month after Penders' resignation, Patricia Ohlendorf was named vice president for administration and legal affairs.

In that capacity, the 44-year-old Ohlendorf, who had been at the university for more than 20 years, would serve as President Larry Faulkner's chief of staff. Ohlendorf was obviously enthusiastic about the promotion. "I am delighted with this opportunity to broaden my university experience, to support Larry Faulkner's presidency, and to help advance the university' s agenda," Ohlendorf told the *American-Statesman*.

Penders in Broadcasting?

In May, just over a month after his departure from Texas and almost two months after first hearing about a position at Host Communications from Bob Utley, Penders acknowledged that broadcasting might be in the near future.

"I'm leaning toward doing something in TV," Penders told the *American-Statesman*. "Broadcasting has always been something I've wanted to do and yet if I do enter that, I don't think it would preclude me from coaching again if I want to go back to it."

Penders, who did spot work for ESPN and other networks during his 10 years at Texas, said he had been asked to audition with ESPN as a color commentator for college basketball telecasts, but he had also discussed a position with Host Communications, the same company he had seen a contract from weeks before he resigned. He said he was leaning toward the Host job.

"The thing that excites me about that situation is that I wouldn' t be doing just color commentating. If the job is just announcing some basketball games, I think I'd be bored," he said. "I could also stay in Austin if I wanted, and I don't feel like uprooting the family at this point."

Jim Host, chairman of the board for the Lexington, Kentucky-based company said Penders could be a solid fit at his company. "I think he'd be good at a lot of different things. We haven't arrived at anything yet, which I can classify as being definitive. But hopefully we will because I've always liked Tom."

"I think he'd be a great addition if we can put it together," Host said. "Nothing in particular is holding it up. We're just talking it through until everybody feels right about it. I hope we get it done fairly quickly and I feel we will."

The following week, Penders signed a four-year, $350,000 a year deal with Host Communications. In the agreement he agreed to serve as a color analyst for basketball games on radio and television that Host farms out, and would serve as consultant to Jim Host. The agreement also allowed him to work with other networks as well. With that, he could audition for a color commentator position at ESPN, which he had planned to do in the coming weeks. It also said he could pursue coaching opportunities if he saw fit to do so. The contract read, "... nothing will prevent you from engaging in additional activities in connection with personal investments, community affairs or meetings with NCAA or NBA institutions to discuss possible coaching positions ... " This clause became most important a month later.

Big 12 Denies Axtell Third Year of Eligibility

At the Big 12 annual spring meetings in Colorado Springs, Colo., Big 12 faculty athletic representatives rejected Luke Axtell's request for a third year of eligibility. By a 10-2 vote, representatives denied the request that would have allowed Axtell to receive a third year of eligibility after he transferred to Kansas. The two votes for the request were from Texas and Kansas. Under Big 12 rules, athletes transferring from one school in the league to another lose a year of eligibility.

Even with the decision, Rasmus said this wouldn't change Axtell's plans. "I doubt this changes anything. Luke's indicated all along that he'll honor his commitment to Kansas and Coach (Roy) Williams."

Rasmus said she and the family expected a different outcome. "If there were ever extenuating circumstances, this was certainly the case. The Axtells are extremely disappointed and dumbfounded that the waiver wasn't granted." She said she planned to meet with UT officials to determine if there was an appeals process.

Big 12 Denies Axtell Eligibility Appeal

In June, the Big 12 Conference board of directors denied Luke Axtell's appeal at the annual meeting of presidents of the league's universities. The board, which consisted of presidents and chancellors of the member schools, upheld the vote of faculty representatives a month earlier.

UT President Larry Faulkner said he voted in Axtell's favor, but Kansas President Robert Hemenway declined to comment on whether or not he cast the other minority vote.

With the ruling, Axtell had two seasons remaining at Kansas after sitting out a year to establish eligibility.

Penders in Running for George Washington Vacancy

A week after publicly expressing his excitement about a future in television and indicating he was not a candidate at George Washington University in Washington, D.C., Penders' name surfaced as a leading candidate for the position.

Penders had said a week earlier that he and longtime friend George Washington Athletic Director Jack Kvancz met at his home in Austin for a couple of days, where he assisted Kvancz in his search of possible replacements for former coach Mike Jarvis, who had left for St. John's.

Kvancz said they did not specifically mention Penders as a replacement. "We didn't get to that point. He's obviously a quality candidate. But I just wanted to see what his interest might be and pick his brain a little about other people out there."

When questioned about the situation Penders said he was still looking forward to his future in television. "I'm not looking for any (coaching) jobs. It would take a situation where I knew and trusted the athletic director to get me to even consider it, but right now I'm excited about the TV thing."

George Washington Names Penders New Head Coach

Just six weeks after signing a four-year deal with Host Communications and a day after canceling a scheduled audition at ESPN Studio headquarters in Connecticut, it was obvious Penders' heart was still in coaching. In a press conference at the Charles E. Smith Center, the 53-year-old Penders put his career in television indefinitely on hold as he was named head coach of the George Washington Colonials.

"Dickie V (Vitale), you don't have to worry for a few years," Penders said to those gathered, after a trumpeter hailed his arrival at the news conference. "I will not be competing for your job. I'm not ready for that. I'm a coach who loves coaching. This is what I do."

Penders had obviously found the GW head coaching situation to be one where he knew and trusted the athletic director – two criteria he had said just days before that were necessary for his return to the profession.

In his press conference he noted that at Texas, Dodds was someone he could not trust near the end of his tenure in Austin. "This past year I just felt quite simply that my athletic director was undermining me. I just felt it was clear to me that I could not work for my athletic director. You cannot succeed without the support of your AD. At Texas, the AD would come into my office maybe once a year. I expect Jack to be in my office or me to be in his office every day.

"I'm working with an athletic director (Kvancz) that I totally trust. I've lost a lot of weight this year ... and I feel like I lost another 50 pounds when I took the steel plate out of my back when I left Texas," added Penders, making a knife-in-the-back reference. "I don't have to worry about that here. I have people that are going to work with me to bring GW the very, very best."

Kvancz said he was quite pleased with the new hire. "We have a great program and we wanted to find a coach to continue that success," he said. "Tom Penders is competitive, he's compassionate, and he's concerned about his players on and off the court."

George Washington President Stephen Joel Trachtenberg was equally enthusiastic about the basketball program's future with Penders. "This is a great day for GW basketball," Trachtenberg said. "We had a great coach. Now we have a wonderful coach."

Penders said he planned to transform the Colonials into his running, pressing style of play that had produced a scoring average of 87 points per game in his first 27 seasons. "We're going to run, we're going to get after people, we're going to play nine or ten people in a rotation."

He said he expected the implementation of his style at George Washington to be an easier transition than past stops in his career because the Colonials program was already in good shape. "Fortunately I'm taking over a program from Mike Jarvis that is fundamentally sound and defensive oriented."

The only potential dilemma at George Washington, he said, would be in calling the eight foreign-born players by name. "The biggest problem I'm going to have is pronunciation."

Penders' six-year contract included a base salary of almost $450,000. Overall, the package including television, radio and shoe deals was reported to be worth at least $600,000.

UT Fans React

Following Penders' news conference in Washington, D.C., which was played repeatedly on television newscasts and radio talk shows throughout Austin, many University of Texas fans were outraged by the former coach's remarks. Still, others believed what he said was true and were happy to see he had landed on his feet.

One caller to a radio talk show expressed disbelief in his remarks. "He's a traitor," the caller said.

Another said Penders' comments specific to Dodds were probably warranted. "Look what Dodds has done to all our coaches recently," he said, referring to the removal of former baseball coach Cliff Gustafson, former football coach John Mackovic, and Penders, all in an 18-month time period.

Despite being months removed from the job and thousands of miles away, the name

"Penders" was still able to get the juices boiling in the veins of many fans. Whether it was pro-Penders or anti-Penders, UT basketball fans were fervent in their beliefs. Many didn't care either way, but just wanted Penders and his controversial departure to just go away.

UT Officials React

The only reaction from University of Texas officials to Penders' press conference came from Dodds and UT President Larry Faulkner.

Dodds declined to respond to the remarks saying "We appreciate the good things he did for the university, and we wish him well in his new challenge."

Faulkner also wished Penders the best in his future endeavors. "I think Tom Penders had a long run at the University of Texas, and I think we still have very positive feelings about the contributions he made to our program."

Smith Transfers to Houston

Several months after Penders had started his new job at George Washington, ripples from his departure were still being felt back in Austin, and the effects were considerable for the Texas basketball program.

After losing Axtell and Goode, Barnes lost another key player in Bernard Smith just days before classes were to resume for the fall semester. Smith, a supporter of Penders and one of the four players who attended the secret meeting at Dodds' house unaware of its nature, announced his intent to transfer to the University of Houston to play for its new head coach, Clyde Drexler.

Smith, who is from Conroe, said he had considered Houston out of high school but wasn't sure about speculation surrounding former coach Alvin Brooks. "The coaching situation was a little shaky but now the coaching situation is perfect for me."

Smith's departure meant Barnes had to fill the shoes of a projected starter who had appeared in all 31 games in the 1997-98 season and averaged better than 22 minutes and nearly six points a game.

New Season, New Coaches

The Longhorns stumbled out of the blocks to a 2-7 start including losses to the likes of San Diego and South Florida. Attendance was also sharply down early in the season as the Erwin Center averaged only 6,590 fans in the nonconference home games, compared to 10,274 under Penders the previous year.

In Washington, D.C., Penders and his Colonials got off to a 6-4 start including losses to North Carolina-Charlotte, DePaul and Stanford.

Although both teams didn't get off to the best of starts, both finished strong in their respective conferences.

Barnes and the Longhorns rebounded nicely to finish the season with an 18-11 overall record, and 13-3 in the Big 12. The 13-3 conference record earned the Horns the Big 12 regular season title, which they won despite playing before their smallest average home crowds since 1987-88, averaging just 9,239 fans per game in the 16,175-seat Erwin Center. The previous low average came in Bob Weltlich's final season when the norm was just 4,028.

Penders and the Colonials also picked up the pace in victories and finished the season with a 19-7, 13-3 record in the Atlantic 10. The 13-3 conference record earned the team its first outright West Division title in the Atlantic 10 Conference.

In the postseason, both teams took similar journeys. The Horns defeated Colorado in the Big 12 Tournament, but bowed out to Oklahoma State in the semifinals. In the Atlantic 10 Conference Tournament, the Colonials defeated Dayton and lost to Rhode Island in the tourney semifinals. Despite losses in the conference semifinals, both teams earned berths in the NCAA Tournament. Unfortunately, for both squads, they exited in the first round.

The Longhorns, a seventh seed in the NCAA East Regional, suffered a 58-54 loss against the 10th seeded Purdue Boilermakers. Texas finished the season with a 19-13 record.

George Washington also bowed out in the first round. As the 11th seed, the Colonials let the game get away early and never recovered against Bob Knight and the sixth-seeded Indiana Hoosiers. The Hoosiers won the South Region first-round contest 108-88. The loss marked only the second time in 10 NCAA appearances that a Penders-led team had bowed out in the first round. The Colonials finished the season with a 20-9 record.

Where are they now?

Eddie Oran – When Rick Barnes took over the reigns at Texas, Oran was not kept on staff like Penders had done for him 10 years earlier. Since that time, Oran has left the basketball coaching profession and is currently a car salesman at Covert Chevrolet in Bastrop, Texas.

Luke Axtell – After transferring to the University of Kansas, Axtell had to sit out a year before regaining his eligibility. Axtell was introduced to Jayhawk fans when he sang a solo in front of 15,800 fans in Allen Fieldhouse during "Late Night," KU's annual festival and abbreviated scrimmage, held to mark the beginning of basketball season. That night, Axtell went on to score eight points, including one three-point field goal.

Vic Trilli – Trilli is entering his third season as head coach at the University of North Texas. In his first two seasons, he compiled a 9-43 record.

Brandy Perryman – Since leaving the University of Texas, Perryman has worked for two seasons as an administrative assistant at North Texas under Vic Trilli where he is also currently working on his master's degree.

Jamie Ciampaglio – Since leaving the University of Texas and the basketball coaching profession, Ciampaglio changed sports moving into the world of golf. He has steadily moved up the ranks and is currently in his second year as a general manager of a country club in Florida.

Travis Mays – After leaving the University of Texas as the school's all-time leading scorer in 1990, Mays played for the Sacramento Kings and Atlanta Hawks of the NBA. Eventually, he made his way to Europe where he is currently under contract with a team in Italy.

Dexter Cambridge - After leaving the University of Texas, Cambridge played with the Dallas Mavericks. He is currently playing in Italy.

Chapter Seventeen

The Axtell Lawsuit

Depositions Requested

In November 1998, just as the Texas basketball team was set to begin the post-Penders era of basketball, the controversy surrounding the former coach's departure reared its ugly head once again – not on the basketball court but in Travis County District Court.

Sherry Rasmus, attorney for Luke Axtell, received clearance to take depositions to pursue possible damages against radio stations KVET-AM and KJFK-FM for defamation of broadcasting an inaccurate academic progress report. KJFK-FM, like KVET-AM, received the report but never broadcast the information.

Through the depositions, Axtell and his representation hoped to discover the circumstances under which the academic progress report was released to the media in March of 1998. According to a report in the *American-Statesman*, Rasmus believed she had the legal right to take the depositions because neither radio station tried to prevent her from doing so. "Right now, we are not targeting anyone," for a lawsuit. "Our goal is to find out the truth about how all this happened."

But attorneys for former assistant Eddie Oran and basketball office administrative assistant Leslie Parks filed papers indicating that their clients should not have to give the depositions because they never received notice regarding a hearing with Travis County District Court Judge Margaret Cooper that was scheduled for November 12. The hearing was canceled when the radio stations failed to oppose the taking of the depositions.

Depositions were also sought from former player Brandy Perryman, current players Kris Clack and DeJuan "Chico" Vazquez, Athletic Director DeLoss Dodds, and KVET-AM sports director Bill Schoening. In a curious move, a deposition was also sought from former coach Vic Trilli, who had left to become head coach at North Texas before Penders' final season and before Axtell ever played at Texas.

Motion Filed to Quash Depositions

Less than a month later, attorneys for Oran and Parks made another legal maneuver as they filed a motion requesting that Judge Cooper quash their depositions which had been scheduled for December 8. Both Oran and Parks failed to appear for the depositions and a hearing date was not set for a ruling by Cooper.

Judge Allows Only One Deposition

A month after the request for quashing of the depositions, Judge Cooper ruled that Rasmus could take depositions from only one of the 10 people she had hoped to depose. Cooper ruled that Rasmus could depose only KVET-AM sports director Bill Schoening because the radio station had agreed to cooperate.

Before Cooper's ruling, attorneys for the nine others had filed motions to quash the depositions. Attorneys for all parties, excluding Schoening and Oran, asserted that the people they represented had little or no relevant knowledge that would benefit Axtell.

According to Chad Geisler, an assistant attorney general for the state of Texas, who was representing Trilli, as well as Perryman and several athletic department employees, the depositions would simply be used as a "fishing expedition" before filing a lawsuit.

With the ruling by Cooper, Axtell essentially had only one option to get depositions from the various parties – file a lawsuit. Rasmus did not discuss whether a suit would be filed against the university or any individuals. "We're contemplating our next move," she told the *American-Statesman*.

Lawsuit Filed

Several days later the contemplation was over and the "next move" was made as Axtell filed a lawsuit against the parent company of radio station KVET-AM, Capstar Texas Limited Partnership, asserting that his right to privacy was violated when the station broadcast his academic status report.

KJFK-FM, inconspicuously, was not included in the suit.

The suit said that KVET failed to "exercise due care to determine whether or not information received was accurate and failed to prevent publication of (Axtell's) academic status."

It asserted that Axtell was not only defamed, but he was subjected to public hatred, contempt and ridicule. Axtell sought damages of more than $50,000.

All's Quiet

For the next six months talk of the Axtell lawsuit was quiet. Behind the scenes, however, the action was heating up. In fact, activities regarding the lawsuit were very active as depositions were taken from the various parties. Penders was not one of them.

During the lull in activity, Penders went through his first off-season at George Washington. Although he focused on his duties as basketball coach of the Colonials, he also kept close tabs on the goings-on back in Austin through his attorney. He said he was just waiting for something to hit the media that would be disparaging toward him and his reputation. "You watch, through these depositions, something is going to come out. They just haven't found something good enough to leak to the media yet."

Depositions Leaked to Media

On August 2, 1999, activities pertaining to the lawsuit went into overdrive.

Between 10 a.m. and 11 a.m., a representative from The Rasmus Firm, Axtell's attorney's office, submitted to the Travis County District Court almost 1,000 pages worth of sworn statements from nine people deposed in the Axtell lawsuit.

To many – including most that read about it in the papers the next several days – this filing of depositions at district court appeared to be standard procedure. It was anything but standard procedure. According to Travis County Chief Deputy Clerk Michelle Brinkman, the depositions should have never been filed.

"The depositions that were submitted by the attorney for Axtell are not filed in our records here," Brinkman said. "They're not supposed to be. We have not accepted depositions in this office for several years."

She said it wasn't until the morning of August 3 when the documents were being processed to the actual case record that they were discovered. At that point in time, Brinkman said she personally cancelled the file mark, called Rasmus and told her that the depositions were not to be filed and they needed to be returned.

"She indicated to me that she would have someone come by or she would come by herself to pick them up," Brinkman said. "I held them in my office through the end of the day. When no one had come that day to pick them up, I had my secretary mail them back." The return of the documents was too late. The damage had already been done.

In less than 12 hours, Penders' suspicions about information being leaked to the media that was disparaging to his character would be validated and he would look more like a prognosticator than a basketball coach.

Penders Tops News at 10

On the evening of August 3, the 10 o'clock news of Austin's ABC affiliate KVUE-24 led off their news with the Penders story. In fact, before the two anchors introduced themselves, they had already pointed the finger at Penders.

"A basketball scandal now points to the man at the top," Walt Maciborski, the news anchor said. Then, Maciborski, along with co-anchor Judy Maggio, introduced themselves.

Maggio then said, "KVUE-24 has new information showing the winningest coach in the program's history, apparently played a much bigger role in the scandal than first thought."

Maggio then reviewed the history of the Axtell case. As she described each stage, headlines were shown on the screen with a picture accompanying each stage.

"Players Complain About Penders."

"Penders Suspends Axtell."

"Axtell's Grades Anonymously Released to Radio Station."

"Penders Claims He is Unaware of the Fax."

Following her description of the last stage, Maggio introduced reporter Joel Thomas, who had investigated the case for months.

"Well, there were no answers about why Penders left or his role in releasing the grades, even after a high-level UT investigation," Thomas said.

Thomas then proceeded to quote from the depositions of Assistant Coach Eddie Oran, Administrative Office Assistant Leslie Parks, and Athletic Director DeLoss Dodds.

With the words from Oran's deposition displayed on the screen, Thomas read from the assistant coach's testimony. In it, Oran said he told Parks to fax the information.

Then, with words of Parks' testimony displayed, Thomas quoted from the secretary's testimony. She said Penders called and asked if she had sent the fax.

Thomas quoted Oran several more times. Oran said in his testimony that he took the blame because he was worried about Parks and he added that UT investigators knew the truth about the situation.

Then quotes from Dodds' deposition were shown on the screen.

In Dodds' deposition, Rasmus asked why was the truth not told once it was determined who authorized the fax.

Dodds: This was a matter of him having a contract and us dealing with legal counsel to resolve those issues.

Thomas, back on camera, said, "That contract not only guaranteed silence, it also guaranteed Penders more than a half-million dollars as he left."

Thomas added that Oran said Penders never asked him to lie, but he never offered to tell the whole story, either. Thomas concluded, "We were unable to contact Penders' attorney."

In an odd addendum to the story, Maggio said, "Joel, one more note to this story. Testimony from the athletic director states that at no time was Luke Axtell ineligible to play basketball because of his grades."

Rasmus' plan had worked. The media had taken the depositions and run with the information. This was just the first of many reports on the depositions and paled in comparison to the attention the story received in the next day's edition of the *Austin American-Statesman.*

Penders' Name Front and Center

On the front page of the August 4 edition of the paper, the top headline read: "The Coach, the Star and the Fax." Pictured were Penders, Dodds, Axtell, Parks and Oran.

The subheadline read "16 months later, newly released court papers help untangle the web surrounding the exit of UT basketball coach Tom Penders."

In the story, written by Suzanne Halliburton and Mark Rosner, the first two paragraphs alone lambasted Penders more than the news story on Channel 24 had done the night before. Not only did the article describe how Penders "orchestrated" the faxing of the grades according to statements filed, it also implied that Penders was unstable.

"The depositions, almost 1,000 pages of sworn statements from nine people, paint a picture of Penders as an erratic and volatile coach who made angry late-night phone calls to players and staff members and who allowed long-time assistant coach Eddie Oran to accept blame for his actions ... " the article stated.

The article then, very much like the story on television the night before, pulled quotes from the depositions of Oran and Parks. It said in Oran's testimony he accepted responsibility for the fax because he was concerned about Parks' health. "I don't think she could have gone through (the stress), so basically, I said I did it. I was thinking about her. Because when she came out of DeLoss' office that day, she was a wreck. And I said, 'I'm going to take care of this.'"

The following are excerpts of the depositions from several individuals including Eddie Oran, Brandy Perryman, DeLoss Dodds and Vic Trilli that ran in the *American-Statesman* article.

Oran's Deposition

In one of the first exchanges between Sherry Rasmus and Eddie Oran in Oran's deposition, Rasmus asked the assistant coach about his knowledge of the Buckley Amendment.

Rasmus: Okay, are you familiar with the Family Educational Rights to Privacy Act that addresses what we've just talked about; that is, before grades can be released, a student must give permission to release the grades.

Oran: I'm not familiar with that.

Rasmus: With the name Family Educational Rights and Privacy Act?

Oran: I'm not familiar with that.

Rasmus: Okay. But just the process?

Oran: Yes.

Rasmus: And before all this stuff blew up, had you ever heard of the Buckley Amendment?

Oran: No.

Rasmus: Okay. Do you know now what the Buckley Amendment is?

Oran: Yes.

Rasmus: What is your understanding of what the Buckley Amendment is?

Oran: The releasing of grades.

Rasmus: Without the student's permission?

Oran: Yes.

Rasmus: Were the coaches and staff at the University informed that grades and academic status were private and not to be released to anyone without permission of the student?

Oran: I can't recall that.

Rasmus: Can't recall ever having any kind of memorandum or any kind of meeting to remind you that you should never release students' grades absent their permission?

Oran: I never recall any meeting like that.

Rasmus: Do you recall hearing or reading that DeLoss Dodds told the press that everybody knows about the Buckley Amendment in college athletics?

(After an objection from Oran's attorney, Rasmus repeated the question.)

Rasmus: Do you recall reading in the press or hearing anywhere where DeLoss Dodds stated that, quote, 'Everybody knows about the Buckley Amendment in college athletics?'

Oran: I don't recall reading that.

Rasmus: But to the best of your recollection, there was no program or meeting, any kind of formal meeting, while you were employed by the University where they sat down and said, This is the Buckley Amendment, or This is Family Educational Rights and Privacy Act, or You should know never to release a student's grades without the student's permission? You don't recall anything like that happening?

Oran: No, I don't.

Rasmus: Do you know if Tom Penders knew what the Buckley Amendment was?

Oran: I don't know if he did or not.

Rasmus then asked Oran what the process was for coaches to receive academic information on student-athletes. Oran said the two men's basketball academic counselors, Curt Fludd and Othell Ballage, would report regularly to Penders.

Rasmus: Well, if Othell would report, for example, that one of the basketball players hadn't been going to study hall, what action would Mr. Penders take, if any?

Oran: He might up their hours for the week.

Rasmus: The study hall requirement hours?

Oran: Uh-huh. (Yes).

Rasmus: Do you know what the minimum requirement was for study hall?

Oran: I'm not sure.

Rasmus: Would Mr. Penders talk with a student athlete himself, or would he have someone else do it?

Oran: He would talk to them.

Rasmus: Is that something as far as you knew he always did?

Oran: Yes. Are you saying that anytime there was an academic problem that Tom – would Tom talk to them every time? Is that what you're saying?

Rasmus: Yes. That's my question.

Oran: There were occasions where maybe we would talk to them about going – they're short on hours, they will have to get their quota or even the academic person. But the majority of the time Tom was aware of and would mention something to them.

Rasmus: Okay. Academic problems – what would you consider to be an academic problem as it related to one of the basketball players?

Oran: Study hall hours, late on assignments, cutting class, low academic achievement on a grade – on their grade point.

Rasmus: Anything else?

Oran: Read those back to me, please.

Rasmus: Study hall hours, late on assignments, cutting class, low academic achievement?

Oran: I guess I could say the progress or their grades that they had – progress report as far as their grade, what their grades were up to that point.

Rasmus: Anything else? Tutoring, or was that with study hall?

Oran: Yeah, I think you'd have to classify that with study hall.

Rasmus: Anything else?

Oran: I may be leaving out something, but that's ...

Rasmus: That's the four things that stand out to you?

Oran: That stands out to me.

Rasmus: And if I understand your testimony, these academic problems would be reported to Tom Penders by either Curt Flud (sic) or Othell?

Oran: Yes.

Rasmus: And most of the time, Tom Penders would speak directly to the player about the academic problem, but sometimes the assistants would talk to the player, or Curt Fludd or Othell would talk to the player?

Oran: That's correct.

Rasmus then proceeded to ask Oran if he remembered, in his time under Penders, if anyone had been suspended from the team for academic reasons.

Rasmus: Last year Tom Penders suspended Luke from the basketball team for academic reasons. Can you – and he said it was because of lots of reasons. One of them was he missed study halls and tutoring, refused to go to tutoring. That was one of the published reasons. Can you remember or think of any player last year who was suspended from the basketball team for academic reasons besides Luke?

Oran: There wasn't anyone else.

Rasmus: Okay. Now, let's go back to the year before last. Can you remember any player being suspended from the basketball team for academic reasons?

Oran: I don't recall anybody.

Rasmus: Okay. Who can you recall being suspended from the basketball team for academic reasons before Luke Axtell last year?

Oran: Terrence Rencher, R-e-n-c-h-e-r.

Rasmus: And can you recall when that was?

Oran: Possibly '96. I would have to go back and look. I'm not sure.

Rasmus: Was he reinstated to the team?

Oran: Yes.

Rasmus: Was he then – I guess it's a natural question maybe or not, but was he suspended during the basketball season?

Oran: Yes.

Rasmus: And then reinstated shortly thereafter?

Oran: Yes.

Rasmus: Other than Luke Axtell, are you familiar with any player who has been suspended from the basketball team for academic reasons outside of the season after the season was over?

Oran: Albert Burditt, but I'm not sure of the timing.

Rasmus: When you say not sure of the timing, whether it was during the basketball season or after the season?

Oran: Right. I'm not sure if it was before the season started or during the season.

Rasmus: Okay. Can you think of any other players that have been suspended from the basketball team for academic reasons besides Terrence Rencher and Albert Burditt?

Oran: There may be more, but that's the two that come to my head.

Oddly, Oran remembered back to the suspensions of Rencher and Burditt, which actually took place in 1992 and 1993, but he forgot the suspension and dismissal of Lamar Wright for academic reasons, which had occurred just the year before.

Rasmus changed her line of questioning to unhappy players in the program.

Rasmus: Were you aware by the end of last season, the '97-'98 basketball season, that there were certain players who were unhappy with things that were going on in the basketball program at UT?

Oran: You're saying at the end of the year?

Rasmus: Uh-huh (Yes).

Oran: End of the season or –

Rasmus: End of the season. March of '98?

Oran: I think – anytime you go through a season that you're not on top or you're not winning, your people are disgruntled.

Rasmus: So did you hear disgruntlement from the players?

Oran: I saw discouragement because we were losing, and the majority of those guys had tasted a great deal of success.

Rasmus: Who did you recognize discouragement from?

Oran: Gabe. Gabe comes to my mind first. It's hard to pinpoint any really one or two guys; although, Gabe is – not contradicting, but Gabe was the guy that seemed to be a little discouraged.

Rasmus: Did he talk to you about it?

Oran: No. I guess it's hard to separate. Did you use the word 'disgruntled?'

Rasmus: No. That was your word.

Oran: Okay.

Rasmus: My word essentially was unhappy with things in the program?

Oran: I never really detected the unhappiness.

Rasmus then asked Oran about his knowledge of Axtell potentially transferring from the program.

Rasmus: Okay. When did you find out that Luke was going to transfer?

Oran: When did I find out that Luke was going to transfer? I'm not sure.

Rasmus: How did you find out about it?

Oran: About Luke? That Luke was going to transfer?

Rasmus: Yes. Or that he wanted to transfer, anyway?

Oran: I don't recall when it was, but I – I don't recall the time period or when it was, but I was told – and by who I was told by, I don't remember – that if Tom was coaching at Texas, Luke would not be back.

Rasmus: Was this before or after Luke was suspended from the team?

Oran: This was before.

Rasmus: Did you know of any kind of meeting between Luke and Tom Penders the week before Spring Break where Tom allegedly told Luke about his academic situation or his academic problems?

Oran: Tom told me he had a meeting with Luke.

Rasmus: When did Tom tell you he had a meeting with Luke?

Oran: Are you asking me when did Tom tell me about the meeting, or when did Tom –

Rasmus: Well, you said that Tom said that he had a meeting with Luke. Was this before the suspension?

Oran: Yes.

Rasmus: Did Tom tell you what the meeting was about?

Oran: No.

Rasmus: Did Tom tell you that he had information that Luke was having academic problems? And this is before everyone breaks for Spring Break.

Oran: I don't remember that.

Rasmus: You don't remember it happening.

Oran: I don't remember it happening.

Rasmus: Okay. Do you recall anyone coming to you and telling you that Luke Axtell was having academic problems at the conclusion of the 1998 basketball season before Spring Break?

Oran: Othell.

Rasmus: And what did Othell tell you?

Oran: Othell sent a memo around, various memos. I remember a memo saying that Luke was having trouble in three of his four courses or ...

Before Oran finished his statement, he was interrupted by Rasmus.

The statement from Oran that Axtell "was having trouble in three of his four courses" according to the memo from Othell Ballage, was contradictory to statements Rasmus made in the future with other witnesses in their depositions, as well as later statements made in Oran's deposition, in which she referred to the report as "inaccurate" or "incorrect." In fact, the wording of the lawsuit was based on this and stated it was to "pursue possible damages against radio stations KVET-AM and KJFK-FM for defamation of broadcasting an inaccurate academic progress report."

Rasmus continued, discussing the actual memo from academic counselor Ballage.

Rasmus: Coach, I want to show you what's been marked as Oran Exhibit No. 1. Have you seen that document before?

Oran: Have I seen this document before?

Rasmus: Yeah. Those four pieces of paper?

Oran: I've seen three of the four.

Rasmus: Okay. Let me ask you to look at the very last page. It's a letter dated March 10th, 1998 addressed to Curt, and it's signed O in quotes. Is that Curt Fludd that it's addressed to?

Oran: Yes.

Rasmus: And the "O" is Othell, correct?

Oran: Uh-huh (Yes).

Rasmus: And then it shows Tom, Eddie, Carlton, Rob and Alex being copied with the memo?

Oran: Right.

Rasmus: Is this a memo you're referring to now that you had received about Luke concerning his academic status?

Oran: Huh-uh (No).

Rasmus: What memo are you talking about?

Oran: I recall a memo that – I recall a memo that stated – yeah, I do remember this memo. This is it.

Rasmus: This is the memo you were just talking about earlier?

Oran: Yeah. About the three – yeah.

Rasmus: Oran: I was thinking there was a memo that stated grades, that classified the four subjects and the grades to each one of them.

Rasmus: Okay. But this is the memo, in fact?

Oran: I remember this memo now.

Rasmus asked Oran again whether or not he knew if Penders and Axtell had met before Penders suspended him.

Rasmus: Okay. If Luke's statement is that, as he was walking down the hall with Mihm to collect his mail, Penders called him in and said, 'You had a great season, work out in the gym; keep up in school; and we'll see you next year,' would you have any personal knowledge that anything different took place?

Oran: Do I have any personal knowledge of anything different?

Rasmus: Yes, sir.

Oran: Only thing that I was – I was told by Tom – I don't know the time frame or when it was. Tom basically told me that his meeting with Luke – now, whether – like I say, I can't tell you the time frame – was if he didn't get his grades up, he was going to suspend him, and that's what Tom is telling me.

Rasmus: Okay. And you don't remember when this conversation took place –

Oran: No, I don't.

Rasmus: – in connection with all the other things that happened?

Oran: It was after the suspension -

Rasmus: Okay.

Oran: – is the only thing I can remember.

Rasmus: Okay.

Obviously, Oran was confused about the time frame of the meeting between Penders and Axtell as he had said earlier in the deposition that the meeting between the two had occurred before the suspension.

Oran was then asked to explain the timing of his gathering Axtell's academic information.

Rasmus: Did Tom Penders tell you to send the fax that morning?

Oran: Not exactly. I mean, did Tom tell me to send the fax?

Rasmus: Yes.

Oran: He told me to gather information.

Rasmus: Okay.

Oran: Solely to send the fax? Is that what you're saying?

Rasmus: Well, my question to you was, did he tell you to send the fax that morning when you talked to him?

Oran: He did not tell me to send the fax.

Rasmus: Okay. He told you to gather information?

Oran: Uh-huh (Yes).

Rasmus: What kind of information did he ask you to gather?

Oran: Well, the information was gathered on the academics prior to that day.

Rasmus: Okay. The information being the Progress Reports Spring 1998?

Oran: Yes.

Rasmus: Study Hall Detailed Report?

Oran: Uh-huh (Yes).

Rasmus: And the memo to Curt from Othell -

Oran: Uh-huh (Yes).

Rasmus: – dated March 10th, 1998?

Oran: Right.

Rasmus: When was this information accumulated or gathered?

Oran: Oh, I don't recall if it was Monday or Tuesday of that week.

Rasmus: The week of Spring Break?

Oran: Yes.

Rasmus: During Spring Break? Okay. And who gathered it?

Oran: I did.

Rasmus: And why did you gather it?

Oran: I was told to gather it.

Rasmus: Who told you to gather it?

Oran: Tom.

Rasmus: Did he tell you why he wanted it gathered?

Oran: No. He just wanted the information on the academics.

Several minutes later, Rasmus asked Oran what he knew about the accuracy of Axtell's academic information.

Rasmus: Okay. Where did you get the document that's attached to this fax as Exhibit 1, Progress Reports Spring 1998?

Oran: Where did I get this?

Rasmus: Yes, sir.

Oran: From Curt Fludd.

Rasmus: Okay. Did you tell – did you know why you were accumulating this information other than Tom said to?

Oran: No.

Rasmus: Okay. Did Curt ask you why you wanted it?

Oran: No.

Rasmus: Okay. Do you know whose writing this is here (indicating)?

Oran: I do not.

Rasmus: Do you know whose writing this is here (indicating)?

Oran: I do.

Rasmus: Whose writing is that?

Oran: Mine.

Rasmus: Okay. Where did you get the information to write?

Oran: That (indicating)?

Rasmus: Yes.

Oran: From Curt Fludd.

Rasmus: Okay. Do you -

Oran's attorney makes a note for the record that the language the witness is pointing to identifies Axtell's first-term grade point average and then has four letters next to it.

Rasmus: Right. And 12 hours total.

Oran: Uh-huh (Yes).

Rasmus: Coach, do you know that this information is incorrect?

Oran: Do I know now that it's incorrect?

Rasmus: Well, sure.

Oran: Did I know that I was writing down wrong information?

Rasmus: Yes, sir.

Oran: I didn't know that.

Rasmus: Okay. Do you know now that it's incorrect?

Oran: You're telling me it is.

Rasmus: Yes, sir. Okay. That's the first time?

Oran: I mean, I'm knowing because you're telling me now, but this was – I wrote down verbatim what Curt Fludd told me.

After several minutes discussing the number of days missed in a semester by players due to travel for basketball games on the road, Rasmus asked Oran about another report.

Rasmus: The next document is the study hall report that's attached. What's the purpose of this report attached to this fax? Why were you asked to compile that information?

Oran: It's the number of hours. As I stated earlier, I'm not sure how many hours they were attending – supposedly to attend in study hall, whether it was eight to 10 to 12 or whatever. This was – this was each week, third week, fourth week, fifth week, sixth week, seventh week, and it totaled the number of hours that he was in study hall for the week.

Rasmus: Okay.

Oran: All right.

Rasmus: Do you know if there were other players at the same time as this schedule shows that failed to meet minimum study hall hourly requirements?

Oran: I don't know if they were or not.

Rasmus: Okay. If the evidence is that there were other players who missed study hall in this same time frame and didn't meet the total number of hours required for study hall, do you know why Luke was singled out?

Oran: No.

Rasmus: Okay. And then this memo we've talked about, were you asked to attach or compile this information by Tom Penders as well to include this memo? Let me rephrase that question, Coach. When Tom Penders asked you to compile academic information about Luke Axtell, why did you include this memo?

Oran: I guess to back up the statement that he was struggling in class.

This statement was conflicting. Instead of Oran saying he included the study hall report on the orders of Penders, which he would say later in his deposition, he acknowledged that he included this information on his own volition. Ironically, this was along the same lines of his statement quoted in March of 1998. "I took it upon myself to let the local media know the truth ... I was never ordered to do this action and never discussed it with anyone until after being interviewed by the (UT) attorneys."

Rasmus continued.

Rasmus: Okay. Tom Penders' statement to the press that that's why he suspended Luke, but this was before – this was compiled before the suspension, correct, Monday or Tuesday?

Oran: What day was the suspension?

Rasmus: Tuesday evening it was published.

Oran: This was compiled before.

Rasmus: Okay. Did you specific – do you remember specifically looking for this memorandum, or was this in Luke's file? Did Luke have a file?

Oran: I don't remember looking for just that. I mean, this was the information that was given to me through Curt Fludd.

Rasmus: Okay. So these three pieces of paper that are attached to the cover sheet of the fax were all provided to you by Curt?

Oran: Yes.

Rasmus: When you asked him for academic information concerning Luke Axtell?

Oran: Yes.

Rasmus: Which you asked at the request and instruction of Tom Penders?

Oran: Yes.

Rasmus then asked Oran why he took the blame for the fax. Oran, as was quoted in the *Statesman* article, said he believed Leslie Parks, the administrative assistant to whom he had given Axtell's academic information, wouldn't be able to handle the turmoil if she had taken responsibility for the actual faxing of the grades. He said Parks, after an earlier miscarriage, had – at the time – discovered she was pregnant again and he didn't want to burden her with any undue emotional stress.

Oran: ...So I was thinking about her. Because when she came out of DeLoss's office that day, she was a wreck. And I said, I'm going to take care of this. So I went in and said I did it. I just didn't want to see her go through ...

Rasmus: Through anymore problems?

Oran: Uh-huh (Yes). But I mean, I just ... I don't think she could have gone through it. So basically I said I did it.

Rasmus: What was happening on the other end with Tom Penders that you couldn't tell DeLoss Dodds that Tom Penders was the one that authorized the transmitting of that academic information?

Oran: DeLoss knew the truth.

Rasmus: And albeit DeLoss knew that Tom Penders had authorized the transmittal of this fax information, he allowed you to accept responsibility for it in the public?

Oran: Uh-huh (Yes). He knew.

Rasmus: How do you know he knew, just if you do? I mean, I know we know a lot, but is there -

Oran: Because I told him.

Rasmus: Okay. So you admitted to DeLoss everything that transpired in connection with compiling that information and faxing it to – or having it for Leslie to fax to Bill Schoening?

Oran nods head affirmatively.

Several questions later, Rasmus asked Oran about his feelings following the release of the article in which Penders said Oran was responsible for sending out the fax.

Rasmus: ...In this article, it goes, 'Tom Penders was calmly explaining that it was his assistant Eddie Oran who sent a fax to the radio station that broadcast the report. In quotes, 'Eddie told me this afternoon,' Penders said from the Caribbean island of St. Martin where he is vacationing, 'I heard from the University lawyer Patty – Patricia Ohlendorf- they wanted to investigate. Eddie just said he didn't know he couldn't do it. He thought that, with all the things that were being written and being said on the radio, he didn't think there was anything wrong with it.' None of that is true, is it, Penders' statements there?

Oran: That's Penders' statements?

Rasmus: Right. Because you didn't tell any of that to Tom Penders, did you?

Oran: I told Tom I did it, you know, after I went into the attorneys.

Rasmus: You told Tom that you gave the information to Leslie as he instructed you?

Oran: He knew. I told him I took the blame.

Rasmus: Did he ask you to take the blame -

Oran: No.

Rasmus: – at any point in time?

Oran: No.

Oran was asked if university attorney Patricia Ohlendorf knew the circumstances surrounding the fax of Axtell's academic progress report.

Rasmus: Did you tell Patricia Ohlendorf the truth about how all this transpired?

Oran: She knew the truth, also.

Rasmus: Do you know from whom she learned of the truth?

Oran: Do I know whom?

Rasmus: Uh-huh (Yes).

Oran: Me.

Rasmus: Did you tell her how all of this transpired?

Oran: With Leslie or just all this?

Rasmus: From the very beginning. From the time you were asked to compile the academic information about Luke Axtell including the time that Tom Penders instructed you to give it to Leslie, including Tom Penders instructing Leslie to fax it to Bill Schoening.

Oran: I'm not sure if I talked to her and told her everything, but my last conversation with her she basically knew and went over some of our conversations that we had had prior to meeting in DeLoss's office.

Several minutes later and nearing the conclusion of Oran's deposition, Rasmus asked about Oran's first meeting with UT officials after the fax was sent.

Rasmus: Okay. Tell me what they talked to you about at your meeting – the first meeting –

Oran: At the Marriott?

Rasmus: – at the Marriott.

Oran: They basically told me that they had talked to a number of people. I don't recall if they really told me who. I remember they said they talked to Leslie. That's the only person I can remember. I remember – I remember them stating, said 'Did Tom Penders tell you to get – send the fax?' And I wouldn't answer. Then at that time I had received a phone call from Tom going to the Marriott, and I did not tell Tom I was going to the Marriott because I didn't know what it was about. I guess I felt like DeLoss was following up on the March 13th, let's get together, let's keep in touch, let's talk. And I really didn't put it all together. So I told them that I didn't feel comfortable in being there because, you know, I – I didn't know what was going on, They said, 'Did Tom tell you to send the fax?' And I just told them – I just – I clammed up. I wouldn't talk. They said, 'Could Tom have told you to send the fax?' And I said yes. They said, 'We know the truth. We know the truth because we've talked to Leslie.' And then they – if they mentioned other people, I don't recall. At that time, I told them 'I just wish that I – you know, right now I wish I was not a coach at The University of Texas,' from what I was, you know, going through. So they said, 'We're going to go back to the office, and here is how the procedures go. Leslie is going to meet; you're going to meet,' blah, blah, blah. So I said okay. So I go back and Leslie is in there, and Leslie is in there forever, it seems like. And when she comes out, that's when I – see her, and that's when I decide. When I walk in, then that starts the second meeting.

Rasmus: And what happened in that meeting?

Oran: Patty said, 'Tell us what you said at breakfast,' and this meeting included W.O. Schultz (sic), and I said, 'I did it.' She says, 'What?' And I said, 'I did it.' I said, 'I take all the responsibility. Punish me.' She said, 'Why are you taking up for Tom? We know he did it.' And I just – we sat there for an hour, and I probably didn't say 10 words. I just said, 'I did it.' So at that time, they told me to go home, get some rest and then talk to them tomorrow. I went home and got rest, and I was able to relax and everything, but the next day at the tower they kept saying, 'Why are you – why are you doing this? Why are you taking up for Tom? Why are you protecting Tom? Would he do it for you? Did you know that he released the grades?' and all – I mean, it was very little conversation. I took the blame.

Rasmus: Do you think they were offering you an opportunity to get out of it, though, and to put the blame where it belonged, on Penders?

Oran: I don't know.

Rasmus: Did you talk with Leslie on how the meeting with her went? I mean, were you concerned?

Oran: No. I just looked her in the eyes. I knew how it went.

Rasmus: Were you concerned about her taking a fall for this?

Oran: She couldn't have handled it.

Rasmus: I understand that. Did you have any indication that she might be subject to some disciplinary action versus Tom Penders?

Oran: Possibly. I didn't really think that much about that as much as I thought about her.

Rasmus: How about, as far as you were concerned if you were to admit releasing this, contrary to what we know now is contrary to the federal law and the privacy acts and several other different things, what concerns, if any, did you have about your well-being in admitting to something that you didn't do?

Oran: Well, I guess – I guess I wasn't thinking in those terms. I was always raised as a coach and as a player to be loyal, and I was thinking of her. I mean, I – I guess if something happened and then maybe I would have changed my story or something. Maybe it came to this – has come to this point here, but ...

Rasmus then cut off Oran.

After asking Oran several questions about the contact he had had with Penders since the incident, the deposition ended.

According to Parks' testimony, Penders was involved. "When I came into the office (March 18), the first thing that happened, Coach Oran told me Tom wanted us to send a fax to Bill Schoening (with KVET) and Bill Simonson (KJFK). ...Penders called at some point in the morning from the Caribbean and asked me if I had sent the fax. And I hadn't sent it at the time and I told him so ... And then he called back again later that day. And again, I don't remember the time. But he asked me if I had sent it.

And at the time, I had, I told him I had sent it."

The article then quoted Rasmus several paragraphs later.

"The goal has been to get both sides of the story out there," Rasmus said. "We've heard what Mr. Penders has had to say. In these depositions, we've found out what really happened in the case of Luke's suspension and the release of his academic records."

The story then stated: "Penders was not asked to give a deposition."

"We've already heard what Mr. Penders has to say," Rasmus said. "He's already been quoted in numerous papers and in the media. We didn't expect his side of the story would change any under oath."

The article then explored the depositions of several players including Kris Clack, Brandy Perryman and DeJuan "Chico" Vazquez.

In the depositions of Clack and Vazquez, both players testified that they were called to Penders' home several days after Axtell was suspended and Penders suggested they hold a press conference to discuss allegations about verbally abusing players.

The article then quoted Vazquez and Perryman, who said that Penders had called them several times late at night after games to criticize their play.

According to the article, Perryman was asked by Rasmus if he was a victim of Penders' verbal abuse, Perryman said: "It was never on the court. It was always off the court. Late night phone calls ... He would call me. 'You lost the game for us. If I could trade you, I would for another player on a different team. Who the hell recruited you? Who the hell gave you a scholarship?' But at the same token, I think there are probably a lot of Division I coaches that do the same."

In the next paragraph, Perryman said Penders "would slur his speech a little bit during the calls."

Perryman's Deposition

In Perryman's deposition, several other key exchanges occurred between Rasmus and the former Texas player that were omitted from the article. In the first, which happened around the midway point of the deposition, Perryman is questioned about a discussion he had with athletic director, DeLoss Dodds.

Rasmus: Did you and DeLoss talk about anything else during that meeting?

Perryman: Yeah. We talked about my family a little bit and what I want to do next year. He brought up the subject of Coach Penders' health.

Rasmus: And what did he talk to you about concerning Coach Penders' health?

Perryman: He –

Rasmus: And this is what he brought up?

Perryman: Yeah. He asked me – basically, he just said his heart wasn't well, and they were going to try and get him some help like they had all season, but try to get him to relax a little bit.

Rasmus: Anything else discussed?

Perryman: The alcohol topic came up.

Rasmus: And under what context, Mr. Perryman, did that come up?

Perryman: I don't even remember. I don't know. I think he brought it up, and he asked me questions about it. And I just – you know, I said the same thing, late night phone calls, and the thought maybe – there was a possibility that he could have been drinking, but I didn't know for sure.

Moments later, the subject of Perryman's discussion with Dodds resurfaced.

Rasmus: He brought up the alcohol topic. But did you have a sense that he knew that there was a problem with respect to Penders and alcohol?

(After an objection from Perryman's attorney, Perryman answered the question.)

Perryman: I'm not sure. I mean, I want to say that he knew, but I don't know. He could have been asking because he has heard other people say it. I don't – I don't really know.

Rasmus: What was your sense?

Perryman: I just answered the question. I didn't think about it.

Rasmus: When it came up, were you surprised that it – the topic came up?

Perryman: A little bit.

Rasmus: Why were you surprised?

Perryman: Because the athletic director was talking to a player about the head coach.

Rasmus: And that topic in particular?

Perryman: Well, all the stuff involved, the health, everything in the meeting.

Several questions later, the line of questioning returned back to the meeting between Perryman and Dodds.

Rasmus: Okay. In the meeting with Mr. Dodds, he talked to you about getting Mr. Penders' help concerning his health?

Perryman: He said that when the season was over, it would be a lot easier. I mean, he had been going seeing doctors while the season was on and missed a lot of practices and things like that, which is totally understandable. But he was saying that, once the season ended that, you know, he could go do what they had to do. I don't know if it was surgery or, you know, get – run a bunch of tests or whatever.

Rasmus: Okay. Did – I mean – but I guess what I'm asking you, did Mr. Dodds say something about, We've got to get the guy help, or Something is wrong, or -

Perryman: No. I mean, he just simply said that, We know he's hurting, physically sick. We need to get him better.

Rasmus then abruptly changed the line of questioning.

Rasmus: Okay. In the past when you – or said at one point in time that DeLoss lets coaches hang themselves, what were you thinking about, or what was your meaning in connection with that?

Perryman: Just that instead of DeLoss stepping up and either firing a coach or whatever, he lets the coaches take care of themselves. I mean, there is two different kinds of ADs in my mind. There is one that lets the coaches go about their business and if they lose and lose, and then they determine their own fate. There is another kind that, you know, if they lose one year or they do one bad thing, then they fire them. So DeLoss is just one of them guys that lets you hang around until you really screw up or you lose a lot.

A few minutes later, Rasmus broached a sensitive subject – involvement of alumni with the program. Two names, familiar to the basketball controversy of March 1998, were mentioned. These same names would also appear later in the depositions of Dodds and Trilli.

Rasmus: Did any alumni give you a hard time about not saying publicly about what was going on?

Perryman: Yes.

Rasmus: Who was that?

Perryman: Russell Douglas (sic)

Rasmus: And do you know why?

Perryman: He wanted me to come out and tell the papers and tell the media the truth. And at that time, I was trying to get a coaching job, and coaches are a pretty tight community.

Rasmus: What was the subject matter that he wanted you to speak out about?

Perryman: I want to assume that it's the alcohol. But I – again. I don't know. I never really talked to him, actually, when all this went down. He just – left a message one time. And he called my dad. And once he talked to my dad, we were done after that. I never talked to him.

Rasmus: Can you think of any other information that he would think – I'm talking about subject matter only. I'm not asking you for details in this question. But can you think of any other topics that he would expect you or ask you to come out about with respect to truth of what was going on, other than what you've just said?

Perryman: Maybe just the well-being of the kids and the people that are in the program now. At that time, a lot of people were – or rumored to transfer. And the guys in alumni, he wanted everybody to stay because we had a pretty good shot this year, everybody with them.

Rasmus: The two topics that you think he wanted you to talk about, maybe the alcohol, maybe the well-being of the kids, did you have any one-to-one conversation with Mr. Douglass about it?

Perryman: No, because when it happened, I was in Colorado, like I said, and he was trying to track me down. Called my father, talked to my father, I don't know how long. But they exchanged words and they got into it, and my father said something, don't ever talk to my son again. I think that's where it was left at.

Rasmus: Okay. I imagine your father would have some concern about putting you in the middle of the controversy?

Perryman: Exactly.

Rasmus: The two subjects, again, that you assume or think that he may have wanted you to come out on, did he leave you messages on your answering machine, or this is just something you think?

Perryman: He just left a message with my parents to call him.

Rasmus: Okay.

Perryman: And I never called him.

Rasmus: Okay. Did you have a conversation with anyone else here in Austin, an alum or anyone not related to the basketball program as a staff member or faculty member?

Perryman: Bill Wendlandt.

Rasmus: And can you tell me what that conversation was about – and concerning this controversy? And the controversy being the faxing of Luke's grades and what developed at the University thereafter.

Perryman: I don't know. You've got one of them on tape. (Perryman is referring to a taped conversation between himself and Wendlandt that Wendlandt taped, and was gathered as evidence in the case.) And then there is only one other time that we went out to lunch, and I really don't recall what we talked about then.

(Rasmus then requests for the deposition to go off the record. After a brief discussion off the record, the deposition continued.)

Rasmus: Mr. Perryman, you indicated you had two conversations with Mr. Wendlandt. Can you tell me – one was at lunch and one was another telephone conversation; is that right?

Perryman: Yes.

Rasmus: Can you tell me with respect to the telephone conversation what you recall discussing in connection with the controversy that arose following the suspension of Luke Axtell and the faxing of his grades from the men's basketball office?

Perryman: There was nothing about faxing the grades. It was about Coach Penders' late night phone calls, was basically it.

Rasmus: Okay. And the lunch that you had with Mr. Wendlandt, what, if anything, did you all discuss concerning, if anything, this controversy?

Perryman: I can't recall. I know we went to Schlotzsky's, but I don't remember what we said.

In one of several quotes from Penders in the *American-Statesman* article, he told the paper that UT officials had been trying to get rid of him for two years by spreading rumors that he had been abusing alcohol. "It's so ridiculous that I don't mind talking about it," Penders said.

Then, the story delved into more information from the depositions that was unrelated to the faxing of grades.

It said: "Rasmus did ask several witnesses under oath about whether Penders had a drinking problem. She asked Dodds whether alumni had expressed concerns that Penders' overuse of alcohol was affecting Penders' ability to coach."

"Dodds responded: 'Over a period of time, several people talked to me about that. And I can't recall when, where, names, but I did have conversations with alums about that.'"

Dodds' Deposition

Although the *American-Statesman* article never quoted Dodds on the specific names of alumni, Dodds mentioned several in his deposition.

Rasmus: During the '97-'98 basketball season, can you recall any other players besides Brandy Perryman coming to you to talk about concerns they have with their situation in the basketball program?

Dodds: During the season?

Rasmus: Yes.

Dodds: No.

Rasmus: How about outside of the season?

Dodds: After the season.

Rasmus: Okay. And tell me about that.

Dodds: I received a call from Bill Wendlandt, who is an alum ex-basketball player, and he told me that there were several student athletes from the basketball team that would like to visit with me, and I told him that I would be happy to do that.

Rasmus: Do you recall when this took place?

Dodds: The telephone call from Bill Wendlandt was sometime before the Big 12 Basketball Tournament last year.

Rasmus: All right, sir. And what else was involved in the conversation of this particular telephone call?

Dodds: He said that the young men would like to talk to me about the basketball program, and he felt that it would do me good to hear them, and I agreed to do that. And we did that, I believe, on the Sunday following the Big 12 Basketball Tournament.

After discussing the meeting with the four players, Rasmus asked Dodds about his conversations with Eddie Oran and the discontent with some players on the basketball team.

Rasmus: During the '97-'98 season, what conversations do you recall having with Eddie Oran concerning the basketball program?

Dodds: I was concerned about unhappy players. Eddie and I had conversations about unhappy players, and Eddie was trying to help correct that during that year, and those conversations were about that.

Rasmus: Can you recall any other player besides Brandy Perryman, then, coming to you before the meeting at the end of the season?

Dodds: I can't.

Rasmus: Do you know the source of your information that there were – when you say 'unhappy players,' I take it that there is more than one. Can you recall the source you had with respect to information you gained that there were unhappy players?

Dodds: I think it was a general rumor that we had unhappy players, and I was hearing it from several places, inside the department and out. I can't recall names of people who would have had those conversations with me.

Rasmus: When you had these conversations with Eddie Oran about unhappy players, did he appear to be aware of it as well?

Dodds: Yes.

Rasmus: What plan, if any, did you and/or Eddie develop to deal with the unhappy player situation?

Dodds: Our conversation pretty much was around the fact that Tom had had some health problems with his heart, and that was the issue. And we thought that as Tom improved on the health side, that the situation would improve with the players. He had been at Texas 10 years and had had happy players for most of those 10 years.

Rasmus: From your perspective, how do you believe Tom's health problems created a situation of unhappy players?

Dodds: I can't – I can't answer that. I'm not a doctor or – to know how that all works, but it seemed that that was the new thing. That was what was different. He had had happy players prior to that. And at this time, he had the health problem, and we had unhappy players. I can't explain why it was the way it was.

Several questions later, the subject returned back to Dodds' meeting with the four players.

Rasmus: When the four players came to meet with you at your home on that Sunday afternoon, did they indicate to you that they didn't believe they could play for Tom Penders any longer?

Dodds: Yes.

Rasmus: Did they talk about transfers?

Dodds: Yes.

Rasmus: Did all –

Dodds: To –

Rasmus: I'm sorry?

Dodds: To different degrees.

Rasmus: Okay. Did Chris Mihm talk to you about transfers at the Sunday meeting?

Dodds: I think his conversation was more, I want to stay at Texas, but I cannot continue if this situation continues. And he talked about transferring with me individually.

Rasmus: When the four players indicated they didn't believe they could play for Penders any longer, what do you think would have been the resolution? For the players to transfer or for there to be a coaching change?

Dodds: Well, you know, I can't guess what way we would have gone because we never got to that point. But when I talked to Coach Penders, I told him we needed to get it fixed.

Rasmus: Gabe Muoneke, did he talk about transferring during the Sunday meeting?

Dodds: I think that he did. I can't recall for sure.

Rasmus: Did Bernard Smith talk about –

Dodds: I don't recall.

Rasmus: – transfer?

Dodds: I'm sorry.

Rasmus: That's all right.

Dodds: I don't recall Bernard speaking much in that meeting, but it was pretty clear that he was thinking about transferring.

Several questions later, Rasmus again broached the subject of conversations with Bill Wendlandt.

Rasmus: After the meeting on Sunday, did you have any follow-up conversations with Bill Wendlandt?

Dodds: There were a lot of conversations in there with a lot of different people, and I'm not going to be able to tell you whether I did or I didn't. I think I probably did. I think he came by my house one night and had a conversation with me about something relative to this. I've even tried to remember what that was, and I can't. So I'm sure I did, but I can't remember what they were.

A few minutes later, Rasmus pursued the conversations between Dodds and Penders prior to the suspension of Axtell.

Rasmus: Okay. And can you tell me the nature of that conversation?

Dodds: We may have talked two or three different times. I know I called him one time in the middle of the afternoon and talked to him for probably an hour, less than an hour, but somewhere in that range. His conversation was that he was going to suspend Luke Axtell. And I tried for an hour to talk him out of doing that. I told him that Luke had told us both that he was transferring and that he should not suspend him. I think it was about an hour conversation. I talked to Susie some about it, too, and told him to talk about it, and that I would call them back in a half an hour or so, hoping that they would – had resolved it and not suspended Luke.

Rasmus: Did Penders say why he intended to suspend Luke?

Dodds: I can't remember exactly what his conversation was. He was – he was upset about Luke saying he was transferring. And he was talking about a person – an individual that he had suspended prior to that for academic reasons, and thought to be consistent, he should do Luke, too.

Rasmus: Are we talking about Burditt?

Dodds: I prefer not to say.

Rasmus: The player who was suspended by Penders prior was actually academically ineligible according to the NCAA rules and Big 12 and Texas, correct.

Dodds: I can't answer that. I don't know.

In this discussion with Rasmus, Dodds, for whatever reason, was hesitant to correct Rasmus and point out that it was Lamar Wright who was dismissed from the team, and who was still academically eligible at the time of his dismissal.

Several questions later, Dodds and Rasmus resumed discussion of the conversation between Penders and Dodds regarding the Axtell suspension.

Rasmus: In the hour conversation or almost hour conversation that you had with Penders with respect to the suspension of Luke Axtell, how did you try to dissuade Penders from suspending Luke? What did you tell him?

Dodds: I talked to him about the other youngsters that were involved in my conversations on Sunday and Thursday and tried to dissuade him to be working on that side of the issue and letting go of the Luke issue. I talked to him about, if he suspended Luke, that would exacerbate the issue, and that it would become – the issue would probably become public, and that would be more harmful to the program and to the individuals involved.

Rasmus: And how did he respond to the concerns you raised with him?

Dodds: Well, he obviously – in my second conversation with him that day, when I called him back to find out if he were or were not going to suspend Luke, he said that he was. And I said to him, Tom, it is your program, and it is your program to run. I disagree with what you're doing, but ...

Rasmus: Is there a written authority given to a coach or is there anything in writing given to a coach that permits them to suspend a student athlete?

Dodds: Those things are in our policy manual, and I would have to go back and look at them. If we have those kinds of issues come up with coaches, they talk to me generally and we talk through it. And most often, or almost always, I allow them to act on their own on those kinds of things.

Rasmus then asked Dodds why he didn't put a stop to the suspension if he believed it was going to be a detriment to the program.

Rasmus: As athletic director, do you have the authority to override the coach's decision if you believe that it's in the best interest of men's athletics?

Dodds: Yes, I do.

Rasmus: In this specific instance with respect to the suspension of Luke Axtell, did you consider overriding Tom Penders' decision to do so?

Dodds: I considered it and did not.

Rasmus: And why not?

Dodds: These coaches run these programs, and I try to let them run their programs, and give them the resources to run them, and I let them run them, and very seldom do I tell them what to do or what not to do. I give them good advice, generally, and that's what I felt I was doing here.

Rasmus: Even though it was your opinion that this suspension would be to the detriment of the program and men's athletics?

Dodds: I thought it would be a detriment to Tom Penders and the program.

Rasmus then focused on Dodds' knowledge of whether Penders and Axtell had met to discuss the student-athlete's academic status.

Rasmus: Do you have any information that Penders talked to Luke about his academic situation?

Dodds: I don't.

Rasmus: When Penders spoke to you for almost an hour on the telephone that day, did he tell you that he had already discussed Luke's academic situation with Luke?

Dodds: I don't recall that.

Rasmus: To the best of your knowledge, then, at this point in time and from information from Penders, you have no information at all that Penders talked to Luke about his academic situation before deciding to suspend him?

Dodds: I don't recall that, no.

Rasmus then asked Dodds about his conversation with Penders and the Buckley Amendment.

Rasmus: Did he say something about what he was going to do, if anything?

Dodds: He said that he was going to see that the media found out what Luke Axtell's academic situation was.

Rasmus: And how did you respond to that?

Dodds: I told him that that was something he could not do because of the Buckley Amendment.

Rasmus: And what did he say?

Dodds: He said that there were – that he could get it out in other ways. And I told him that he could not get it out, that it was a violation of the Buckley Amendment, and he could not do that.

Rasmus: And how did he respond to that?

Dodds: I don't recall how the conversation ended, other than me telling him that he could not put out any academic information on Luke Axtell.

Rasmus: Did you have concerns as to whether or not he would go along with you on that?

Dodds: Not until the end of the day.

Rasmus: As far as you were concerned, when your conversation ended on that telephone call, you didn't have any concerns that Penders would find a way to get the information out to the media?

Dodds: Well, I had thoughts about it, but I thought I had covered it with him.

Several questions later, Rasmus returned to the same conversation between Penders and Dodds.

Rasmus: All right. Let's back up, and let's go back to the morning. You had a telephone conversation with Tom Penders wherein he was expressing his upset about the article that occurred in the – that was presented in the paper on Wednesday, March 18th. Do you know how he saw that article?

Dodds: No, I do not.

Rasmus: What time of day did you have that conversation with Mr. Penders?

Dodds: It would have been sometime probably early morning, 9 o'clock, sometime in that range.

Rasmus: Okay. And at that point in time, Tom Penders threatened to get the information about Luke Axtell's academic status out to the media?

Dodds: That's accurate.

Rasmus: And you specifically told him that to do that would be a violation of the Buckley Amendment?

Dodds: I did.

Rasmus: Did you use the terms 'Buckley Amendment?'

Dodds: I did.

Rasmus: When you used the term "Buckley Amendment" and the provision of Luke's academic status being a violation of that amendment, did Penders understand what you were saying?

(After an objection from Dodds' attorney, Dodds answered the question.)

Dodds: I don't know the answer.

Rasmus: Did Mr. Penders respond to you when you told him that the release of Luke's academic status would be a violation of the Buckley Amendment?

Dodds: Say it one more time.

Rasmus: Did Tom Penders respond to you that the release of Luke Axtell's grades to the media would be a violation of the Buckley Amendment?

Dodds: He responded that there were other ways to get it out. And I told him that there were no other ways to get it out, that any of that would be a Buckley Amendment violation.

Rasmus: Were you clear and concise to him about that?

Dodds: Yes.

Rasmus: Were you unequivocal that any release of Luke Axtell's academic status by him would be a violation of the Buckley Amendment?

Dodds: Yes.

Rasmus: Were you unequivocal to him that any such release by him would be unacceptable to you as athletic director and his boss?

Dodds: I don't remember whether I said those words.

Rasmus: What was your tone or – about it?

Dodds: Firm.

When asked about this particular conversation, Penders said essentially with Dodds' remarks, he was admitting that he knew a violation of the Buckley Amendment was going to be committed before it ever happened, and did nothing to stop it.

"He's got control of the department and all the fax machines and computers," Penders said. "I'm down there (in St. Martin) and I'm supposed to have done this, and he can't put a stop to it. He's saying if he knew this was against the law, then he was an accessory to it."

Penders said if this conversation with Dodds had actually happened, why didn't Dodds ever mention any of it when everything occurred back in March 1998. "Why didn't he bring up this discussion back then (about violating the Buckley Amendment)?" Penders asked. "Because he's talking about a conversation that never existed," he said, answering his own question.

Later in the deposition, there is another brief exchange between Dodds and Rasmus regarding Axtell's academic status and the policy surrounding his suspension.

Rasmus: As far as school policy, The University of Texas school policy, Big 12 rules, or the NCAA rules were concerned, there was no basis for Penders to suspend Luke Axtell for academic reasons, was there?

Dodds: Those are team matters that coaches establish their own criteria for.

Rasmus: But as far as school policy, Big 12 rules, and NCAA rules, there was no basis for Luke to be suspended?

Dodds: Right.

Several questions later Rasmus asked Dodds about the incident when Penders reported the parents of Chris Mihm may have violated NCAA rules by taking a flight to a basketball game.

Rasmus: My question is, what was the background to Penders turning in The University of Texas to the NCAA about a flight that Chris Mihm's parents took to Oklahoma State? Do you recall that controversy coming up?

Dodds: I recall Penders contacting Barbara Walker and meeting with her and giving her that information.

Rasmus: Did you look into the situation yourself?

Dodds: Barbara talked to me about it. She looked into the situation.

Rasmus: And did she report to you her findings after looking into that situation?

Dodds: It's a long, drawn-out scenario, but yes, she did.

Rasmus: Okay. And what was the conclusion?

Dodds: The conclusion, as I recall it, is that the Mihms had to pay back to the people that provided the airplane for their transportation money for the flight.

Rasmus returned to the topic of Penders and the release of Axtell's grades. Dodds was asked if Penders was indeed responsible for the fax, why wasn't he punished?

Rasmus: Mr. Dodds, under the circumstances where you specifically instructed your employee, Tom Penders, to not release any academic information concerning Luke Axtell and specifically warned him that it would violate the Buckley Amendment and there was no way in which he could get around it to release that information to the media, when he ignored your warning and went on against your direct order and authorized the release of Axtell's academic report, as athletic director, would that be grounds for termination from your standpoint?

Dodds: Tom had a contract, and because of that contract and I needed legal advice on that, I went to attorneys to work through the process.

Rasmus: Okay. Within the contract itself, it provides that the coach will adhere to school policy, does it not?

Dodds: That's correct.

Rasmus: And that failure to do so may be grounds for termination?

Dodds: That's correct.

Based on these words by Dodds and his previous explanation that he told Penders it would be a violation of the Buckley Amendment if he released Axtell's academic information, Dodds, conceivably would have had grounds to terminate Penders.

Rasmus then asked Dodds about the broadcasting job for Penders with Host Communications.

Rasmus: What, if anything, can you tell me about Penders interviewing for a TV commentator's job with USA Collegiate formerly known as Host Communications.

Dodds: That he did do that, that he did interview with them.

Rasmus: Was that opportunity arranged by The University of Texas and/or men's athletics?

Dodds: We were part of the arrangement. We were part of the conversation –

Rasmus: Okay.

Dodds: – about that.

Rasmus: Can you tell me what that conversation involved, then?

Dodds: We have a relationship with Host, and felt that Tom had some abilities in that area, and I talked to Host about that. And it was his call whether he did or didn't do, was the agreement with him.

Rasmus: Did this – did this involvement take place before or after the release of Axtell's grades?

Dodds: For the job?

Rasmus: Yes, sir.

Dodds: It was after.

Rasmus: How did it come about that men's athletics would be involved in providing an opportunity to Penders for a TV commentator's job with Host?

Dodds: I don't understand the question.

Rasmus: Well, how did – how did you get involved as a director of – athletic director? How did you get involved with Host in promoting Tom Penders or at least setting up an opportunity for Penders to interview for a TV commentator's job?

Dodds: It was part of the conversations that I had with attorneys during that process.

(After Dodds' attorney instructed him not to disclose any contents of any conversations he had with counsel, Rasmus continued.)

Rasmus: Mr. Dodds, absent guidance and direction from legal counsel, is there any other reason why you would advance the interest of Tom Penders when he had so obviously violated school policy and put men's – the men's athletics department in a difficult situation by releasing Axtell's academic information?

Dodds: No.

(After Dodds' attorney objected after the fact, Rasmus went on to another topic.)

Rasmus: Can you tell me, Mr. Dodds, why it took so long for the investigation conducted by the University to be completed when you knew as of Wednesday evening from Leslie Parks that Tom Penders had been the one that authorized the release of the fax?

Dodds: This investigation was done by legal counsel and not by the department.

Rasmus: Do you know why it was necessary to interview 20 people in the course of the two-week investigation when you knew Wednesday night from Leslie Parks that the fax had been authorized by Tom Penders and had that confirmed by Eddie Oran the next day?

Dodds: I prefer not to get into the investigation.

As Dodds' deposition concluded, just as it had begun, a familiar name was the topic of discussion.

Rasmus: Going back to the meeting that occurred on Sunday afternoon before all this broke loose, do you recall having conversations with Tom Douglass about concerns that he had as an alum with the basketball program?

Dodds: I had conversations – yes, I have had conversations with Tom Douglass.

Rasmus: Did you also have conversations about concerns about the basketball program with Russell Douglass?

Dodds: Yes.

Rasmus: Did either of them talk to you about the meeting with the four players?

Dodds: I don't recall that.

Last, the *American-Statesman* article used quotes from the deposition of Vic Trilli, the former assistant coach who was a year-removed from the University of Texas, but was still deposed.

"Rasmus asked Trilli, 'With respect to the knowledge of people in men's athletics and those connected with the basketball program in men's athletics, was it your belief that they were aware of the problems in connection with the use of alcohol and Coach Penders."

"Trilli responded: 'I mentioned a discussion (to) you with an associate athletic director by the name of Chris Plonsky (who) had approached me after the (1997) Colorado game (and) said it was going to be taken care of.'"

Vic Trilli's Deposition

When Trilli's deposition began, he questioned Rasmus as to why he had been deposed.

Trilli: ... I'm still trying to figure out why I'm here.

Rasmus: Okay, Well, you're here because you may have some information that may be important to Luke's situation in connection with the suspension and his grades release.

Trilli: I wasn't even there.

In another of the early exchanges, Trilli answered what he believed to be the knowledge and familiarity of athletic department staff with the Buckley Amendment. It was similar to that of Oran, and the exact opposite of Dodds.

Rasmus: Were you aware of the Buckley Amendment itself as it's described or named Buckley Amendment while you were at The University of Texas?

Trilli: Yes.

Rasmus: To your knowledge, were UT coaches and staff informed by the University that grades and academic status of the student-athlete were private and not to be disseminated to anyone without permission of the student?

Trilli: I would say no.

Rasmus: Okay.

Trilli: I became aware because of my involvement with academics through Curt Fludd.

Rasmus: Okay. Do you have an opinion one way or the other as to whether or not the other members of the coaching staff in the men's basketball program were aware of the Buckley Amendment?

Trilli: I wouldn't – I have no opinion. I don't how they would or why they would –

Rasmus: Okay. DeLoss Dodds testified in this case, and he indicated that everybody in men's athletics was aware of the Buckley Amendment. Would you agree or disagree with that?

Trilli: I personally would disagree.

Rasmus: Okay. And what is that based upon?

Trilli: I don't know when it occurred. Now, I may have missed a meeting or something where we – where it was discussed or a memo that was sent out. But the only way I was made aware of it, to the best of my knowledge, was through my dealings with Curt Fludd.

Rasmus: Okay. How involved was Tom Penders in the academic side of the program?

Trilli: He was very involved. That was – I mean, I had to – I had to let him know what was going on. And we – he got daily reports on study hall as I did.

Rasmus: Those were copied out of Curt Fludd's office, correct?

Trilli: Yes.

Rasmus: Okay. When you say he was very involved, that he got daily reports on – from the academics office concerning study hall, then —

Trilli: Let me – can I change that?

Rasmus: Sure.

Trilli: Let me say, instead of involved, I would say informed, very informed.

Rasmus: You say if Tom Penders became aware of study hall issues, it reached a different level. Explain that for me.

Trilli: Well, if we had a problem with the guy either going to class or making study hall, and it became one that I couldn't – we couldn't fix or change, and then either myself or Curt Fludd and I together would approach Tom.

Rasmus: And then what would occur?

Trilli: Either a meeting would be set up with the parents or with the individual or both. In some cases, maybe phone calls to the parents if they are not – you know, if we can't get them in, you know.

Rasmus: If they live away?

Trilli: Yes.

A few questions later, Rasmus asked about any other players who had been suspended without being academically ineligible.

Rasmus: Are you aware of any player prior to Luke Axtell who was suspended for academic reasons but at the time was not academically ineligible, either under Texas – the

University of Texas policy or NCAA rules?

Trilli: They were still eligible, but they –

Rasmus: Yes.

Trilli: – still got suspended? Yes.

Rasmus: Yes, you're aware of that?

Trilli: Uh-huh (Yes.)

Rasmus: Okay, how many – how many instances?

Trilli: One.

Rasmus: Okay.

(Rasmus then requested they go off the record.)

After going back on the record, Rasmus began discussing with Trilli his opinion of the event that led to Penders' resignation. She asked him what he had heard about the situation while in Denton.

Rasmus: ... Have you had any conversations with anyone else here in Austin that you used to associate with, like any alumni, for example?

Trilli: Like?

Rasmus: I don't know. To talk about this particular incident, how about Russell Douglass? Have you had any contact with Mr. Douglass?

Trilli: No. I had contact with Russell Douglass when the thing – I made a comment in the newspaper, in the *Dallas Morning News*.

Rasmus: What was the comment?

Trilli: Something that I – I was the guy that did the verbal abuse.

Rasmus: That you were the one that did verbal abuse?

Trilli: Yeah. It was a joke. It was kind of a joke. And we haven't talked since that day. He was one of my best friends.

Rasmus asked Trilli who else he spoke with during the controversy.

Rasmus: Okay. Did you talk to any other alums or people here from Austin besides Mr. Douglass that you can recall about the circumstances or the situation involving the controversy between Tom Penders and his suspending Luke and faxing the grades out?

Trilli: I talked to Bill Wendlandt.

Rasmus: And when did you and Mr. Wendlandt talk?

Trilli: That's a good question. It was sometime in there. I'm not sure as to when.

Rasmus: Okay.

Trilli: But my purpose – my reason to talk to him was he is real close friends with Russell Douglass, and I was hoping he could help me with, you know, the relationship with Russell – our families were close. We were real close until all this happened.

Rasmus: Have you been –

Trilli: I haven't heard since.

Rasmus: You haven't heard from him since?

Trilli: No.

After a myriad of questions on topics including verbal abuse and late-night phone calls, Rasmus returned to discussions about Wendlandt and Douglass.

Rasmus: In the 1997-98 season, did Mr. Douglass or Mr. Wendlandt or anyone from Austin call you and talk to you about concerns that there were players on the team here at UT that were thinking about transferring?

Trilli: Is that while I was at North Texas?

Rasmus: While you were at North Texas?

Trilli: Yeah, Russell.

Rasmus: Okay.

Trilli: Oh, I don't know about their – he had concerns.

Rasmus: Okay. What were his concerns?

Trilli: That -

(After Trilli's attorney objected, Trilli answered the question.)

Rasmus: His concerns were that things weren't going good.

Rasmus: And?

Trilli: That they should have been winning more games and just basically unhappy with the overall.

Rasmus: Things not going good, and he thought he – he thought, in his opinion, that they should be winning more games. What other – what other concerns, if any, did he pose to you?

Trilli: Oh, boy. I don't know. That players weren't getting developed the way they thought they should have been.

Rasmus: Did he talk to you about any players talking about being transfered?

Trilli: Well, I don't – I can't recall that.

Rasmus: Okay. What other concerns did he talk to you about?

Trilli: Just basically Tom.

Rasmus: And what did he say about Tom?

Trilli: Just not happy, not happy at all with what was going on with the basketball program. The record wasn't good. They felt like they had enough talent to win. Basically, the same team back that had gone to the Sweet 16 prior. And added, you know, what we thought we needed all along, which was two big guys, you know.

Rasmus: Chris Mihm and Luke Axtell?

Trilli: And Luke Axtell. Not to mention the two – Marlon Drakes and Wendell Carter. That's more size than we've ever had, more talent than we've probably ever had.

Rasmus: Okay. Did anyone call you, Mr. Russell or Mr. Douglass or anyone from Austin – and I'm talking about general public now. I'm not talking anyone from UT or coaching staff calling and visiting about anything. But to talk to you about four of the players – Bernard Smith, Gabe Muoneke, Chris Mihm, or Luke Axtell – talking about transferring?

Trilli: Did anybody call me and tell me about that?

Rasmus: Yeah, or visit with you about it?

Trilli: I think Russell mentioned something to me about it, not just general public.

Rasmus: Okay.

Trilli: But I didn't believe him, to be honest with you.

Rasmus: What did he tell you?

Trilli: He said it's bad.

Rasmus: Did he tell you how bad, or is that —

Trilli: No, he didn't. And then I watched him play in the tournament, you know, and they were winning. I'm talking about in the – what's it called – the Big 12 tournament.

Rasmus: Big 12?

Trilli: And Brandy was – hit a shot that won a game, and I couldn't tell that there was any problem.

Rasmus: Okay.

Trilli: And when I left, which wasn't that long between that time, there wasn't any problem. And I had talked to Eddie on the phone, and the biggest problem that ever came up was Gabe Muoneke.

Rasmus: And what was told to you about any problem involving that player?

Trilli: Gabe?

Rasmus: Uh-huh (Yes).

Trilli: Nothing. Just that he – Gabe was Gabe. He's a different culture. He is African. His daddy is from Africa, and he was raised in a different culture, and he is hard to deal with. I knew that, though, because I recruited him.

Rasmus: Where -

Trilli: But that was – you know, Eddie was always frustrated with that. That was it.

Rasmus: Was there any conversation in particular about Gabe from his concerns about his own development as a basketball player in this program?

Trilli: By?

Rasmus: By Mr. Douglass or anybody you may have talked to?

Trilli: Not specifically. Russell did mention to me about the development of the kids, and he was really worried about Luke, and he was worried about Chris.

Rasmus: Did any –

Trilli: Particularly Chris being a big guy.

Rasmus: Did Mr. Douglass or anyone talk to you about a plan to have players meet with DeLoss Dodds to express their concerns about the basketball program and the direction that the basketball program was taking?

Trilli: He had said that, that that was going to occur at the end of the season, but I couldn't see it. I couldn't see about what was going on in the field – I mean, on the floor, that that was a legitimate deal, because they played well when I watched. It's hard, you know, when you sit there and you watch and you know these guys, and you hear this, and you're going – you know, I just didn't believe them, to be honest with you. That's why I did the joke thing in the newspaper.

Several minutes after the discussion about Douglass and Wendlandt's involvement, Rasmus went to the topic of Penders and his use of alcohol.

Rasmus: You were aware that Mr. Penders did use alcohol, correct?

Trilli: Uh-huh (Yes), as I did.

Rasmus: You were aware that there were times that he overused alcohol, correct?

(After an objection from Trilli's attorney, Rasmus rephrased her question.)

Rasmus: Were you aware there were times Mr. Penders overused alcohol?

Trilli: I've never seen him.

Rasmus: Okay. Did you ever go to DeLoss Dodds and express concern to him about

Tom Penders' use of alcohol and its effect on his ability to act as head basketball coach at The University of Texas?

Trilli: No. DeLoss came to me.

Penders and his consumption of alcohol remained the focus of Rasmus' questions. At one point, Mollie Axtell was overcome with emotion and the deposition was interrupted.

Rasmus: Do you recall Tom Penders – I'm sorry. Do you recall DeLoss Dodds telling you that there was nothing he could do about Tom Penders' alcohol program – or I'm sorry, alcohol problem, because Tom Penders was the winningest coach?

Trilli: No. That never occurred.

Rasmus: In your opinion, did Penders' alcohol use affect his ability to coach?

Trilli: No.

Rasmus: As you sit here today, are you telling me that you never told or said that everyone in men's athletics knew about Tom Penders' alcohol program – or problem, including DeLoss Dodds?

(After an objection from Trilli's attorney, Chad Geisler, the session was halted.)

Geisler: Are you okay, Ms. Axtell? Do you need to take a break?

Rasmus: Excuse me, Counsel.

Geisler: Well, it's distracting for me as an attorney for this witness to have to watch Ms. Axtell apparently be really uncomfortable and express verbally and with her body language her discomfort at some of the answers and questions, and it's distracting for me. And if she needs a break, we should take a break.

Rasmus: I'm sorry you're distracted.

Geisler: Well, so am I, and that's why -

Rasmus: So if -

Geisler: – that's why I'm objecting.

Rasmus: If she's – she's fine, Counsel.

Geisler: Well, it doesn't look that way.

Rasmus: Your objections to form are inconsistent with form questions. But we're not going there, okay? Now, let's go back to my last question, please. Ms. Axtell is fine. If she needs a break, she'll tell me, and we'll accommodate her.

After the disruption, Rasmus continued in her line of questions about Penders and alcohol.

Rasmus: Okay, do you remember Mollie Axtell confronting you about not telling her about Penders' alcohol problem?

(After an objection from Trilli's attorney, Trilli answered the question.)

Trilli: Yeah, I've had plenty of conversations with Mollie Axtell.

Rasmus: Okay. Specifically, I'm referring you to her confronting you about a failure to tell her about Penders' alcohol problem.

(After an objection from Trilli's attorney, Trilli answered the question.)

Trilli: I don't know that Tom has an alcohol problem.

Rasmus: Okay. But for you not being any kind of a medical expert, Coach, or any kind of an alcohol treatment expert, I'm not asking for an expert opinion. I'm asking for your own observations and your opinions, your own beliefs?

Trilli: Right.

Rasmus: Did – let me ask you this question. Did Mollie Axtell confront you about, from her perspective, your failure to inform her about a alcohol problem of Coach Penders?

Trilli: Yes.

Rasmus: And what, if anything, did you say to her?

Trilli: I don't recall.

Rasmus: Okay. Did you say anything to her about, I don't know that Penders has an alcohol problem?

Trilli: I don't recall. I can't remember what I said to her.

Rasmus: Okay.

Trilli: I would also – I think in regards to Mollie, probably in the 25 years that I've been coaching, I don't know that anyone has ever zeroed in on a program as much as Mollie had the opportunity to and took the opportunity to. I know that she made many, many, many practices, both at the Erwin Center, as well as the Berger Center, I think, or whatever. She was very proactive with what was going on the year-and-a-half prior to Luke, I guess, coming to school here.

The questions on alcohol continued. Rasmus asked Trilli if he was ever confronted about an alcohol problem with Penders by outside sources. Two familiar names appeared, yet again.

Rasmus: Did any alumni close to the program talk to you about Penders' drinking problem?

(After an objection from Trilli's attorney, Trilli answered the question.)

Trilli: Yes.

Rasmus: And who were those alumni?

Trilli: Oh -

Rasmus: Can you remember?

Trilli: Probably Russell Douglass. Bill Wendlandt may have said something to me, Tom, Russell's brother, David Walter. I don't know.

Rasmus: And how would you respond to them when they would talk to you about this concern?

Trilli: Somewhat concerned?

Rasmus: And how were you concerned?

Trilli: That this was going on. This was becoming a public deal.

Rasmus: And why were you concerned about that?

Trilli: What do you mean?

Rasmus: Well, why – I mean, that it was a public deal. What about the truth or falsity of it?

Trilli: See, the problem I have with it is, I don't know that it is the truth. That could very easily just be somebody that's mad.

Rasmus: Did you tell that to these people?

Trilli: I don't know. I don't recall. In what we do for a living, we're scrutinized on everything we do.

Rasmus: I understand.

Trilli: I mean, somebody can look at me and see me somewhere off and have a drink and said that, you know, the night before a game, and I make bad decisions, and base that on the fact that I was out having a drink the night before. I've never been drunk in my life, ever.

Rasmus: We're talking about situations or circumstances much greater than that, though, aren't we, for these four people that you named to express concerns to you about Penders' alcohol use, correct?

Trilli: I don't know that that is correct.

Rasmus: Okay.

Trilli: It was easy to sit and talk and say this and say – but to actually know is a different deal.

Rasmus: Okay. Did you ever concern yourself about Mr. Penders' use of alcohol and its effect on his ability to coach these young athletes?

Trilli: I never worried about Tom's ability to coach the kids, no.

Rasmus: Did you ever worry about his use of alcohol?

Trilli: No. That's his own personal deal. That's between him and himself alone and his family.

Rasmus: Okay.

As the deposition reached its conclusion, Trilli was asked about his working relationship with Penders.

Rasmus: Did you have any difficulty working with Tom Penders in his basketball program here at The University of Texas?

Trilli: Tom allowed me a tremendous opportunity to be me.

Rasmus: Did you —

Trilli: And if there is something wrong with me being me, then that's the problem. I thought I did a great job representing the University, representing the basketball program, and that opportunity was presented to me solely by Tom Penders. I am where I'm at right now because of the opportunity he gave me.

Rasmus: And your performance as his assistant coach, I would think, had some play in it, correct?

Trilli: Had some play in me leaving?

Rasmus: No, sir. I would think that your receiving a head coaching position was the result of —

Trilli: I wouldn't know.

Rasmus: — your performance?

Trilli: I wouldn't know that. I couldn't comment on that. I would hope that it would be.

Rasmus: Did Tom Penders get you the job at North Texas?

Trilli: He gave me the opportunity to get the job by allowing me to be here and perform and do what – like you just said. Did he get me the job?

Rasmus: Yes, sir.

Trilli: No. I got the job.

Rasmus: Were you happy to get out from underneath Tom Penders?

Trilli: I was happy to get on my own again. I had been a head coach and an athletic director once.

Finally, as the deposition concluded, Trilli, had grown weary of the questions, indicative by his final response.

Trilli: ... I was elated to be the assistant basketball coach at The University of Texas. If that's what you want me to crawl down to, that's what I'll say I was.

Rasmus: No, sir. I don't want you to crawl down. Stand up straight and be tall and be proud of everything you accomplished.

Trilli: It sounds like it. Are you going to do the same thing? Are you going to stand up tall and be proud of what this is? That's what I want to know. Just me and you, face to face.

Rasmus: Yes, sir. We can talk about that.

Trilli: And so you guys – this is the way you conduct business on a daily basis?

Rasmus: We can talk about that. I don't have any more questions at this time. I'll pass the witness.

The Controversy Relived

That evening became a complete flashback to the days of the original controversy, which led to Penders' departure, as switchboards of radio station talk shows across the city lit up and bulletin boards on the Internet were filled with endless chatter. Everyone had something to say – positive or negative – about Penders, Axtell, Oran, Dodds and the countless others involved.

One post on the Internet read:

"What does Tom Penders' alcohol problems, or verbal abuse have to do with it?!? Why print it if it has nothing to do with it? Why didn't the article, or the depositions point out the fact that certain testimonies debunked the other? ... This is so obviously a setup it isn't even funny, and the paper is jumping right on. I mean, why sue a radio station, and then just ask questions not related to the case? Why did the lawyers from the radio station let it happen? ... The saddest thing about this is that it is so blatantly done to smear Penders and that it has nothing to do with anything else. The journalists don't mention this at all."

Ohlendorf Speaks

Although Penders was seen and heard on almost every television and radio station in town defending his character that night, it was one interview that followed Penders on KLBJ-AM's Sports Talk radio show that left the biggest impression with those who heard it.

Patricia Ohlendorf, former vice provost and general counsel at the university and current vice president for administration and legal affairs, spoke with KLBJ's Ed Clements and Jeff Ward. After Ohlendorf denied that Penders' records of his employment were destroyed or misplaced as he had claimed in his interview just moments before, Ohlendorf spoke for the first time about the two-week investigation into the release of Axtell's grades. Ohlendorf said after they had interviewed the 20 people and the university had released its single-page report that consisted of three steps the school would take, which were detailed in Penders' resignation press conference, the records of the investigation were then destroyed.

"Verbally it was decided that we would not issue a written report and so the handwritten notes that I had were sent through the shredder," Ohlendorf told the two talk show hosts.

Ward, Clements, and the rest of the listening audience were in shock. Ward expressing his disbelief, asked Ohlendorf if she realized at any point that the documents might be needed for later use. Ohlendorf repeated that it was agreed the report would be verbal and no written documents were necessary.

Many followers of the situation, who had seen the report the night before on Channel 24, could only think back to Joel Thomas' remarks of a "high-level UT investigation." High-level? Shredded? Something was amiss.

Besides her remarks on shredding documents, Ohlendorf said some stories, such as Oran's, had changed between the previous year and the depositions. "Some statements in the depositions are different than what some individuals said at the time Mr. Penders resigned, but that's something that we're just going to have to accept." She said at the time, the issue with Penders was resolved "in the best way possible for everyone."

UT Defends Itself

A week after the depositions were leaked to the media and the public responded with questions about why Penders received $900,000 when he left, the University of Texas defended itself in the buyout of Penders' contract.

"I personally may believe certain things happened. But we didn't have proof. Some people said different things in the depositions than they said at the time (of the investigation)," Ohlendorf said in the August 14 edition of the *American-Statesman*.

Axtell's attorney, Sherry Rasmus, was also quoted in the article. When asked what the Axtells' plans were in the future, Rasmus said the Axtells "still are looking at (their) options as to whether or not to go forward and add Penders and the University of Texas to the lawsuit."

About the author

Kyle Dalton graduated from the University of Texas in 1992 with a degree in journalism. Since that time he has served as managing editor for two national trade magazines – *High-Tech Coaching & Training* and *AutoCAD World*, and written numerous articles for both the high-tech and sports industries. For four years he was also a regular contributor to the sports section of the *Austin American-Statesman*. Today, he serves as Internet Editor for a state agency and freelances for several different publications.

Photo Credits

Allsport – cover, insert page 9 bottom, insert page 11 top

AP/Wide World – insert page 1 top, insert page 12, insert page 11 bottom, insert page 15

Dallas Morning News – insert page 8, back cover

Houston Chronicle – insert page 10

Susie Penders – insert page 1 bottom, insert page 2 all, insert page 3 all, insert page 4 all, insert page 5, insert page 6 all, insert page 7 all, insert page 9 top, insert page 13 all, insert page 14 all, insert page 16 all